Access to Higher Educati

How do we understand and explain who has access to higher education? How do we make sense of persisting and new forms of inequality? How can global, national and institutional policymakers and practitioners make higher education more inclusive? *Access to Higher Education: Theoretical perspectives and contemporary challenges* seeks to update thinking on these questions, combining new voices and emerging perspectives with established writers in the field.

This novel text highlights the contribution of social theory to issues of access to education, with chapters introducing and drawing on the works of key interdisciplinary thinkers including Pierre Bourdieu, Margaret Archer, Amartya Sen and Herbert Simon. It then moves to examine how theoretical perspectives can be applied to the contemporary challenges of forging more equal access, with examples drawn from a wide range of contexts, including the UK, the US, Australia, South Africa and Japan.

Global in scope, this book documents the shared nature of the access challenge in a period when higher education is growing rapidly, but inequalities continue to be stark. It concludes by proposing a new direction for research and a reassertion of the role of the researcher as a social activist for disconnected and disadvantaged groups, equipped with the thinking tools needed to move the agenda forward.

Access to Higher Education is a rigorous text for the global research community, with relevance to policymakers, practitioners and postgraduate students interested in social justice and social policy. It provides those with an academic interest in access and a commitment to enhancing policy with theoretical and practical ideas for moving the access agenda forward in their institutional, regional or national contexts.

Anna Mountford-Zimdars is a senior lecturer in Higher Education and Head of Research at King's Learning Institute, King's College London, UK.

Neil Harrison is a senior lecturer in the Department of Education at the University of the West of England, UK.

The Society for Research into Higher Education (SRHE) is an independent and financially self-supporting international learned Society. It is concerned to advance understanding of higher education, especially through the insights, perspectives and knowledge offered by systematic research and scholarship.

The Society's primary role is to improve the quality of higher education through facilitating knowledge exchange, discourse and publication of research. SRHE members are worldwide and the Society is an NGO in operational relations with UNESCO.

The Society has a wide set of aims and objectives. Amongst its many activities the Society:

* is a specialist publisher of higher education research, journals and books, amongst them Studies in Higher Education, Higher Education Quarterly, Research into Higher Education Abstracts and a long running monograph book series.

The Society also publishes a number of in-house guides and produces a specialist series "Issues in Postgraduate Education".

* funds and supports a large number of special interest networks for researchers and practitioners working in higher education from every discipline. These networks are open to all and offer a range of topical seminars, workshops and other events throughout the year ensuring the Society is in touch with all current research knowledge.

* runs the largest annual UK-based higher education research conference and parallel conference for postgraduate and newer researchers. This is attended by researchers from over 35 countries and showcases current research across every aspect of higher education.

SRHE *Society for Research into Higher Education*
Advancing knowledge Informing policy Enhancing practice

73 Collier Street
London N1 9BE
United Kingdom

T   +44 (0)20 7427 2350
F   +44 (0)20 7278 1135
E   srheoffice@srhe.ac.uk

www.srhe.ac.uk

Director: Helen Perkins
Registered Charity No. 313850
Company No. 00868820
Limited by Guarantee
Registered office as above

Society for Research into Higher Education (SRHE)

Series Editors: Jennifer M. Case, *University of Cape Town*
Jeroen Huisman, *University of Ghent*

Published titles:

**Writing in Social Spaces: A social processes approach
to academic writing**
Rowena Murray

**Digital Technology and the Contemporary University:
Degrees of digitization**
Neil Selwyn

**Stepping up to the Second Year at University: Academic,
Psychological and Social Dimensions**
Clare Milsom, Martyn Stewart, Mantz Yorke and Elena Zaitseva

Culture, Capitals and Graduate Futures
Ciaran Burke

**Researching Higher Education: International perspectives
on theory, policy and practice**
Jennifer M. Case and Jeroen Huisman

**Freedom to Learn: The threat to student academic freedom
and why it needs to be reclaimed**
Bruce Macfarlane

Student Politics and Protest: International Perspectives
Rachel Brooks

Theorising Learning to Teach in Higher Education
Brenda Leibowitz, Vivienne Bozalek and Peter Kahn

**Access to Higher Education: Theoretical perspectives
and contemporary challenges**
Edited by Anna Mountford-Zimdars and Neil Harrison

Access to Higher Education

Theoretical perspectives
and contemporary challenges

Edited by Anna Mountford-Zimdars
and Neil Harrison

Routledge
Taylor & Francis Group

LONDON AND NEW YORK

First published 2017
by Routledge
2 Park Square, Milton Park, Abingdon, Oxon OX14 4RN

Together with the Society for Research into Higher Education
73 Collier Street
London, N1 9BE
UK

and by Routledge
711 Third Avenue, New York, NY 10017

Routledge is an imprint of the Taylor & Francis Group, an informa business

British Library Cataloguing in Publication Data
A catalogue record for this book is available from the British Library

Library of Congress Cataloging in Publication Data
A catalog record for this book has been requested

ISBN: 978-1-138-92410-9 (hbk)
ISBN: 978-1-138-92411-6 (pbk)
ISBN: 978-1-315-68457-4 (ebk)

Typeset in Galliard
by Apex CoVantage, LLC

Contents

Contributors   x

Preface   xii

SECTION I
Access to higher education   I

1 Global trends of access to and equity
  in postsecondary education   3
  CHIAO-LING CHIEN, PATRICK MONTJOURIDÈS AND HENDRIK
  VAN DER POL

2 The stratification of opportunity in high participation
  systems (HPS) of higher education   33
  SIMON MARGINSON

SECTION 2
Theoretical perspectives   49

3 Capitals and habitus: a Bourdieusian framework
  for understanding transitions into higher education
  and student experiences   51
  CIARAN BURKE

4 Explaining inequality? Rational action theories
  of educational decision making   67
  RON THOMPSON

5 Student choices under uncertainty: bounded rationality
  and behavioural economics   85
  NEIL HARRISON

6 Higher education: too risky a decision?   101
   MALCOLM BRYNIN

7 Widening access with success: using the capabilities
   approach to confront injustices   113
   MERRIDY WILSON-STRYDOM

8 Reflexivity and agency: critical realist and Archerian
   analyses of access and participation   128
   PETER KAHN

SECTION 3
Contemporary challenges   143

9 Framing and making of access policies: the case of
   Palestinian Arabs in higher education in Israel   145
   AYALA HENDIN, DALIA BEN-RABI AND FAISAL AZAIZA

10 Widening access in a vast country: opportunities
    and challenges in Australia   158
    ANN JARDINE

11 Accessing postgraduate study in the United States
    for African Americans: relating the roles of family, fictive
    kin, faculty, and student affairs practitioners   171
    CARMEN M. McCALLUM, JULIE R. POSSELT
    AND ESTEFANÍA LÓPEZ

12 Participation and access in higher education in Russia:
    continuity and change of a positional advantage   190
    ANNA SMOLENTSEVA

13 Can Holistic and Contextualised Admission (HaCA) widen
    access at highly selective universities? Experiences from
    England and the United States   205
    ANNA MOUNTFORD-ZIMDARS

14 Diversifying admissions through top-down entrance
    examination reform in Japanese elite universities:
    what is happening on the ground?   216
    BEVERLEY ANNE YAMAMOTO

15 The mobility imperative: English students and 'fair' access
to international higher education 232

RACHEL BROOKS AND JOHANNA WATERS

Conclusion 244

NEIL HARRISON AND ANNA MOUNTFORD-ZIMDARS

Index 251

Contributors

Faisal Azaiza – University of Haifa, Israel

Dalia Ben-Rabi – Myers-JDC-Brookdale Institute; Ben-Gurion University of the Negev, Israel

Rachel Brooks – University of Surrey, England, UK

Malcolm Brynin – Institute for Social and Economic Research; University of Essex, England, UK

Ciaran Burke – Ulster University, Northern Ireland, UK

Chiao-Ling Chien – UNESCO Institute for Statistics, Montreal, QC, Canada

Neil Harrison – University of the West of England, Bristol, England, UK

Ayala Hendin – Myers-JDC-Brookdale Institute; Ben-Gurion University of the Negev, Israel

Ann Jardine – University of New South Wales, New South Wales, Australia

Peter Kahn – University of Liverpool, England, UK

Estefanía López – University of Michigan, Michigan, USA

Carmen M. McCallum – Eastern Michigan University, Michigan, USA

Simon Marginson – UCL Institute of Education; University College London, England, UK and Centre for the Study of Higher Education, University of Melbourne, Australia

Patrick Montjouridès – UNESCO Institute for Statistics, Montreal, QC, Canada

Anna Mountford-Zimdars – King's College London, England, UK

Julie R. Posselt – University of Southern California, California, USA

Anna Smolentseva – National Research University; Higher School of Economics, Moscow, Russia

Ron Thompson – University of Huddersfield, England, UK

Hendrik van der Pol – UNESCO Institute for Statistics, Montreal, QC, Canada

Johanna Waters – University of Oxford, England, UK

Merridy Wilson-Strydom – Centre for Research on Higher Education and Development (CRHED); University of the Free State, Bloemfontein, South Africa

Beverley Anne Yamamoto – Osaka University, Japan

Preface

Supporting access to and successful participation in higher education is a shared global challenge. While some of the private benefits or returns to higher education have come under scrutiny recently, by and large, globally the story still seems to hold that graduates usually enjoy better health, more stable employment, more autonomous jobs, higher life-time earnings and are more engaged in civic life than non-graduates. For most, higher education is a life-changing experience that opens new horizons, while there are gains for their communities, their nations and across the globe.

However, there is ample evidence from around the world that the opportunities to access higher education are not equally distributed. In the developing world, access is generally still reserved for a privileged few. In the developed nations, where mass systems of higher education predominate, access for disadvantaged groups is stronger but social elites still dominate, often with a saturated market for those at the top. Fair access to high-status universities is a particular concern for such countries.

This is the backdrop for this book. We have used the term 'higher education' in the title, this preface and the conclusion. We use it to mean education which follows compulsory schooling and which generally leads to the award of a degree (or similar), regardless of the route or the nature of the awarding institution. Other terms used in this book include 'post-secondary' and 'tertiary' education. Given the diversity of national systems and new emergent forms of higher education (e.g. online/distance delivery or workplace-based), it is impossible to find a catch-all term. Authors have used the terminology most appropriate in their own context, while confirming that we are (as far as is possible) talking about the same thing. Similarly, the words 'institution' and 'university' are used interchangeably while appreciating that higher education may be delivered through a college or private provider as well as university.

Another clarification is that the focus of the book is firmly on access to higher education directly from (or soon after) secondary schooling. This is not to deny the importance of higher education for mature students, especially from disadvantaged backgrounds – indeed, this would need a whole book to do it justice. However, progression from school comprises an overwhelming share of access to higher education in most countries thus justifying focused attention.

This book aims to make a novel contribution. It was born of a belief that the field has been insufficiently theorised and that there has been a tendency for theoretical camps to be inward-looking rather than expansive and open to alternative perspectives. Sociologists, economists and psychologists all contribute to the field, but the disciplines rarely interact and there is a danger of losing valuable insights from a creative synthesis. We have therefore aimed to produce a volume that gives voice to a wide range of theoretical perspectives from renowned thinkers.

The book falls naturally into three parts. The **first section** sets the scene with two chapters providing a broad overview of the field of access in higher education. Chien and colleagues draw on UNESCO data to examine progress in equality across a broad array of countries, while Simon Marginson explores 'high participation' systems in the developed world in more detail, highlighting trends and challenges that still need our collective attention.

The **second section** is at the heart of what this book is seeking to achieve. Each chapter is written by an enthusiast who provides an introduction for the novice, as well as an example of how the theory has been (or might be) applied in either research or practice. From an editorial perspective, these are offered neutrally, with the intent of providing an entry point for readers wishing to expand their theoretical repertoire. The field has been dominated largely by perspectives grounded in the work of Pierre Bourdieu (and, indeed, this is ably represented here by Ciaran Burke's opening chapter), but there is a danger that this has dominated to the exclusion of other useful perspectives. The five other chapters in this section therefore provide a showcase of theories drawn from the work of renowned international thinkers such as Margaret Archer, Amartya Sen, Martha Nussbaum, Herbert Simon, Daniel Kahneman, Raymond Boudon and Ulrich Beck. These six theoretical chapters address access issues both from the macro level of whole societies (e.g. Ron Thompson's chapter on rational action and Merridy Wilson-Strydom's on the capabilities approach), through a meso level of labour markets (Malcolm Brynin's chapter on risk) down to the micro level of understanding the internal dialogues of individuals and the decisions they make (Neil Harrison's chapter on bounded rationality and Peter Kahn's on reflexivity). Similarly, the theories presented also straddle a broad philosophical palette, from Bourdieusian structuralism, through the 'third way' thinking of Archer and Beck, to Sen's classical liberalism.

The **third section** then provides a showcase for chapters addressing contemporary challenges in the real-world of access as experienced by practitioners and academics. Unlike some books on access to higher education, we have tried not to simply describe 'country case studies'. Instead, this section comprises a mixture of empirical studies and 'think pieces' grounded in theory. These are deliberately wide in their scope, taking in examples from the United States, Japan, Australia, Israel/Palestine, Russia and the United Kingdom. Some of these address particular social groups for whom access to higher education remains problematic, including Ann Jardine's chapter on rural communities in Australia and Carmen McCallum and colleagues' exploration of equality of access to postgraduate education for African Americans. Others examine the particular challenges presented by shifting geopolitics and inter-community strife, with Anna Smolentseva's examination of post-communist Russia and Ayala Hendin and colleagues' look at efforts to extend higher education to Palestinian Arabs in Israel. Finally, the chapters from Anna Mountford-Zimdars and Beverley Yamamoto look at high-status higher education and how social elites benefit from highly hierarchical systems, while Rachel Brooks and Johanna Waters examine how their ability to be geographically mobile provides a positional advantage.

The shared nature of the access challenge has given rise to a global social movement pushing for greater educational access and more inclusion of disconnected or historically disadvantaged groups. The first *World Congress on Access to Post-Secondary Education* held in Montreal in 2013 focused the shared commitment of over 250 delegates from nearly 40 countries. It amply illustrated how bottom-up grassroots practitioners and top-down national policy initiatives are increasingly supporting opportunities for higher education access. The event and the existence of so many groups committed to making a difference also highlight the appetite for learning from each other.

This book was very much conceived in the spirit of this global access movement and we hope that it will be useful to policymakers, practitioners, teachers and students, as well as to the researchers at which it is primarily aimed. We believe that a dialogue between disciplines and between theoretical perspectives will support the next wave of policy and practice, seeding greater insight into contemporary challenges and new approaches to delivering a fairer distribution of the benefits that higher education can offer.

Section 1

Access to higher education

This section explores recent trends in global higher education during a period of rapid expansion, but where participation rates continue to vary widely between countries, along with the extent to which access to elite forms of higher education are available to all.

Chapter I

Global trends of access to and equity in postsecondary education

Chiao-Ling Chien, Patrick Montjouridès and Hendrik van der Pol

Worldwide, access to postsecondary education[1] has improved significantly over the last two decades. In 2013, global postsecondary enrolment reached 210,245,000, nearly 3 times higher than 20 years ago (Figure 1.1). Participation in postsecondary education, measured by the gross enrolment ratio,[2] increased from 14% in 1990 to 33% in 2013 (Figure 1.2). However, such measures of the global growth in enrolment can mask stark disparities in progress within and between countries. Given the importance of advanced education to lifelong opportunities, inequality in educational opportunities raises serious concerns for underrepresented or underserved groups. Therefore, it is essential to investigate the sources of educational disadvantages and the extent to which inequality in access to postsecondary education can intensify the disadvantages faced by those lagging behind.

The purposes of this chapter are twofold: first, to identify the recent trends in access to postsecondary education; and second, to examine wealth-related inequality in access to postsecondary education both within and between countries. Assessing wealth-related inequity is particularly imperative because most countries worldwide have experienced greater internal disparities between rich and poor (Piketty, 2013/2014), making balancing the dual policy goals of access and equity challenging.

This chapter draws data from three sources to illuminate critical patterns shaping education inequalities: the UNESCO Institute for Statistics and two international household survey programmes (DHS, MICS) to measure and compare rates of participation in postsecondary education across countries. It also used the Concentration Index to quantify wealth-related inequality in different levels of education.

Expansion and massification

The massive growth of postsecondary enrolment has been driven by both individual and social demand. On the individual level, thanks to the numerous efforts made towards achieving the Millennium Development Goals of universal primary education and gender equality in education by 2015, most countries have

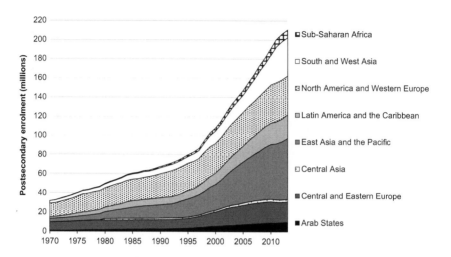

Figure 1.1 Postsecondary enrolment by region, 1970–2013

Note: Country groupings by region can be seen in the UIS (2015a).

Source: UNESCO Institute for Statistics (2015b).

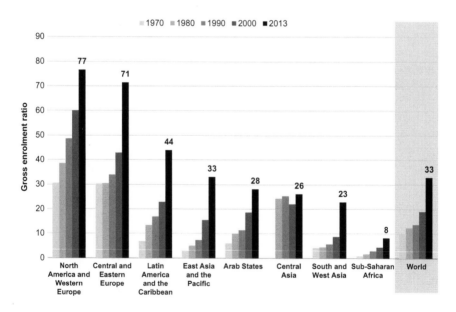

Figure 1.2 Gross enrolment ratios for postsecondary education by region, 1970–2013

Notes: 1. Enrolments in postsecondary, non-tertiary education programmes (the International Standard Classification of Education Level 4, or ISCED 4) are excluded from the calculation because the data on relevant age population for ISCED 4 programmes are unavailable. 2. Country groupings by region can be seen in the UIS (2015a).

Source: UNESCO Institute for Statistics (2015b).

invested heavily in primary and secondary education, resulting in massive numbers of learners qualified and seeking postsecondary education. On the social level, increased public investment in postsecondary education is justified by the belief that higher-level education and training is needed to ensure sustained economic growth in the knowledge economy (Altbach et al., 2009). Postsecondary education systems in many countries thus are entering a massification or even universalization phase (see Trow, 2006, for classification). The postsecondary education systems of China, Colombia, Egypt, India, Malaysia, Mexico, and South Africa took less than two decades to leap from the elite phase to the massification phase.

Middle-income countries have been the largest contributors to the explosive growth of global postsecondary enrolment. In the 1970s, postsecondary enrolment was concentrated in high-income countries, accounting for 70% of global enrolment, as opposed to only 29% in middle-income countries (Figure 1.3). The current picture, however, is very different: postsecondary enrolment in middle-income countries now represents the largest share (66%) of the global total, driven largely by progress in Brazil, China, India, and Indonesia. Their large populations and significant investment in postsecondary education have

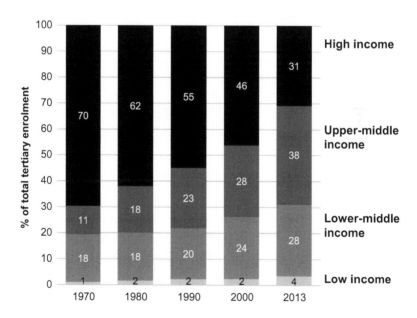

Figure 1.3 Distribution of postsecondary enrolment by income groups, 1970–2013

Notes: 1. National income groupings are according to the World Bank's classification of July 2014. 2. Enrolments in postsecondary, non-tertiary education programmes (ISCED 4) are excluded from the calculation.

Source: UNESCO Institute for Statistics (2015b).

made middle-income countries the leaders in postsecondary enrolment. Conversely, high-income countries' share of postsecondary enrolment went down to 31% in 2013. Despite this decrease in their global share, enrolments in high-income countries remain disproportionately overrepresented in postsecondary education compared with their share of youth population of the world (31% versus 14%).

Particularly in the last decade, low-income countries have made the most impressive gains in terms of postsecondary enrolment, albeit from a low basis. Their postsecondary enrolment nearly tripled from 2,500,000 in 2000 to 7,200,000 in 2013. Among all regions, Sub-Saharan Africa – where more than half of its countries remain low income – lags behind with a very low gross enrolment ratio of 8% for postsecondary education (2013). Given its growing youth population and increasing rate of completion for secondary education, Sub-Saharan Africa has the potential for a rapid increase in the number of people eligible for, and demanding access to, postsecondary education.

The rise of private postsecondary education and international mobility

Private institutions (see Levy, 2009, for classifications) have mushroomed in response to unmet demand (both qualitative and quantitative) for postsecondary education. In countries where student demand for postsecondary education has exceeded supply, the private sector has expanded to accommodate students who cannot attend public institutions. In addition to addressing quantitative demand, private universities are founded to address students' need for better quality and efficiency. In Kenya and Nigeria, students are choosing to attend private universities because of both limited availability and declining quality in the public sector, as well as that some private universities offer preferred programmes relevant to workplace (O'Hara, 2010).

East Asia and Latin America have strong traditions of private postsecondary education, where the majority of students attend private institutions (Levy, 2009). Even in countries where the establishment of private institutions was a new initiative, many governments allowed and encouraged the expansion of private postsecondary education in an effort to shift students away from the heavily subsidized public sector (UIS, 2014). For instance, private universities were not permitted in Cambodia until 1997, and now over two-thirds of its postsecondary enrolment is in private institutions[3] (Figure 1.4). Sub-Saharan Africa came even later to modern private postsecondary education, but its growth there is also marked (Varghese, 2006).

The growth of private postsecondary education has a number of implications that concern stakeholders such as students, their families, and policymakers. Among those concerns are affordability, accessibility, and quality. While public universities and colleges are highly subsidized by governments, private institutions need to recover most of their costs from tuition and other services (e.g. consulting). Tuition

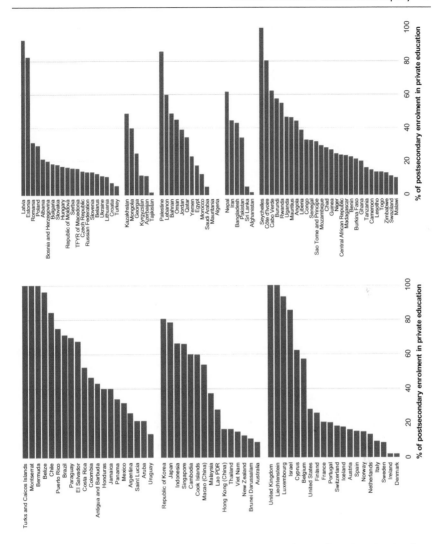

Figure 1.4 Share of enrolment in private postsecondary education institutions by country, 2012

Notes: 1. Private enrolment includes that in government-dependent private institutions and independent private institutions, according to the UNESCO/OECD/Eurostat (2014) manual on concepts, definitions, and classifications. 2. Enrolments in postsecondary, non-tertiary education programmes (ISCED 4) are excluded from the calculation.

Source: UNESCO Institute for Statistics (2015b).

fees charged by private institutions are relatively higher, which may not be afford-able for people from all socioeconomic backgrounds. Thus, students enrolled in private institutions are more likely to be from families that are able to pay the fees or from lower-income families relying on financial assistance (e.g. loans) or taking part-time jobs to finance education. This pattern is found across both developed and developing countries. In Egypt, for instance, nearly two-thirds of students in private universities come from highest quintile wealth families (Buckner, 2013). Private postsecondary education also raises concerns about accessibility. Private institutions tend to locate in populous cities and urban areas, suggesting that rural students may find it hard to attend because of costs associated with travelling and higher living expenses (Buckner, 2013; Fielden & Cheng, 2009).

Another concern about private postsecondary education involves the issue of quality (Lemaitre, 2009; United Nations, 2014). Certainly there are not-for-profit, creditable, and even world-class private universities. However, in many emerging economies, demand-absorbing private institutions are established but quality assurance mechanisms are feeble or non-existent. Private education thus becomes a black box making it difficult for governments and parents to identify practices beneficial to students.

The global expansion of postsecondary education is also reflected in the growing numbers of students who study abroad. In 2013, over 4,060,000 students pursued postsecondary education outside their home countries,[4] representing 2% of global enrolment at the postsecondary level. Besides individual aspirations, numerous national initiatives (e.g. Brazil Science Without Borders and Saudi Arabia King Abdullah Scholarship Programme) and regional initiatives (e.g. Erasmus Plus programme in Europe, and ASEAN International Mobility for Students in Asia) have contributed to international student mobility. Additionally, the global development agenda through the Sustainable Development on Education (Goal 4) aims by 2020 to substantially expand the number of scholarships available to developing countries for enrolment in higher education. The growing trend of cross-border mobility of students is set to continue.

Across regions and countries, there is great variation in demand for overseas education, as measured by the outbound mobility ratio. The Arab States, Central Asia, Sub-Saharan Africa, and Western Europe have relatively high outbound mobility ratios (Figure 1.5). At the country level, China, India, Germany, and the Republic of Korea have the highest number of students enrolled abroad (712,200, 181,900, 119,100, and 116,940, respectively), whereas countries with the highest ratio of student mobility include Andorra, Seychelles, San Marino, Luxembourg, and Liechtenstein, which are all microstates with limited to no provision of higher education and with more than half of their students studying abroad.

In many societies, opportunities to study abroad remain limited to socioeconomically advantaged groups (Hauschildt et al., 2015). First-generation college students and those from lower-income families are less likely to study abroad. The financial burden and a lack of information about opportunities to study abroad deter these students from studying abroad.

Recent developments in regional cooperation on postsecondary education and training in Africa and Asia show countries with more developed education systems assist their neighboring countries with less developed systems. Fifteen countries of the Southern Africa Development Community (SADC) agreed to

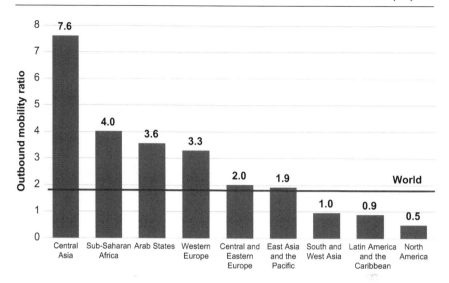

Figure 1.5 Outbound mobility ratio by region, 2013

Note: Outbound mobility ratio is calculated by dividing the number of students from a given region enrolled in tertiary educational programmes abroad by total tertiary enrolment in that region and multiplying the result by 100.

Source: UNESCO Institute for Statistics (2015b).

reserve at least 5% of their enrolment capacity at tertiary education institutions for students from other SADC countries. To facilitate student mobility within the subregion, mechanisms have been initiated such as standardising entrance requirements, harmonizing academic years, easing of credit transfer, and providing in-state tuition fee rates to students from other SADC countries (Chien & Chiteng, 2011). Consequently, a high proportion (50%) of international students from SADC countries remain in their own region to study. Similarly, the launch of the Association of Southeast Asian Nations (ASEAN) International Mobility for Students programme in 2009 initiated an increase in the number of students pursuing postsecondary education from a neighboring country. For instance, Thai and Malaysian universities enrol over 4,000 students from Lao PDR, Myanmar, and Cambodia, where domestic postsecondary enrolment ratios are the lowest among the ASEAN countries.

Postsecondary education financial austerity and access challenge

Financing postsecondary education has become challenging as a result of two intertwined developments: the rapid growth of enrolment and the rising costs of postsecondary education (Johnstone, 2015). Postsecondary education is usually financed by a combination of sources, including governments, students and their families, and business and non-profit organizations; and generally, it is highly subsidized by governments. In many countries, the rate of increase in the costs of postsecondary education has exceeded the inflation rate and is faster than governments can keep pace with.

The extent of government spending on tertiary education[5] in individual countries varies, ranging from as low as 0.1% of GDP in Liberia to as high as 2.4% in Denmark, and even higher (4.5%) in Cuba in 2013. Overall, government spending on tertiary education has grown partly because of the expansion of the postsecondary education system. Between 2000 and 2013, government tertiary expenditure as a percentage of GDP has increased in three-quarters of the countries with trend data available (74 of 97 countries) (Figure 1.6). However, even in countries with an increase in government funding for tertiary education, the rapid growth in the number of students has led to a lower per-student allocation. Comparing the government expenditure per tertiary student as a percentage of GDP per capita, the per-student allocation has declined in two-thirds of the countries with trend data available (49 out of 71 countries) (Figure 1.7).

Worldwide there is an increasing reliance on private spending by students and their families and by private entities, which has led to a decreasing share of government funding in total tertiary education expenditure. This trend is particularly evident in the member states of the Organisation for Economic Co-operation and Development (OECD), where 21 countries (out of 26) with comparable data available for 2000 and 2011 show an increase in the share of private funding for tertiary education (OECD, 2014).

To meet decreasing shares of government funding, postsecondary education institutions look for other non-government revenue sources, such as tuition fees, research grants, selling university services, and providing fee-charging programmes. Among all the available means, one common strategy that institutions and governments adopt is to shift some of the increasing cost burden from governments and taxpayers to students and their families – so-called cost sharing (Johnstone, 1986, 2004). Cost sharing takes various forms, including the introduction of or increases in tuition fees and the elimination or reduction of student grants or scholarships. Additionally, governments' strategy for cost sharing can involve restricting capacity in public universities while simultaneously officially encouraging the growth of tuition-dependent private postsecondary institutions (Altbach et al., 2009).

Countries differ significantly in terms of how the costs of postsecondary education are shared among the government, students and their families, and other private entities (e.g. companies and non-profit organizations), as well as in the financial support they provide to students, such as scholarships, grants, and study loans. The OECD (2014) report shows that some of its member states charge no or low tuition fees and have sound student financial support systems, such as the Nordic countries. Some countries have high tuition fees accompanied with well-developed student financial support systems, such as Australia, Canada, the Netherlands, New Zealand, the United Kingdom, and the United States. Other countries, by contrast, have relatively less-developed student support systems, such as Chile, Japan, and the Republic of Korea.[6]

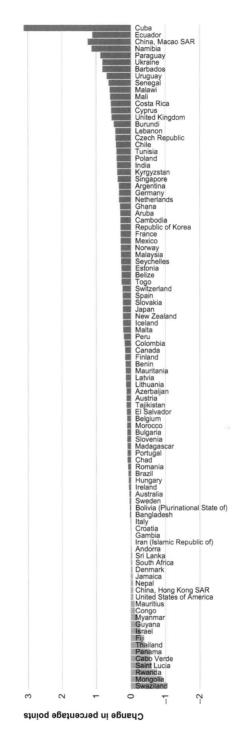

Figure 1.6 Change in government expenditure on tertiary education as a percentage of GDP between 2000 and 2013

Source: UNESCO Institute for Statistics (2015b).

Figure 1.7 Change in government expenditure per tertiary student as a percentage of GDP per capita between 2000 and 2013

Source: UNESCO Institute for Statistics (2015b).

Cost sharing initiatives have successfully expanded access to postsecondary education as found in many countries (European Commission, 2014; Nyahende, 2013; Pillay, 2009). However, the prevalence of cost sharing raises concerns about inequality in education opportunities when not all students have equal access to the means to finance their education. Rises in tuition fees tend to have been accompanied by increased need-based financial aid that offset the costs of tuition to varying extents, as observed in certain European countries and China (Dong & Wan, 2012; European Commission, 2014). Despite a growing body of research on cost sharing in postsecondary education, existing research is inconclusive on the impact on low socioeconomic groups.

Empirical studies in OECD countries found that cost sharing does not significantly reduce the proportion of students from low-income families to participate in postsecondary education. However, cost sharing does influence these students' selections of educational programmes. In the United States, average college costs have nearly doubled between 1990 and 2013, and the net price of attendance (i.e. the cost of attendance minus all grant aids) for low-income students has increased. Consequently, students in second, third, and bottom family income quartiles faced greater unmet financial need for their participation in postsecondary education, whereas students in the highest quartile have a surplus in expected family contribution. The rising costs of attending postsecondary education have affected low-income students more likely to choose studying in two-year institutions (with lower average costs) over four-year institutions (Cahalan & Perna, 2015). Similarly, in Canada, rises in tuition fees are found associated with decreases in lower-income students enrolled in professional programmes (with relatively higher tuition fees) (European Commission, 2014).

Continued concerns about equity

The importance of equal access to postsecondary education has been emphasized repeatedly in international documents. The *Universal Declaration of Human Rights* and the *International Covenant on Economic, Social and Cultural Rights* clearly state that higher education shall be equally accessible to all on the basis of merit and individual capability (United Nations, 1948, 1966). This was reinforced in 2015 with the Incheon Declaration, in which the world's ministers of education and leading development institutions committed to addressing all forms of exclusion, marginalization, disparities and inequalities in access, participation, and learning outcomes (UIS, 2015c). By definition, equity does not mean that all must be treated exactly the same or that there should be precise equality of representation in all fields of education (Martin, 2010). Instead, equity in postsecondary education is usually examined through the lens of equality of opportunity for all. As such access and success in postsecondary education should not be affected by the circumstances that one cannot control (e.g. gender, birthplace, ethnicity, disability, or parental income) (Salmi & Bassett, 2014). Attaining equity therefore requires interventions to promote equality of opportunity (Salmi & Bassett, 2014).

Previous studies on equity in education have identified a number of background characteristics that may affect individuals' participation in postsecondary education, including parents' educational attainments, income or wealth, gender, location (rural/urban), ethnicity, religion, and people with disability (e.g. see Breen & Jonsson, 2005; Chankseliani, 2013; Hout & DiPrete, 2006; Salmi & Bassett, 2014; Wawire et al., 2010). The following explores gender disparities in postsecondary education participation, followed by wealth-related inequalities.

Unlike before the 1990s, women now represent the majority of the postsecondary student population in most countries. In 2013, in two-thirds of the 161 countries with available data, more women than men participated in postsecondary education (Figure 1.8), and this is attributed to three reasons. First, higher levels of schooling are required for women to attain social mobility (Takyi-Amoako, 2008).

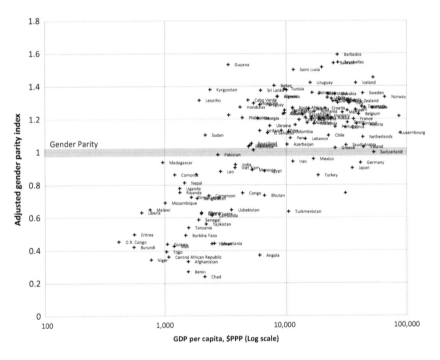

Figure 1.8 Adjusted gender parity index for gross enrolment ratio for postsecondary education in relation to GDP per capita ($PPP), 2013

Notes: 1. The gender parity index (GPI) is a measure used to assess gender differences in education indicators. It is defined as the value of a given indicator for females divided by that for males. UNESCO has defined a GPI value of between 0.97 and 1.03 (after rounding) as the achievement of gender parity. A GPI less than 1 indicates that the value of the indicator is higher for males than for females, and the opposite is true when the GPI is greater than 1. In this figure, the GPI is adjusted to present disadvantages symmetrically for both genders. 2. Enrolments in postsecondary, non-tertiary education programmes (ISCED 4) are excluded from the calculation.

Source: UNESCO Institute for Statistics (2015b).

Second, though postsecondary education leads to individual returns in the form of higher incomes, women need to have more years of education than men to secure jobs of comparable pay – a pattern found in both developed and developing countries. Finally, there has been an ongoing diffusion of ideas on the subject of gender egalitarianism across countries (UIS, 2010). In contrast, in one-third of the 161 countries analyzed, women face barriers to access that keep their rate of participation lower than that of men. Women's underrepresentation in postsecondary education is typical of lower-income countries, except for Angola, Germany, Japan, Liechtenstein, and Turkey, which are middle- or high-income countries but have a lower rate of women's participation. Regionally, Sub-Saharan Africa has the lowest female participation rate (6.7%). In Benin, Chad, and Niger, the male participation rate is 2.5 to 4 times higher than that of females (the gross enrolment ratios for females are 8.4%, 0.9%, and 0.9%, respectively).

Postsecondary education remains hardly accessible for the poorest

Income disparities have intensified sharply in most countries over the past three decades (Piketty, 2013/2014), but how does this affect access to postsecondary education? This section first examines the disparity in access to postsecondary education in relation to household wealth, and then investigates how that disparity has changed over time.

Earlier studies on equity in access to postsecondary education point to two main findings: an overall reduction of inequalities in access to postsecondary education over time (though the situation differs across countries); and the persistent over-representation of individuals from high socioeconomic backgrounds in postsecondary education, despite improvements in the equality of educational opportunity (Koucký & Bartušek, 2013; Santiago et al., 2008; Shavit et al., 2007). For poor families, sending a child to university represents a significant financial burden. In the United States, there is still a gap of 37 percentage points in postsecondary participation between individuals (18–24 years old) from the richest quartile families and those from the poorest quartile (Cahalan & Perna, 2015). Financial burden remains one major obstacle for young people from poor families, as the average net price of participating in postsecondary education accounts for over 84% of their annual family income (Cahalan & Perna, 2015). Similarly, in Thailand and Viet Nam, household spending on postsecondary education is about 60% of total annual income of the poorest, and less than 30% for the richest (World Bank, 2012a).

To date, most research on inequality in access to postsecondary education is limited to developed countries.[7] Much less has focused on developing countries, despite the dynamic and rapid development of their postsecondary education systems. To fill the information gaps, this section assesses how household wealth affects their children's chances of attending postsecondary education and utilizes household surveys from 68 middle- and low-income countries across different regions. Specifically, data from two household survey programmes (DHS and

MICS) – have been standardized based on the ISCED 1997.[8] The target population of ages 20 to 24 years old is analyzed.

We find large disparities in access to postsecondary education across household wealth quintiles. In 9 out of every 10 countries analyzed, students from the two bottom quintiles (i.e. the poorest 40%) represent less than one-fifth of all of those who had access to postsecondary education (Figure 1.9). This is particularly striking in Sub-Saharan Africa. In Burkina Faso, Côte d'Ivoire, and Tanzania, which are generally considered to be good performers in the Education for All monitoring framework,[9] the share of young people from the poorest quintile households who had attended postsecondary education is almost nil. In Burkina Faso, Rwanda, and Malawi, young people from the richest quintile households account for over 90% of those who had attended postsecondary education.

The distribution of educational opportunities also reflects the equalitarian nature of societies in general. Table 1.1 provides an indication of the degree of inequality in the distribution of income within countries, by region and income groups. Central Asia, and Central and Eastern Europe which have less pronounced income inequalities, also have less skewed distributions of opportunities in access to postsecondary education. In these regions, students from the second and third richest quintiles are well represented in postsecondary education. This situation is also the product of decades of socialist policies which put the emphasis on quality

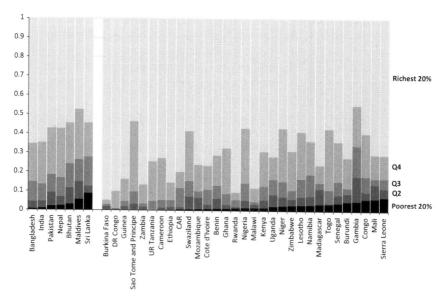

Figure 1.9 Distribution of the population aged 20–24 years old who has ever attended postsecondary education by wealth quintile in selected countries, 2011 or most recent year available

Notes: 1. Countries are ranked in an ascending order according to the share of individuals from the poorest quintile. 2. The data year for each country can be seen in Figure 1.10.

Sources: DHS and MICS, authors' calculations.

Table 1.1 Gini Index by income group and region, circa 2012

	Gini Index	StdDev	n
Arab States	36.04	(6.60)	4
Central and Eastern Europe	30.49	(5.05)	9
Central Asia	31.81	(5.50)	5
East Asia and the Pacific	38.06	(3.83)	8
Latin America and the Caribbean	50.08	(4.43)	14
South and West Asia	34.82	(3.87)	6
Sub-Saharan Africa	43.28	(8.41)	20
World	37.76	(8.62)	66
Low income	41.20	(8.27)	17
Lower middle income	39.83	(8.81)	23
Upper middle income	40.04	(9.89)	26

Note: The Gini Index of 0 represents perfect income equality, while an index of 100 implies perfect inequality.

Source: Poverty and Equity Database, World Bank (2015).

primary and secondary education for all (Salmi & Bassett, 2014), resulting in more students eligible for college or universities.

The disparity in postsecondary educational opportunities between the richest and the poorest is enormous. In one-third of the countries analyzed, the access rate (i.e. those who attended postsecondary educational institutions divided by the corresponding population) for the richest quintile households is over 20 times higher than that for the poorest and second poorest quintiles (Figure 1.10). In Tanzania in 2010, for instance, postsecondary education was almost exclusively reserved for students from the most affluent households. Financial burden was a prominent barrier for the poor, as costs incurred in applying for universities (e.g. application fees, travel costs, and other associated expenses) could go up to the equivalent of the current per capita GDP (World Bank, 2012b). As a result, the access rate for the poorest quintile households is over 500 times lower than that for those from the richest quintile. Similarly, in Ethiopia the access rate for the poorest quintile is over 100 times lower than that for the richest quintile; in Bangladesh, Cameroon, Haiti, and Togo, the difference in the access rate between the richest and the poorest is more than 60 times; and in Timor-Leste, Bolivia, and India, the difference is more than 30 times.

Have inequalities in access to postsecondary education been reduced over time?

Earlier studies found that many developed countries have managed to improve equality in access to postsecondary education over time, including Australia, France, Japan, Sweden, the United States, the United Kingdom, and the Republic of Korea (Koucký & Bartušek, 2013; Koucký et al., 2007, 2010; OECD, 2008; Santiago et al., 2008; Shavit et al., 2007). However, the relationship

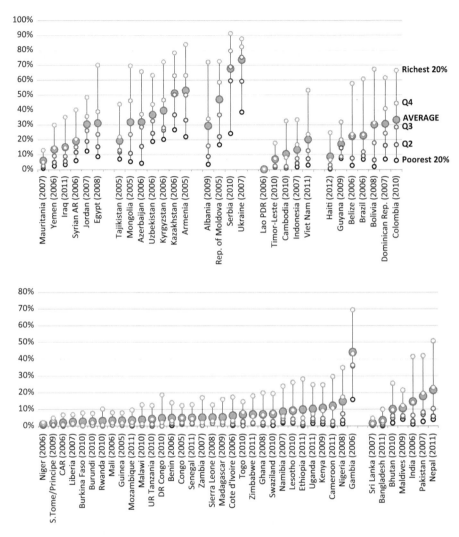

Figure 1.10 Share of the population aged 20–24 years old who has ever attended postsecondary education by household wealth quintile in selected countries, 2011 or most recent year available

Sources: DHS and MICS, authors' calculations.

between the expansion of postsecondary education systems and improvement in the equality of educational opportunity is not linear. In France and Germany, a sustained increase in access to postsecondary education has been accompanied by irregular progress in equity over the past 20 years (OECD, 2008). By contrast, only a handful of countries, such as Czech Republic and Hungary, have experienced an increase in inequality of opportunities between individuals with high socioeconomic background and those with low socioeconomic background (OECD, 2008).

Middle- and low-income countries tell a mixed story – the expansion of the postsecondary education system does not necessarily go hand in hand with the improvement of equity in access (e.g. see Darvas et al., 2014; Torche, 2010). Our analysis employed odds ratios to assess the relative chances for the rich and the poor to attend universities or colleges. The results reveal at least three distinct developments across countries. First, certain countries show expanded access to postsecondary education with a growing disparity in educational opportunity between the rich and the poor. For instance, in Bolivia, the access rate increased from 23.6% in 2005 to 30.1% in 2010 (Table 1.2). However, this increase has not benefitted the poorest quintile households; their chances of attending colleges or universities went from being 75 times lower to over 100 times lower than those from the richest quintile households. Likewise, in Haiti, the access rate has almost doubled, but inequity between the richest and the poorest grew by almost 70%. A similar development is also evident in Cameroon, Ethiopia, Kenya, Mozambique, and Nigeria.

At the other end of the spectrum, certain countries have successfully managed to increase both access and equity in postsecondary education. In Nepal, the access rate to postsecondary education increased by almost 4 times, from 4.5% in 2005 to 21.5% in 2010. During the same period of time, the relative advantage of young people from the poorest 20% of households improved by a quarter. Cambodia, Colombia, Guyana, Lesotho, and Togo exhibit a similar development, having made progress in terms of both access and equity. Finally, in countries including Indonesia and Burkina Faso, though not much progress was made in expanding access to postsecondary education, equality in access improved. In Indonesia, the access rate increased slightly from 11.8% to 13.3%, while the disparity between the rich and the poor in terms of the chances of attending postsecondary education reduced by a third over a decade.

While the odds ratio quantifies the difference in the outcome variable (i.e. the access rate) between top and bottom wealth quintiles, it does not take into account the situation faced by middle quintiles. We thus employed the Concentration Index[10] as a means to include all wealth quintiles to assess the magnitude of wealth-related inequalities. An index value close to one implies that educational opportunities tend to favour wealthy households, whereas an index value close to zero implies that educational opportunities are equally distributed across households by wealth quintiles.

Table 1.2 Share of the population aged 20–24 years-old who has ever attended postsecondary education and the odds ratio richest/poorest wealth quintile in selected countries, circa 2000, 2005, and 2010

	2000	2005	2010		2000	2005	2010	% of the population aged 20–24 who has ever attended postsecondary education (Q1 vs Q5 odds ratio)
Egypt	11.8 (42.1)	29.0 (23.5)	31.1 (24.5)	Burundi	3.1 (2.5)	#N/A	2.7 (10.5)	
Indonesia		#N/A	13.3 (28)	Burkina Faso	2.2 (52.3)	1.8 (28.1)	2.5 (27.2)	
Cambodia		5.2 (64)	10.4 (49.7)	Cameroon	5.2 (24.1)	6.4 (28.1)	12.0 (129)	
Bolivia		23.6 (75.2)	30.1 (103.1)	DR Congo		5.4 (22.7)	4.7 (28.1)	
Colombia		28.1 (40.2)	33.3 (30.7)	Ethiopia		2.5 (72.4)	9.8 (142.5)	
Guyana		14.1 (11.8)	17.1 (5.8)	Kenya	7.5 (12.2)	#N/A	10.7 (26.7)	
Haiti		4.7 (51.5)	8.7 (86.8)	Lesotho		4.6 (73.8)	9.2 (19.4)	
Bangladesh		3.5 (31.8)	3.4 (75.9)	Mozambique	1.1 (25)	2.1 (20)	3.4 (59.8)	
Nepal		4.5 (35.6)	21.5 (25.7)	Malawi		1.6 (28.5)	3.7 (41.3)	
				Nigeria	11.3 (17.8)	8.6 (35.5)	14.7 (37.7)	
				Rwanda		1.0 (23)	2.9 (44.8)	
				Senegal		2.7 (4.7)	4.9 (10.8)	
				Swaziland		7.6 (30)	7.1 (68.5)	
				Togo		4.9 (21.7)	6.9 (8)	

Notes: 1. Numbers in parentheses are odds ratios. An increase in the odds ratio over time indicates the chance of accessing postsecondary education (vs. not accessing it) improves faster for the richest 20% than for the poorest 20%. 2. Countries are selected with available data for at least two data points between 2000 and 2010. 3. The first row for each country is the % and the second is the odds ratio.

Sources: DHS and MICS, authors' calculations.

Table 1.3 Concentration Index in postsecondary education by income group and region

	Concentration		
	Index	StdDev	n
Arab States	0.38	(0.08)	7
Central and Eastern Europe	0.27	(0.14)	5
Central Asia	0.29	(0.08)	7
East Asia and the Pacific	0.48	(0.11)	6
Latin America and the Caribbean	0.41	(0.10)	7
South and West Asia	0.45	(0.07)	7
Sub-Saharan Africa	0.52	(0.09)	7
World	0.4	(0.12)	46
Low income	0.52	(0.10)	10
Lower middle income	0.38	(0.11)	24
Upper middle income	0.34	(0.10)	12

Note: An index value close to one implies that educational opportunities tend to favour wealthy households, whereas an index value close to zero implies that educational opportunities are equally distributed across households by wealth quintiles.

Sources: DHS and MICS, authors' calculations.

Wealth-related inequalities in access to postsecondary education differ between countries and regions. Such inequalities are particularly prominent in low-income countries, where the Concentration Index has a high value of 0.52, suggesting severe wealth-related inequalities (Table 1.3). Regarding regional differences, Central and Eastern Europe, as well as Central Asia, have low levels of wealth-related inequalities, while Sub-Saharan Africa has the highest.

Inequalities formed prior to postsecondary education

Focusing research on inequality in a single level of education ignores the process of accumulating disadvantage throughout the education cycle (Reisberg & Watson, 2010; Santiago et al., 2008). Inequalities of opportunity in access to postsecondary education are affected by policy decisions and other factors related to earlier schooling. This association is evident in Sweden and France, where reforms in secondary education have led to significant diminution of inequality at the postsecondary level (OECD, 2008). For this reason, the existing literature (Duru-Bellat, 2012; Shavit et al., 2007; Vallet, 2006) suggested the importance of a conditional analysis to disentangle inequalities generated in postsecondary education from those generated earlier in the educational cycle. Figure 1.11 shows Concentration Index values for each transition point in education. The disparities in wealth-related equality in attending a postsecondary educational institution are the worst in Rwanda, Malawi, Cambodia, and Lao PDR; in these countries, such inequalities have constantly increased, starting with primary education and continuing through postsecondary education. At the other end of the spectrum, in countries in Central Asia or Central and Eastern Europe, educational opportunities at the primary and secondary levels tend to be

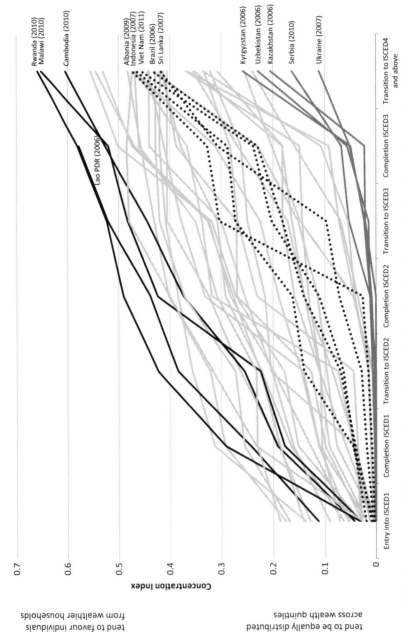

Figure 1.11 Concentration Index at each transition point in the education cycle in selected countries, 2011 or most recent year available

Sources: DHS and MICS, authors' calculations.

distributed equally between the rich and poor. In these countries, significant wealth-related inequalities do not form until the start of postsecondary education attendance.

How much does each transition point contribute to the inequalities observed at the point of postsecondary education attendance? Taking the example of Mauritania, by the end of primary education, the level of wealth-related inequality is already three-quarters of its final level (observed at postsecondary education attendance). The additional increase in this level during postsecondary education is relatively minimal (Table 1.4). This pattern is found in a number of low-income

Table 1.4 Contribution of various transition points in the education cycle to the inequalities observed at the entry to postsecondary education

	Acc. ISCED 1	Compl ISCED 1	Trans. ISCED 2	Compl. ISCED 2	Trans. ISCED 3	Compl. ISCED 3	Trans. ISCED 4+	Concentration Index at the entrance into post-secondary education
Maldives (2009)	2%	5%	16%	3%	77%	0%	−3%	0.33
Uganda (2011)	6%	43%	18%	18%	17%	1%	−2%	0.47
Mauritania (2007)	33%	42%	10%	7%	6%	3%	0%	0.42
Bhutan (2010)	39%	20%	4%	23%	11%	2%	0%	0.43
Yemen (2006)	32%	15%	18%	15%	20%	0%	0%	0.41
Pakistan (2007)	40%	9%	15%	7%	9%	21%	0%	0.44
Nepal (2011)	21%	16%	9%	12%	10%	32%	0%	0.44
Senegal (2011)	40%	9%	0%	16%	9%	23%	2%	0.47
Zimbabwe (2011)	1%	8%	13%	8%	10%	56%	4%	0.50
Morocco (2004)	36%	24%	6%	17%	6%	5%	5%	0.48
Mongolia (2005)	7%	17%	7%	35%	0%	28%	6%	0.41
Congo (2005)	4%	21%	7%	43%	10%	7%	7%	0.44
Iraq (2011)	15%	24%	14%	17%	4%	17%	9%	0.42
Haiti (2012)	6%	22%	5%	17%	8%	33%	10%	0.56
India (2006)	27%	8%	7%	10%	9%	28%	11%	0.53
Rwanda (2010)	5%	39%	20%	10%	5%	9%	12%	0.66
Cambodia (2010)	7%	25%	11%	20%	12%	14%	13%	0.60
Lao PDR (2006)	20%	22%	25%	9%	14%	10%		0.58
Bangladesh (2011)	10%	13%	13%	15%	8%	27%	14%	0.55
Syrian AR (2006)	8%	2%	2%	56%	11%	4%	15%	0.33
Turkey (2004)	10%	3%	51%	4%	10%	4%	19%	0.32
Malawi (2010)	5%	23%	7%	31%	9%	6%	20%	0.65

(Continued)

Table 1.4 (Continued)

	Acc. ISCED 1	Compl ISCED 1	Trans. ISCED 2	Compl. ISCED 2	Trans. ISCED 3	Compl. ISCED 3	Trans. ISCED 4+	Concentration Index at the entrance into post-secondary education
Rep. of Moldova (2005)	1%	1%	2%	15%	40%	21%	21%	0.25
Belize (2006)	3%	7%	6%	52%	4%	6%	22%	0.47
Dominican Rep. (2007)	5%	20%	5%	8%	9%	27%	24%	0.36
Sri Lanka (2007)	1%	3%	2%	10%	6%	50%	27%	0.42
Guyana (2009)	3%	12%	8%	13%	12%	25%	27%	0.26
Albania (2009)	1%	1%	1%	2%	58%	5%	31%	0.47
Kenya (2009)	5%	7%	5%	10%	18%	24%	31%	0.46
Timor-Leste (2010)	11%	13%	7%	9%	7%	18%	34%	0.47
Jordan (2007)	1%	1%	1%	12%	14%	37%	34%	0.24
Indonesia (2007)	1%	8%	20%	5%	24%	3%	38%	0.47
Philippines (2003)	1%	18%	17%	16%	7%	0%	41%	0.31
Bolivia (2008)	1%	17%	5%	4%	9%	18%	47%	0.43
Brazil (2006)	2%	7%	7%	17%	9%	11%	47%	0.43
Viet Nam (2011)	4%	5%	4%	10%	20%	8%	48%	0.46
Colombia (2010)	1%	10%	13%	15%	7%	5%	48%	0.35
Ukraine (2007)	1%	1%	1%	5%	12%	27%	54%	0.11
Serbia (2010)	1%	0%	2%	3%	25%	9%	59%	0.16
Egypt (2008)	19%	9%	1%	6%	3%	1%	60%	0.37
Tajikistan (2005)	2%	2%	1%	8%	4%	16%	68%	0.34
Armenia (2005)	1%	0%	0%	1%	25%	1%	72%	0.23
Azerbaijan (2006)	2%	1%	1%	8%	8%	5%	75%	0.37
Uzbekistan (2006)	0%	0%	0%	5%	1%	18%	75%	0.23
Kyrgyzstan (2006)	0%	0%	0%	3%	5%	10%	81%	0.26
Kazakhstan (2006)	0%	0%	0%	0%	10%	1%	89%	0.21
Average	10%	12%	8%	14%	13%	15%	29%	0.40

Notes: 1. The contribution is calculated by assessing the variation in the Concentration Index value at the given transition point as a percentage of the Concentration Index value at the point of attending postsecondary education. 2. The headings of the columns can be seen in X-axis labels in Figure 1.11.

Sources: DHS and MICS, authors' calculations.

countries with low access rates for postsecondary education, including Bhutan, Iraq, Mauritania, Mongolia, Nepal, Pakistan, Senegal, and Yemen.

By contrast, countries in Central Asia and Central and Eastern Europe demonstrate another pattern: wealth-related inequalities start to form significantly at the point of postsecondary education attendance. In Ukraine, for instance, more than half of the final level of inequality is generated at the entrance to postsecondary education. In Kazakhstan, Kyrgyzstan, and Uzbekistan, the proportion is even higher, at more than two-thirds.

Finally, a noticeable pattern is observed in Cambodia, Lao PDR, Malawi, and Rwanda, where wealth-related inequities are generated continually during the whole education cycle, and each transition point contributes around 10% to the level of inequality observed at access to postsecondary education. In Brazil, Colombia, Indonesia, and Viet Nam, which have some of the largest and most quickly expanding postsecondary systems, over 40% of the level of inequality is generated at the point of entering postsecondary education, which suggests that while access to postsecondary education has expanded, equality of educational opportunity has been sacrificed.

The need to look beyond access for greater equality

To achieve greater equality in education, ensuring equal access to postsecondary education is necessary but insufficient. Other factors and variables also require careful examination, including which subgroups of students attend different institutions and educational programmes, whether all students progress to completion, and the degree to which students' learning outcomes meet a certain standard. First, abundant evidence has shown that disadvantaged populations (e.g. first-generation colleges students, minority groups, and those with low socioeconomic status) tend to be enroled part time, and in two-year colleges or short-cycle postsecondary education programmes (Cahalan & Perna, 2015; Hauschildt et al., 2015). These programmes typically offer fewer opportunities for employment and further education afterwards. This pattern is particularly evident in countries where the expansion of the postsecondary education system has been accompanied by institutional diversification and stratification. In such systems, various types of postsecondary education institutions (e.g. research universities or first-tier universities, second-tier universities, and less selective colleges) have emerged in response to fast-growing demand, and most of the growth in enrolment has been absorbed by second-tier institutions (Shavit et al., 2007). Thus, while attendance at first-tier postsecondary education institutions enhances socioeconomic status and labour market outcomes (e.g. wages), previous research shows that such educational opportunities remain limited to the most affluent or elite groups, further maintaining social and employment-related inequalities (Duru-Bellat, 2012).

To ensure that students succeed in postsecondary education, research and educational planning must account for inequalities in not only access, but also retention, completion, and outcomes. Research shows consistently that once enrolled, students with low socioeconomic status are more likely to drop out and thus less likely to complete degrees, when compared with their peers with high socioeconomic status (Cahalan & Perna, 2015; Jerrim & Vignoles, 2015).

There is a broad consensus within the international community on the need to look beyond access to education in order to improve the educational opportunities and learning outcomes of all youth. The Sustainable Development Goal 4 of the United Nations' post 2015 development agenda aims to "ensure inclusive and equitable quality education and promote lifelong learning opportunities for all." This entails that by 2030, "all girls and boys complete free, equitable and quality primary and secondary education leading to relevant and effective learning outcomes" and that countries "ensure equal access for all women and men to affordable and quality technical, vocational and tertiary education, including university" (United Nations, 2015). While including the monitoring of learning outcomes in the upcoming global education agenda signals a major advancement by the international community, the new challenge is how to measure learning outcomes.

Implications and conclusions

The expansion of the postsecondary education systems in most countries has allowed more students to attend universities and colleges than ever before. While certain countries (e.g. Burkina Faso, Cambodia, Colombia, Guyana, Indonesia, Lesotho, Nepal, and Togo) have managed to improve both access and equity, many others (e.g. Bolivia, Cameroon, Ethiopia, Haiti, Kenya, Mozambique, and Nigeria) have expanded access with deterioration of equity. Therefore, not all young people have benefited equally from this expansion of opportunity. Socioeconomic factors, such as household wealth, affect individuals' chances of attending universities or colleges. Though the participation rate of students from low-wealth families has increased significantly over the past two decades, they have been, and still are, poorly served at all levels of education.

Some postsecondary education systems have expanded with improvement in equity. It remains, however, quite difficult to disentangle the mechanisms or causes behind such improvement: is it due to effective policies (or interventions) which aim at promoting equity, or simply due to the fact that the most advantaged socioeconomic groups have reached their "saturation point"?

On the one hand, many countries have implemented outreach and bridge interventions that aim at reducing barriers (in academic, aspirational, informational, and personal aspects) to participating in postsecondary education among underserved or underrepresented populations.[11] Previous research suggests that effective policies and practices generally include a combination of financial support with interventions to overcome non-financial barriers; early interventions; collaborative partnerships between postsecondary education providers, primary and secondary schools, and employers; and well-targeted programmes (e.g. see Salmi & Bassett, 2014; Savitz-Romer et al., 2010).

On the other hand, another explanation of improvement in equity could be found in social stratification theories. Reduced inequality in educational opportunity can be attributed to the fact that education expansion naturally leads to a decline in inequalities in access once the rate for the most advantaged socioeconomic groups reach "saturation point", as formulated as the hypothesis of Maximally Maintained Inequality (MMI) (Raftery & Hout, 1993; see also chapter by Thompson). At that point, these advantaged groups are also better placed to take up qualitatively better types of educational opportunity, as hypothesized in Effectively Maintained Inequality (EMI) (Lucas, 2001).

Tackling the inequalities of opportunity in postsecondary education is like hitting a moving target. The root of the issue can be found at any educational level depending on the stage of development of a country's education system and will move along as the system continues to expand. In particular, significant inequalities may have formed in earlier schooling prior to postsecondary education. As found in our analysis, in a number of lower-income countries (e.g. Bhutan, Iraq, Mauritania, Mongolia, Nepal, Pakistan, Senegal, and Yemen), a great disparity in educational opportunity between the rich and poor has already been generated in primary education attendance. Thus, focusing measures at the postsecondary level may not effectively solve the problem of inequality. It is necessary for educational planners to take an integrated approach to investigating disadvantages accumulated at each transition point between educational levels and to develop aligned policies and measures.

Postsecondary education policy and planning also needs to focus on student success (instead of access only) to ensure that students who attend universities and colleges successfully complete their education and attain relevant learning outcomes. Departing from the previous global education agenda stressing access to education, measuring students' learning outcomes has indeed become the centre of the agenda, as seen in the United Nations' post-2015 Sustainable Development Goals. This meaningful shift suggests that monitoring progress made in student success requires well-developed data management systems at the institutional, national, and international levels that capture students' background characteristics and their postsecondary education experience.

Notes

1 According to the International Standard Classification of Education (ISCED) 2011, postsecondary education includes both postsecondary non-tertiary education and tertiary education. Data from the UNESCO Institute for Statistics show that among 210,245,000 postsecondary enrolment in 2013, tertiary enrolment accounts for 95%. This chapter focuses on education at the tertiary level.

2 The gross enrolment ratio is the number of students enrolled in tertiary education programmes, regardless of age, to the school-age population corresponding to tertiary education and multiplying the result by 100. The standard age range of five years (starting from the official secondary school graduation age) is used as the denominator. Limitations occur when comparing the actual population coverage across countries due to the diversity of the duration of postsecondary

education programmes and the lack of typical ages of people who participate in postsecondary education.

3 Definitions of "public" and "private" vary by countries and regions. The UNESCO Institute for Statistics, OECD, and Eurostat (UOE) classify educational institutions into public or private depending on the body which has overall control of the institution and not according to which sector provides the majority of the funding. Figure 1.4 presents enrolment in private institutions, controlled and managed by non-governmental organizations (e.g. a church, a trade union or a business enterprise, foreign or international agency), or with governing boards consisting mostly of members not selected by a public agency.

4 Degree-seeking students, excluding those in short-term exchange programmes.

5 Public spending analyzed here includes funding for university research and development (R&D), which are not directly allocated to students, thus potentially overestimating overall public expenditure per tertiary student in countries with a high level of university R&D spending.

6 Japan and the Republic of Korea have recently implemented reforms to improve their student support systems.

7 See, for instance, Chapter 6 of Santiago, Tremblay, Basri, and Amal (2008) for a good review of issues and trends in equity at the tertiary level in developed countries.

8 For the purpose of this analysis, using ISCED 1997 or ISCED 2011 does not have any implications because noted differences between these two classifications start at the tertiary level.

9 The Education for All (EFA) movement is a global commitment, led by UNESCO, to provide quality basic education for all children, youth, and adults. At the World Education Forum in Dakar in 2000, 164 governments pledged to achieve EFA and identified six goals to be met by 2015.

10 For the methods of the Concentration Index of education, see p. 28 in UIS (2014).

11 Savitz-Romer, Rowan-Kenyon, Weilundemo, and Swan (2010) provide a good review of outreach and bridge programmes and policies that promote successful participation in baccalaureate programmes.

References

Altbach, P. G., Reisberg, L., & Rumbley, L. E. (2009). *Trends in Global Higher Education: Tracking an Academic Revolution.* A report prepared for the UNESCO 2009 World Conference on Higher Education. Retrieved from http://www.uis.unesco.org/Library/Documents/trends-global-higher-education-2009-world-conference-en.pdf

Breen, R., & Jonsson, J. O. (2005). Inequality of Opportunity in Comparative Perspective: Recent Research on Educational Attainment and Social Mobility. *Annual Review of Sociology, 31*, 223–243. doi: 10.1146/annurev.soc.31.041304.122232

Buckner, E. (2013). Access to Higher Education in Egypt: Examining Trends by University Sector. *Comparative Education Review, 57*(3), 527–552.

Cahalan, M., & Perna, L. (2015). *Indicators of Higher Education Equity in the United States.* 45 Year Trend Report. 2015 Revised Edition. Pell Institute for the Study of Opportunity in Higher Education. Retrieved from http://www.pellinstitute.org/downloads/publications-Indicators_of_Higher_Education_Equity_in_the_US_45_Year_Trend_Report.pdf

Chankseliani, M. (2013). Rural Disadvantage in Georgian Higher Education Admissions: A Mixed-Methods Study. *Comparative Education Review, 57*(3), 424–456. Special Issue on Fair Access to Higher Education. doi: 10.1086/670739

Chien, C.-L., & Chiteng, F. (2011). New Patterns in Student Mobility in the Southern African Development Community. In P. Kotecha (Ed.), *Building Regional Higher Education Capacity through Academic Mobility* (pp. 4–22). Retrieved from http://www.sarua.org/?q=publications/vol-3-no-1–2011-building-regional-higher-education-capacity-through-academic-mobilty

Darvas, P., Ballal, S., & Feda, K. (2014). Growth and Equity in Tertiary Education in Sub-Saharan Africa. *International Journal of African Higher Education, 1*(1), 85–137.

Dong, H., & Wan, X. (2012). Higher Education Tuition and Fees in China: Implications and Impacts on Affordability and Educational Equity. *Current Issues in Education, 15*(1). Retrieved from http://cie.asu.edu/ojs/index.php/cieatasu/article/view/811

Duru-Bellat, M. (2012). Appréhender les inégalités dans l'enseignement supérieur: spécificité des processus, spécificité des mesures? [Understanding inequality in higher education: specificity of the process, specific measures?] In Martin Benninghoff, Farinaz Fassa, Gaële Goastellec & Jean-Philippe Leresche (Eds.), *Inégalités Sociales et Enseignement Supérieur* [Social Inequality and Higher Education] (pp. 17–29). Brussels, Belgium: De Boeck.

European Commission (2014). Do Changes in Cost-Sharing Have an Impact on the Behaviour of Students and Higher Education Institutions? *Evidence from Nine Case Studies. Volume I: Comparative Report.* Retrieved from http://ec.europa.eu/education/library/study/2014/cost-sharing/comparative-report_en.pdf doi: 10.2766/74065

Fielden, J., & Cheng, K.-M. (2009). Financial Consideration. In S. Bjarnason, K.-M. Cheng, J. Fielden, M.-J. Lemaitre, D. Levy, & N.V. Varghese (Eds.), *A New Dynamic: Private Higher Education* (pp. 29–49). Paris: UNESCO.

Hauschildt, K., Gwosć, C., Netz, N., & Mishra, S. (2015). Social and Economic Conditions of Student Life in Europe. *Synopsis of Indicators, EUROSTUDENT V 2012–2015.* Retrieved from http://www.eurostudent.eu/download_files/documents/EVSynopsisofIndicators.pdf doi: 10.3278/6001920bw

Hout, M., & DiPrete, T. A. (2006). What We Have Learned: RC28's Contribution to Knowledge about Social Stratification. *Research in Social Stratification and Mobility, 24,* 1–20.

Jerrim, J., & Vignoles, A. (2015). University Access for Disadvantaged Children: A Comparison across Countries. *Higher Education, 70,* 903–921.

Johnstone, D. B. (1986). *Sharing the Costs of Higher Education: Student Financial Assistance in the United Kingdom, the Federal Republic of Germany, France, Sweden, and the United States.* New York: College Entrance Examination Board.

Johnstone, D. B. (2004). *The Economics and Politics of Cost Sharing in Higher Education: Comparative Perspectives.* Retrieved from http://gse.buffalo.edu/org/inthigheredfinance/files/Publications/foundation_papers/(2004)_The_Economics_and_Politics_of_Cost_Sharing_in_Higher_Education_Comparative_Perspectives.pdf

Johnstone, D. B. (2015). *Financing Higher Education: Worldwide Perspectives and Policy Options.* Retrieved from http://gse.buffalo.edu/org/inthigheredfinance/

Koucký, J., & Bartušek, A. (2013). Access to a Degree in Europe. Inequality in Tertiary Education Attainment 1950–2011 (Working Paper). Education Policy Centre: Charles University in Prague. Retrieved from http://www.strediskovzde lavacipolitiky.info/

Koucký, J., Bartušek, A., & Kovařovic, J. (2007). Inequality and Access to Tertiary Education: European Countries 1950–2005 (Working Paper). Education Policy Centre: Charles University in Prague. Retrieved from http://www.strediskovzde lavacipolitiky.info

Koucký, J., Bartušek, A., & Kovařovic, J. (2010). Who Gets a Degree? Access to Tertiary Education in Europe 1950–2009 (Working Paper). Education Policy Centre: Charles University in Prague. Retrieved from http://www.strediskovzdelavacipoli tiky.info

Lemaitre, M. J. (2009). Quality Assurance for Private Higher Education. In S. Bjarnason, K.-M. Cheng, J. Fielden, M.-J. Lemaitre, D. Levy & N.V. Varghese (Eds.), *A New Dynamic: Private Higher Education* (pp. 91–109). Paris: UNESCO.

Levy, D. C. (2009). Growth and Typology. In S. Bjarnason, K.-M. Cheng, J. Fielden, M.-J. Lemaitre, D. Levy & N.V. Varghese (Eds.), *A New Dynamic: Private Higher Education* (pp. 1–27). Paris: UNESCO.

Lucas, S. R. (2001). Effectively Maintained Inequality: Education Transitions, Track Mobility, and Social Background Effects. *American Journal of Sociology, 106,* 1642–1690.

Martin, M. (2010). Equity and Quality Assurance: Can They Come Together? An Introduction to the Problematic. In M. Martin (Ed.), *Equity and Quality Assurance: A Marriage of Two Minds* (pp. 23–36). Paris: UNESCO International Institute for Educational Planning. Retrieved from http://unesdoc.unesco.org/images/0018/001871/187184e.pdf

Nyahende, V. R. (2013). The Success of Students' Loans in Financing Higher Education in Tanzania. *Higher Education Studies, 3*(3), 47–61. doi:10.5539/hes.v3n3p47

O'Hara, S. (Ed.). (2010). *Higher Education in Africa: Equity, Access, Opportunity.* New York: Institute of International Education.

OECD (2008). *Higher Education to 2030.* Volume 1. Demography. Paris, France: Center for Educational Research and Innovation. Retrieved from http://www.oecd.org/education/skills-beyond-school/highereducationto2030vol1demography.htm#3

OECD (2014). *Education at a Glance 2014: OECD Indicators.* Paris: OECD.

Piketty, T. (2014). *Capital in the Twenty-First Century* (A. Goldhammer, Tran.). Cambridge, MA: Harvard University Press. (Reprinted from *Le Capital au XXIe siècle, 2013*, Paris: Éditions du Seuil).

Pillay, P. (2009). Challenges and Lessons from East and Southern Africa. In J. Knight (Ed.), *Financing Access and Equity in Higher Education* (pp. 19–39). Rotterdam/Taipei: Sense Publishers.

Raftery, A. E., & Hout, M. (1993). Maximally Maintained Inequality: Expansion, Reform, and Opportunity in Irish Education, 1921–75. *Sociology of Education, 66*(1), 41–62.

Reisberg, L., & Watson, D. (2010). Chapter 11: Access and Equity. In *Leadership for World-Class Universities: Challenges for Developing Countries.* Chestnut Hill: Boston College. Retrieved from http://www.gr.unicamp.br/ceav/revista/content/pdf/Watson_Reisberg-Access_and_Equity_en.pdf

Salmi, J., & Bassett, R. M. (2014). The Equity Imperative in Tertiary Education: Promoting Fairness and Efficiency. *International Review of Education, 60*, 361–377.
doi: 10.1007/s11159–013–9391-z

Santiago, P., Tremblay, K., Basri, E., & Amal, E. (Eds.). (2008). *Tertiary Education for the Knowledge Society. Special Features: Equity, Innovation, Labour Market,
Internationalisation*. Volume 2. Retrieved from http://www.oecd.org/edu/skills-
beyond-school/41266759.pdf

Savitz-Romer, M., Rowan-Kenyon, H., Weilundemo, M., & Swan, A. K. (2010). *Edu-
cational Pathways to Equity: A Review of Global Outreach and Bridge Practices and
Policies that Promote Successful Participation in Tertiary Education*. Washington,
DC: The World Bank. Retrieved from http://siteresources.worldbank.org/EDU
CATION/Resources/278200–1099079877269/547664–1099079956815/
547670–1128086743752/Jamil_OutreachandBridge2011_Nov.4.pdf

Shavit, Y., Arum, R., & Gamoran, A. (Eds.). (2007). *Stratification in Higher Education: A Comparative Study*. Stanford, CA: Stanford University Press.

Takyi-Amoako, E. (2008). Poverty Reduction and Gender Parity in Education:
An Alternative Approach. In S. Fennell & M. Arnot (Eds.), *Gender Education
and Equality in a Global Context Conceptual Frameworks and Policy Perspectives*
(pp. 196–210). London: Routledge.

Torche, F. (2010). Economic Crisis and Inequality of Educational Opportunity in
Latin America. *Sociology of Education, 83*(2), 85–110.

Trow, M. (2006). Reflections on the Transition from Elite to Mass to Universal
Access: Forms and Phases of Higher Education in Modern Societies since WWII.
In J. J. F. Forest & P. G. Altbach (Eds.), *International Handbook of Higher Educa-
tion* (pp. 243–280). Dordrecht: Springer.

UNESCO Institute for Statistics (UIS) (2010). *Global Education Digest 2010: Comparing Education Statistics across the World*. Montreal: UNESCO Institute for Statistics. http://www.uis.unesco.org/Library/Documents/GED_2010_EN.pdf

UNESCO Institute for Statistics (UIS) (2014). *Higher Education in Asia: Expanding
Out, Expanding Up. The Rise of Graduate Education and University Research*. Retrieved
from   http://www.uis.unesco.org/Library/Documents/higher-education-asia-
graduate-university-research-2014-en.pdf

UNESCO Institute for Statistics (UIS) (2015a). *UIS Data Centre, Regional
and Country Profile*. Retrieved May 2015 from http://www.uis.unesco.org/
DataCentre/Pages/regions

UNESCO Institute for Statistics (UIS) (2015b). *UIS Data Centre*. Retrieved
May 2015 from http://www.uis.unesco.org/datacentre

UNESCO Institute for Statistics (UIS) (2015c). *Incheon Declaration Education
2030: Towards Inclusive and Equitable Quality Education and Lifelong Learning
for All*. Retrieved from http://www.uis.unesco.org/Education/Documents/
education_2030_incheon_declaration_en.pdf

UNESCO/OECD/Eurostat (2014). *UOE Data Collection on Formal Education.
Manual on Concepts, Definitions and Classifications*. Retrieved from http://www.uis.
unesco.org/UISQuestionnaires/Documents/UOE2014manual_05092014.docx

United Nations (1948). *Universal Declaration of Human Rights*. Retrieved from
http://www.un.org/en/documents/udhr/

United Nations (1966). *International Covenant on Economic, Social and Cultural
Rights*. Retrieved from http://www.ohchr.org/EN/ProfessionalInterest/Pages/
CESCR.aspx

United Nations (2014). *Report of the Special Rapporteur on the Right to Education.* Retrieved from http://www.right-to-education.org/sites/right-to-education. org/files/resource-attachments/UNSR_Report_to_UNGA_Privatisation_2014. pdf

United Nations (2015). *Sustainable Development Goals. Goal 4 targets.* Retrieved from http://www.un.org/sustainabledevelopment/education/

Vallet, L.-A. (2006). *What Can We Do to Improve the Education of Children from Disadvantaged Backgrounds?* Retrieved from http://www.pass.va/content/dam/ scienzesociali/pdf/es7/es7-vallet.pdf

Varghese, N. V. (Ed.). (2006). *Growth and Expansion of Private Higher Education in Africa.* Paris: UNESCO International Institute for Educational Planning.

Wawire, V., Elarabi, N., & Mwanzi, H. (2010). Higher Education Access and Retention Opportunities for Students with Disabilities: Strategies and Experiences from Selected Public Universities in Egypt and Kenya. In S. O'Hara (Ed.), *Higher Education in Africa: Equity, Access, Opportunity* (pp. 117–134). New York: Institute of International Education.

World Bank (2012a). *Putting Higher Education to Work: Skills and Research for Growth in East Asia.* Retrieved from http://siteresources.worldbank.org/EASTASIAPA-CIFICEXT/Resources/226300-1279680449418/7267211-1318449387306/ EAP_higher_education_fullreport.pdf

World Bank (2012b). *Increasing Access to Higher Education for the Poor in Tanzania.* Retrieved from http://www.worldbank.org/en/news/feature/2012/10/24/ increasing-access-to-higher-education-for-the-poor-in-tanzania

World Bank (2015). *Poverty and Equity Data.* Retrieved from http://povertydata. worldbank.org/poverty/home/

Chapter 2

The stratification of opportunity in high participation systems (HPS) of higher education

Simon Marginson

Introduction

As measured by UNESCO and discussed in Chapter 1, the worldwide Gross Tertiary Enrolment Rate (GTER) is increasing very rapidly by historical standards, at 1 per cent a year, and now constitutes one third of the nominal school leaver age group. Participation is expanding significantly in most countries, whatever the level of their GTERs. The tendency towards high participation systems (HPS) of higher education, systems in which the GTER exceeds 50 per cent, has spread from the high-income and post-Soviet zones to include most of the emerging ('developing') countries with GDP per capita of $5,000 or more. The growth of higher education is accompanied by economic modernisation, but economic demand is not sufficiently consistent to explain the very widespread expansion of educational participation, which is occurring in countries with very different rates of growth and industry-skill profiles (Marginson 2016a). Rather, as suggested by Trow (1973) in his essay on the transition from elite to mass to universal systems, the ongoing dynamism of higher education is powered by the ambitions of families for social position and of students for self-realisation. These ambitions have no limit and feed on themselves. As participation grows it becomes mandatory for all middle-class families to enrol, for states to respond to the demand for opportunities and for participation to extend further into the urban population. Over time social demand accumulates and tends towards the universal, and higher education becomes ubiquitous.

HPS are more socially inclusive than elite higher education, by definition. But does high participation education provide all persons with equal educational opportunity? Does it render countries more open and mobile, more socially and economically equal? States and higher education institutions (HEIs) together structure HPS, stratifying the forms of provision and their cost and value. In the interaction between on one hand structural forms and regulatory processes, and on the other hand the active agency of families – who have little scope to directly influence forms of educational differentiation, but work the structures as well as they can in their own interest – higher education sifts and sorts the population.

Its role in social allocation, which varies from HPS to HPS, and is affected by patterns of equality/inequality in the larger society, determines the extent to which higher education renders society more equal, facilitating upward social mobility, or tends to reproduce pre-existing social inequalities. This chapter reviews the patterning of social outcomes in HPS, drawing on recent research into social and educational stratification, and social, economic and educational inequalities. It focuses on forms of educational differentiation and the implications for social equality of opportunity.

Social inclusion and stratification

Not just education but prior social inequalities determine whether people from low-income families, remote locations or excluded minorities can improve their social circumstances. Table 2.1, drawn from Thomas Piketty's *Capital in the Twenty-first Century* (2014) indicates the wide variations in place and time in the extent of income inequality. Scandinavian societies in the 1970s/1980s were more enabling of upward social mobility than is the highly unequal United States today, and this affect the potentials of education.

In education itself, not all participation is of equal value. Higher education provides a stratified structure of opportunity, from elite universities and high status degrees to the much larger number of places in mass education with uncertain outcomes. Students from affluent families often dominate the high value positions within higher education. Populations are socially stratified, HPS higher education is stratified and outcomes are stratified. The objective of equity strategy is to modify the extent to which these forms of stratification reproduce each other, opening up the potential for upward social mobility through the HPS. Countries vary. The design of the HPS makes a difference.

Table 2.1 Income shares of top 1 per cent and bottom 50 per cent, various years

	Europe 1910 High inequality	Scandinavia 1970s/1980s Low inequality	Europe 2010 Medium inequality	USA 2010 High inequality
TOP 1%				
Share of labour income	6%	5%	7%	12%
Share of capital income	50%	20%	25%	35%
Share of total income	20%	7%	10%	20%
BOTTOM 50%				
Share of labour income	n.a.	35%	30%	20%
Share of capital income	5%	10%	5%	5%
Share of total income	20%	30%	25%	20%

Source: Adapted by the author from data in Piketty (2014), pp. 247–249.

Family background and educational stratification

In HPS the principal intrinsic limit to social equality of opportunity is the persistence of irreducible differences between families in economic, social and cultural resources. Policy can partly compensate for economic differences but cannot eliminate the potency of the family in cultural capital and social networks (Mountford-Zimdars and Sabbagh 2013). In a comparison of 11 European countries, Triventi (2013a) finds that 'individuals with better educated parents have a higher probability of attaining a degree from a top institution, of a higher standard, and with better occupational returns' (p. 499). In another four-nation study he notes that the effects of social background on graduates' occupational outcomes vary by country in the extent of educational expansion, the social selectivity of education, the connections between education and the labour market, and 'the degree of institutional stratification in higher education' (Triventi 2013b, pp. 47–48).

> [S]tratification of higher education refers to the degree of variation in selectivity, quality/prestige and labour market value of different courses, fields of study and institutions. All else being equal, the higher is the stratification of higher education, the more important is the role of social background in the occupational attainment process.
>
> (Triventi 2013b, pp. 48–49)

The HPS trend increases the pool of graduates but does not increase the number of high value social outcomes that graduates can reach, which is determined by relations of social power and equality/inequality beyond education. Expansion exacerbates social competition in education (Arum et al. 2007, pp. 7–8) and this in turn enhances the effects of prior social inequalities. 'All else being equal, countries with a mass higher education system may be characterised by stronger competition among graduates in the transition to the labour market and, thus, by a larger effect of social background on occupational returns' (Triventi 2013b, p. 48). The trend to HPS, which enhances equity as inclusion, also increases the regressive effects of family background on educational and social outcomes. Thus research on the growth of participation finds that as systems expand, class inequalities in access to elite higher education and career outcomes are not reduced (Arum et al. 2007, p. 3). Stratification effects trump the equalisation of educational quantity through growth, except in unusual times of high social mobility such as the 1960s/1970s in the US (Marginson 2016b). 'Qualitative differentiation replaces inequalities in the quantity of the education obtained' (Arum et al. 2007, p. 4). The national cases in *Stratification in Higher Education* (Shavit et al. 2007) demonstrate that as higher education expands, affluent families dominate the elite institutions. Newly participating social layers are largely confined to the sub-elite institutions where participation alone is not enough to generate strong social outcomes.

Why does educational stratification tend to reinforce prior social inequalities, and why does expansion enhance the effects of social background, or make no difference? Here the point about the growth of HPS being driven by family aspirations for social position, rather than by the state responding to the needs of the economy, gains significance. HPS are populated by families that apply active agency to the contest for educational and social success, at every stage. Families with financial, social, cultural or political capitals bring those capitals to bear on education and continue to do so in the transition to work and beyond (Borgen 2015). Oxfam refers to 'opportunity hoarding', whereby 'social disparities become permanent'. Privileged groups 'take control of valuable resources and assets for their benefit', such as 'access to quality education' (Oxfam 2014, p. 20). The formal stratification of opportunities on the basis of institutional hierarchies and/or financial barriers provides points of purchase for family strategies. Whenever there is a hierarchy of value, families with prior social advantages are best placed to compete for scarce places or pathways that confer the greatest positional advantages (Lucas 2001, 2009; Triventi 2013b, p. 47). HPS are regulated by the degree and type of selectivity and closure, within a common social regime of openness and inclusion. Social competition at the key points of transition and selection – entry to higher education, entry to professions and occupations – enables a fine-grained differentiation of the population, maximising scope for stratified family capacities and strategic acumen.

Nevertheless, the institutional reproduction of prior social inequalities is punctuated by moments (more of them in some systems than others) when state policy, educational practices and student effort broaden the potential for upward mobility via education.

Stratification between and within institutions

The mechanisms of social and educational stratification are now examined more closely.

Schooling

Some nations pursue a comprehensive approach to schooling with low stratification of quality. Affluent families in the United Kingdom (UK) can invest in high fee private schools, which are successful in accessing selective universities. Spending per student is three times that in state schools (Cheung and Egerton 2007, p. 218; Dorling 2014, p. 28 and pp. 40–41). Boliver (2011, 2013) traces unequal social access to selective UK universities since the 1960s. Applicants for leading Russell Group universities from state schools, and from black and South Asian ethnic backgrounds, 'were much less likely to receive offers of admission from Russell Group universities, in comparison with their equivalently qualified peers from private schools and the White ethnic group' (Boliver 2013, pp. 344–345). Private school students had an advantage equivalent to 'an additional B-grade A-level' over state school students with the same marked achievement (p. 358).

Fields of study in higher education

In HPS in which the institutional hierarchy is relatively 'flat', field of study can be more determining than institution attended of graduate earnings and status. Overall, field of study is more likely than institution to be associated with earnings differentials, especially in early years after graduation, while institutional prestige is more likely to be associated with occupational status and the likelihood of moving into managerial functions (e.g. Triventi 2013b, pp. 54–57; Hu and Vargas 2015), which may translate into later earnings advantages (Roksa and Levey 2010). Wolniak and colleagues (2008) suggest that the STEM disciplines reinforce the effects of prior family backgrounds, while business and education degrees provide more scope to change inherited inequalities (p. 135). Borgen (2015, p. 36) notes that when a high proportion of credentials are generic without clear vocational pathways, the hierarchy of institutions is more important as a distinguishing factor in driving family positional strategies. Significantly, this finding applies to both the market-driven, mixed funded and stratified US system, and the publicly financed and 'flatter' Norwegian system.

Vertical and horizontal diversity

In contrast with schooling, in higher education some institutional stratification is inevitable, even in Nordic societies. Concentrations of top researchers, and student places in high status professional programmes, are scarce by nature. Bourdieu (1988) sees higher education systems as structured on a binary basis between selective institutions with high prestige that ration their places, and demand-driven mass institutions without prestige that build volume in order to maximise their revenues and social presence. Sitting between is a layer of ambiguous middle institutions, aspiring to the elite but lacking status and resources. States can use parcels of funding, the location of specific programmes or mission designations to expand the size of this group; for example spreading middle level value by designating them as research universities.

National HPS vary in the 'steepness' of vertical stratification, and the extent to which horizontal distinctions based on institutional mission also function as vertical distinctions of status and resources. Emerging mass higher education often takes a binary form, partly to protect the mission (and clientele) of the academic universities. The second sector may emphasise technical-vocational education related to manufacturing, as in Germany, Korea or Taiwan; or middle professions such as teaching and/or local employment, as in the Netherlands. System expansion is also associated with a counter-tendency to academic drift whereby growing second sectors seek to widen their horizons by acquiring a research role. In HPS vertical diversity tends to trump horizontal diversity: given a choice, most institutions will move beyond the bounds of a non-research mission to the extent necessary to upgrade status. The movement of erstwhile second sectors into research helped to trigger the dissolution of binary systems in Australia (1988) and the UK (1992). At present there are unresolved pressures for upward drift in the Netherlands. On the other hand policy, regulation and custom may retain a stable division of labour, as in Germany and the California State University (CSU) campuses. The US CSUs are modeled as a ladder to the University of California (UC). German binary diversity is more horizontal. The *fachhochschulen* tend to have strong labour market outcomes (Teichler 2009).

If they choose, states can manage HPS on the basis of near equality of resources and a common mission, blurring the tendency to stratification of value by distributing capacity on a broad basis. Egalitarian system design has shaped universities in the Nordic world, Belgium, the Netherlands and the German-speaking countries. All sustain a rough equality in graduate standing and research missions, though there is a moderate informal prestige hierarchy. However, except for Switzerland none have the world' top 30 universities (ARWU 2015). Here egalitarian HPS design conflicts with the logic of 'World-Class Universities', concentrations of global research strength designed to attract status, academic migrants and industry innovation (Altbach and Salmi 2011; Hazelkorn 2011; Marginson 2011). Germany's Excellence Initiative and the state-induced mergers in Denmark (Salmi 2009) were important departures from egalitarian HPS design. The WCU model is especially attractive to emerging countries that need to link to the world research system as soon as possible. Given the high investment required, there is a danger that WCU building will associate with neglect of mass higher education, or encourage strategies of expanding provision using Massive Open Online Courses (MOOCs) and low-cost online distance learning, or for-profit sectors.

Public/private diversity

Private sectors have more than one implication for social stratification. The US Ivy League universities are engines of social advantage. Soares (2007) finds that in 1988–2000, 64 per cent of the students of Tier 1 institutions were from the top 10 per cent American families in income (p. 167). This social composition reflects not just academic competition but high tuition and the use of supplementary entry criteria in the form of middle-class cultural capital, for example applicants' records in music, elite sports and 'leadership'. Both modes of differentiation, finance and bio, are strategic opportunities for affluent families. The public sector UC Berkeley is equally selective in academic terms but runs a progressive tuition policy based on family income. Entry is free for 45 per cent of students. Only 28 per cent are from top 10 per cent of households in income terms (Soares 2007, pp. 166–167; Douglass 2013, pp. 4–5). However, it is Ivy League degrees, not UC Berkeley degrees, that provide graduate entry into elite American firms in law, financing and business services (Rivera 2011, 2015).

The private sector is positioned differently outside the US. Most HPS—Korea and the Philippines are partial exceptions – have few elite private institutions. National research universities are the focus of family ambition. Where there are large private sectors, as in Brazil, they provide mass education that expands freely in response to social demand without the constraint of public fiscal cost. While there are some rapidly growing public sectors, as in China, on average sectoral diversification facilitates the growth rate of HPS. However, mass private sectors carry problems of low and variable quality, especially for-profit colleges, which spend less of their revenue on teaching, and whose degrees lack potency in the labour market as the US case shows (Mettler 2014, pp. 87–110). There are also quality problems in mass public sectors in the many countries that underfund them, but there at least states can readily intervene, and they can be held to public account.

Effects of competition

As suggested, in competitive HPS stratification tends to 'stretch' over time. Davies and Zarifa (2012) use Gini coefficients, Lorenz curves and other measures of inequality to compare the level of stratification in financial resources across four-year institutions in Canada and the US over 1971 to 2006 (p. 143). There is a moderate to strong association between resource concentration and selectivity. In both nations, 'policy-makers are urging universities to remake themselves into highly differentiated, competitive, responsive, and entrepreneurial hubs of activity', with 'greater competittion for revenue, whether in the form of tuition-paying clients, fund-raising, or research grants, and . . . less bountiful and reliable government support' (pp. 144–145). Competition for status and resources is subject to cumulative advantage: strong institutions improve their relative position over time. 'Universities that are already older, established and wealthy enter new competitions for resources with prominent alumni networks, sizeable endowments, favorable locations, and strategic corporate ties' (p. 145). The US HPS is 'strikingly more stratified' than the Canadian in financial terms, and 'dominated by a small number of super-resourced, elite institutions that are highly distinct from the masses' and 'have pulled away from the pack' (p. 150 and 154). However, in both HPS stratification has notably increased, especially in the last decade.

Stratified structure and self-stratified agency

Family agency is not constant over time, or between countries, or between socioeconomic status (SES) groups. Confronted by the stratified structure of provision, families respond in a differentiated fashion that reflects their varying circumstances. Whereas upper-middle class families may put great effort into achieving the highest possible position within the HPS, low SES and remote students are less likely to nurture high ambitions (Hoxby and Avery 2013), more likely to be deterred by cost (Roksa et al. 2007; Mettler 2014), more likely to focus on secure and predictable employment-related paths rather than diffuse intellectual forma-tion (Thomsen et al. 2013), more likely to believe they lack the cultural capital to survive and perform at university (Thomsen et al. 2013) and less familiar with performance and application strategies (Hoxby and Avery 2013).

It is important to recognize that self-stratification happens even in free Nordic HPS (Thomsen et al. 2013, p. 457 and pp. 471–474) as well as in the more hier-archical American system. However, all else being equal, highly vertically strati-fied HPS with price barriers tend to evoke larger self-stratification effects, and are more likely to empty out degree completion altogether in the bottom SES layers (Stiglitz 2013). In 2012 in the United States the Gross Tertiary Enrolment Ratio was 94.3 per cent, while the Gross Graduation Ratio at degree level was only 40.1 per cent (UNESCO 2015). Most people in the bottom half of the income dis-tribution graduate below degree level, drop out or never enroll (Mettler 2014). The gap between participation and degrees increased from 41.0 per cent in 1999 to 54.2 per cent in 2012 (UNESCO 2015), while income inequality was worsen-ing (Saez 2013). Self-stratification will now be examined more closely.

'Under-matching' in applications

In a census-level study of all 2008 applicants to US higher education Hoxby and Avery (2013) track the applications of 'high-achieving' school students, ranked in the top 4 per cent by SAT scores and grade point averages (p. 2). These stu-dents number 25,000–35,000 each year. In 2008, 17 per cent were in the bottom family income quartile (pp. 14–15). The vast majority of these low-income high achievers did not apply to a selective college, though selective colleges charged lower tuition than many non-selective colleges, due to financial aid (pp. 5–6). The researchers found the application behavior of most of the low-income high achiev-ers differed greatly from that of their high-income counterparts. High-income high achievers followed advice to apply to a mix of highly selective and less selec-tive colleges. Low-income high achievers opted for uniformly safe choices. Typi-cally they were from districts too small to support selective public high schools or a mass of fellow high achievers, and/or were unlikely to encounter a teacher, counselor or student who had attended a selective college.

Hoxby's and Avery's finding on the 'under-matching' of poor and remote students are replicated in Chankseliani's (2013) study of rural students in Geor-gia. 'Of two applicants with the same general aptitude', the odds for an appli-cant from a mountainous village to apply to a least prestigious institution rather than a most prestigious one' are about '12 times as high as the odds for an applicant from the capital' (pp. 438–439). In the UK Boliver (2013) finds that 'applicants from lower class backgrounds and from state schools remained much less likely to apply to Russell Group universities than their comparably qualified counterparts from higher class backgrounds and private schools' (p. 344). Boliver refers to widespread perceptions that prestige universities are for the privately educated white upper middle class (p. 347). When education is seen to belong to someone else, family aspirations and agency are diminished (Wilkinson and Pickett 2010, p. 113).

Tuition-based stratification

In HPS with tuition barriers the external price structure is internalised as self-stratification, accentuating prior social differences and shaping access, field of study and completion (Arum et al. 2007, pp. 24–25). Free or low tuition, as in most of Northwest and Central Europe, eliminates this form of stratification. When tuition is managed on the basis of income-contingent loans, as in Australia and the UK, the effects in self-stratification are minimised. Students do not pay at enrolment, and only discharge the loan as increased tax obligations when their earnings exceed the repayment threshold. This greatly reduces the disincentive effects of tuition, and its socio-economic bias, except for earning students who pay in the year of study (Callender 2013; Chapman 2014). This facility is not available in the US. The consequences for American equality are explored in a large body of research and commentary on tuition barriers.

Mettler (2014) notes that whereas in 1971 the average cost of attending four-year public college was 42 per cent of the income of bottom quintile families, by 2011 the figure was 114 per cent. For top income quintile families that average cost rose from 6 to 9 per cent of income (p. 121). In many community colleges families meet more than half the costs (p. 122) though the qualifications are often marginal (Roksa et al. 2007; Hansen 2011). Federal PELL grants cover a declining share of tuition (PELL Institute 2015, pp. 19–20). The US GTER hovers around 90 per cent but there is steep stratification inside this. In 2013, 77 per cent of persons in the top family income quartile completed a degree by age 24 years, almost double the 40 per cent in 1970. In the bottom quartile the graduation rate rose from 6 to 9 per cent between 1970 and 2013. In the second bottom quartile it rose from 11 to 17 per cent (p. 31). Less than 40 per cent had a degree by 24 years. Others dropped out, had two-year diplomas of low value or gained degrees slowly. US higher education 'stratifies people by income group rather than providing them with ladders of opportunity' (Mettler 2014, p. 8). Financial disincentives and self-stratification in the US are compounded by the regressive character of taxation, compared to most countries (Smeeding 2005). OECD data on for 2012, using Gini coefficients, show that while in most countries state taxes and transfers reduced market-generated income inequality by 35–45 per cent, in the US the effect was only 24 per cent, and Mexico 3 per cent (OECD 2015).

The highly unequal social outcomes of education in the US are unsurprising. As suggested, they parallel the extreme inequality of income distribution in the US (Table 2.1) and are both produced by that inequality and contribute to its reproduction. When social inequality is very high, people from low SES backgrounds invest less in education and skills. They have less capacity to meet educational costs, less prospect of entering high value institutions, and less prospect of turning degrees into careers. Over the generations their relative position deteriorates (OECD 2014b, p. 12). The comparison by Cingano (2014) across the OECD countries suggests that a rise in income inequality of 6 Gini points reduces the probability of individuals with parents of low educational background being in tertiary education by 4 percentage points. However, 'inequality does not have any impact on the probability of graduating from tertiary education in the case of individuals with medium or high family background' (pp. 24–26).

Social mobility and higher education

What then is the extent of social mobility in different countries and what role does higher education play? Corak (2012) measures social mobility in terms of the 'intergenerational elasticity in earnings' (IEE), the percentage difference in earnings in the child's generation associated with the percentage difference in the parent generation.

> An intergenerational elasticity in earnings of 0.6 tells us that if one father makes 100 per cent more than another then the son of the high income father will, as an adult, earn 60 per cent more than the son of the relatively lower income father.
>
> (p. 2)

Denmark, Norway and Finland each have an IEE of less than 0.20. Canada is at 0.18. Germany 0.32, France 0.41. The US is at 0.47, indicating relatively low social mobility (p. 10). Corak (2012) plots OECD nations' Gini coefficients against their IEEs. The line of best fit indicates a clear association between (a) high income inequality, and (b) high IEE, meaning relatively low social mobility. However, these data do not clarify the role of higher education in social mobility.

The OECD measures intergenerational educational mobility by comparing the odds of enrolling in tertiary education for two groups: those with at least one parent who attended tertiary education, and those neither of whose parents attended tertiary education. Americans from tertiary educated families were 6.8 times more likely to access tertiary education than those from non-tertiary families. England (6.3) was similar. Scandinavia ranged from Finland (1.4) to Denmark (3.0). In South Korea mobility was 1.1 (OECD 2014a, p. 93). But these data on educational mobility are not linked to income or occupational status outcomes. Table 2.2 summarises the OECD and Corak (2012) data.

There is no study that establishes the role of higher education in social mobility. All that can be stated with confidence is that this role varies by country; and the societies with egalitarian income distribution and high social mobility have HPS of higher education, low investment of private funding to secure positional advantage, and school systems with high and distributed learning achievement (OECD 2014c). This includes the Nordic countries, Benelux, Canada and South Korea. In contrast, the US has an exceptionally unequal income structure

Table 2.2 Income inequality (2012), two indicators of social mobility (2000s and 2012), and spending on tertiary education (2011), OECD countries with available data

	Gini income coefficient after tax/ transfers (2012)	Ratio of post-tax income at 90/10 percentiles (2012)	Social mobility: intergenerational elasticity in earnings (2000s)	Educational mobility: generational odds ratios (2012)	Private funding of tertiary education as a % of GDP (2011)
					%
Denmark	0.249	2.8	0.15	3.0	0.1
Slovak Republic	0.250	3.2	n.a.	n.a.	0.2
Norway	0.253	3.0	0.17	2.0	0.1
Czech Republic	0.256	3.0	n.a.	n.a.	0.3
Finland	0.260	3.1	0.18	1.4	0.1
Sweden	0.274	3.3	0.27	2.3	0.2
Austria	0.276	3.5	n.a.	5.1	0.1
Netherlands	0.281	3.3	n.a.	2.8	0.5
Switzerland	0.285	3.5	n.a.	n.a.	n.a.
Germany	0.289	3.5	0.32	5.1	0.2
Poland	0.298	3.9	n.a.	9.5	0.3
Ireland	0.304	3.8	n.a.	3.3	0.3
France	0.306	3.6	0.41	6.0	0.2
South Korea	0.307	n.a.	n.a.	1.1	1.9
Canada	0.315	4.2	0.19	2.6	1.2
Australia	0.326	4.4	0.26	4.3	0.9
Italy	0.327	4.4	0.50	9.5	0.2
Spain	0.335	4.9	0.40	3.9	0.3
Estonia	0.338	4.7	n.a.	4.7	0.3
United Kingdom	0.350	4.2	0.50	6.4*	0.3
United States	0.390	6.2	0.47	6.8	1.8
Japan	n.a.	n.a.	0.34	5.1	1.0
Chile	n.a.	n.a.	0.52	n.a.	1.7

n.a. = data not available

* England and Northern Ireland only

IIE = Intergenerational Elasticity in Earnings. 'For example, an intergenerational elasticity in earnings of 0.6 tells us that if one father makes 100 per cent more than another then the son of the high income father will, as an adult, earn 60 per cent more than the son of the relatively lower income father'. These data are not specifically dated but are from the 2000s (Corak 2012, p. 2).

'Odds ratios' compare the odds of enrolling in tertiary education for two groups of 20- to 34-year-olds—those with at least one parent who attended tertiary education (the numerator) and those neither of whose parents attended (the denominator) (OECD 2014a, p. 93).

Sources: Table prepared by author. Data from OECD (2014a, p. 93 and p. 232); OECD (2015) and Corak (2012).

(Table 2.2, OECD 2014b; Piketty 2014; Saez 2013), low social mobility, and weak school learning achievement stratified by social background, plus very stratified higher education, high private sector tuition fees and growing public sector fees, and an HPS with high entry but a weaker and social skewed pattern of achievement.

National variations

There are structural variations in the high social mobility countries. Nordic HPS have fairly 'flat' stratification, high public spending and no tuition. Canadian stratification and tuition are higher than in Europe but more modest than in the US. There is high spending both public and private, while public policy emphasises citizen rights as in Europe. In South Korea high social mobility (Table 2.2) is joined to a stratified HPS with emphasis on elite universities and high private costs in other institutions. The tendency of the highly stratified HPS to exacerbate unequal social outcomes is cushioned by Korean equality in income determination and regional growth (Lee et al. 2012), a school system that ensures all graduates have advanced literacy, and East Asian not European/American educational culture (Marginson 2013). The results of the OECD (2014c) Programme of International Student Assessment show that all East Asian societies place exceptional value on learning; and the desire for educational success runs so deep in low SES families that private costs stratify ambition, participation and completion less than is the case in Europe and the US.

Conclusions

The larger social inclusion brought about by growth in participation is not enough in itself to secure a broadening of lifetime opportunities. What matters is the capacity of an HPS to contribute to expanded social mobility. Higher education systems located in societies in which mobility is relatively high have a number of common features:

1   Funding is largely from public sources. If tuition fees are charged, income contingent loans are used and there is extra support for under-participating social groups. (The exception is higher fee higher education in East Asia, where strong state supervision ensures that private investment in higher education is less liable to compromise the merit principle.)
2   Any private sector provision is closely regulated to ensure social inclusion and maintain quality of learning.
3   Institutional stratification is modest. Research and professional training functions are broadly distributed. WCU development may be necessary (or inevitable), to strengthen national science and elevate university prestige but WCUs are coupled with policies that ensure a strong second tier and healthy

mass higher education. (East Asia is again a partial exception – the top HEIs enjoy great prestige – but a feature of Korea and Taiwan is the strength of second tier and vocational HEIs.)

4   HEIs and state authorities value rigorous learning and ensure that autonomous institutions, and assessment and selection, are free from manipulation by powerful families (directly or via the state) seeking competitive advantage. This maximises opportunities for low SES students to move up through their own hard work.

5   The scope of social regulation is extended to improve equity at the point of graduate selection into the labour market.

However, it is hard to achieve more equal educational outcomes or greater mobility in highly unequal societies. Higher education is not the only driver of social mobility. It is necessary but not sufficient, one part of a chain of institutional effects and not the most important. If income is the measure of equality, then income determination, tax and transfers have more direct effects. Perhaps higher education can have larger effects in relation to social status and personal agency, provided that these are not confined largely to students from advantaged backgrounds. However, education can only function in an equalising manner when this is supported by social consensus. Nordic egalitarianism in higher education and elsewhere is sustained by broad agreement on the continuing goals of social equality and social mobility, grounded in a threshold level of trust and equality of respect, and actively supported by consistent state policy (Gärtner and Prado 2012).

Acknowledgements

The term 'high participation systems' was coined by Anna Smolentseva. Thank you also to Brendan Cantwell.

References

Academic Ranking of World Universities, ARWU (2015). *2015 Academic Ranking of World Universities*. Shanghai Jiao Tong University. http://www.shanghairanking.com

Altbach, P. and Salmi, J. (eds.) (2011). *The Road Academic Excellence: The Making of World-Class Research Universities*. Washington, DC: World Bank.

Arum, R., Gamoran, A. and Shavit, Y. (2007). More inclusion than diversion: Expansion, differentiation and market structures in higher education. In Y. Shavit, R. Arum and A. Gamoran (eds.), *Stratification in Higher Education: A Contemporary Study* (pp. 1–35). Stanford: Stanford University Press.

Boliver, V. (2011). Expansion, differentiation, and the persistence of social class inequalities in British higher education. *Higher Education*, 61, 229–242.

Boliver, V. (2013). How fair is access to more prestigious UK universities? *The British Journal of Sociology*, 64 (2), 344–364.

Borgen, N. (2015). College quality and the positive selection hypothesis: The 'second filter' on family background in high-paid jobs. *Research in Social Stratification and Mobility*, 39, 32–47.

Bourdieu, P. (1988). *Homo Academicus*. Trans. P. Collier. Stanford: Stanford University Press.

Callender, C. (2013). The funding of part-time students. In D. Heller and C. Callender (eds.), *Student Financing of Higher Education: A Comparative Perspective* (pp. 115–136). London: Routledge.

Chankseliani, M. (2013). Rural disadvantage in Georgian higher education admissions: A mixed-methods study. *Comparative Education Review*, 57 (3), 424–456.

Chapman, B. (2014). Income contingent loans: Background. In B. Chapman, T. Higgins and J. Stiglitz (eds.), *Income Contingent Loans: Theory, Practice and Prospects* (pp. 12–28). Basingstoke and New York: Palgrave Macmillan.

Cheung, S. and Egerton, R. (2007). Great Britain: Higher education expansion and reform – changing educational inequalities. In Y. Shavit, R. Arum and A. Gamoran (eds.), *Stratification in Higher Education: A Contemporary Study* (pp. 195–219). Stanford: Stanford University Press.

Cingano, F. (2014). *Trends in Income Inequality and its Impact on Economic Growth*. OECD Social, Employment and Migration Working Papers, No. 163. Paris: OECD.

Corak, M. (2012). *Inequality from Generation to Generation: The United States in Comparison*. Ottawa, Canada: Graduate School of Public and International Affairs, University of Ottawa.

Davies, S. and Zarifa, D. (2012). The stratification of universities: Structural inequality in Canada and the United States. *Research in Social Stratification and Mobility*, 30, 143–158.

Dorling, D. (2014). *Inequality and the 1%*. London: Verso.

Douglass, John (2013). *To Grow or not to Grow? A Post-Great Recession Synopsis of the Political, Financial, and Social Contract Challenges Facing the University of California*. Research and Occasional Paper CSHE 15.13. Berkeley: Center for Studies in Higher Education, University of California Berkeley.

Gärtner, S. and Prado, S. (2012). *Inequality, Trust and the Welfare State: The Scandinavian Model in the Swedish Mirror*. Högre seminariet, 7 November. Ekonomisk-historiska institutionen, Göteborgs universitet.

Hansen, H. (2011). Rethinking certification theory and the educational development of the United States and Germany. *Research in Social Stratification and Mobility*, 29, 31–55.

Hazelkorn, E. (2011). *Rankings and the Reshaping of Higher Education: The Battle for World-Class Excellence*. Houndmills: Palgrave Macmillan.

Hoxby, C. and Avery, C. (Spring 2013). *The Missing 'One-Offs': The Hidden Supply of High-Achieving, Low-Income Students*. Brookings papers on economic activity.

Hu, A. and Vargas, N. (2015). Horizontal stratification of higher education in urban China. *Higher Education*. DOI 10.1007/s10734-014-9833-y.

Lee, H., Lee, M. and Park, D. (2012). *Growth Policy and Inequality in Developing Asia: Lesson from Korea*. ERIA Discussion Paper 2012–12.

Lucas, S. (2001). Effectively maintained inequality: Education transitions, track mobility, and social background effects. *American Journal of Sociology*, 106 (6), 1642–1690.

Lucas, S. (2009). Stratification theory, socioeconomic background, and educational attainment: A formal analysis. *Rationality and Society*, 21, 459–511.

Marginson, S. (2011). Imagining the global. In R. King, S. Marginson and R. Naidoo (eds.), *Handbook of Higher Education and Globalization* (pp. 10–39). Cheltenham: Edward Elgar.

Marginson, S. (2013). Emerging higher education in the Post-Confucian heritage zone. In D. Araya and P. Marber (eds.), *Higher Education in the Global Age* (pp. 89–112). New York: Routledge.

Marginson, S. (2016a). High participation systems of higher education. *Journal of Higher Education*, 87 (2), 243–271.

Marginson, S. (2016b). *The Dream is Over: The Crisis of Clark Kerr's California Idea of Higher Education*. Berkeley: University of California Press and the Centre for Studies in Higher Education, University of California Berkeley.

Mettler, S. (2014). *Degrees of Inequality: How the Politics of Higher Education Sabotaged the American Dream*. New York: Basic Books.

Mountford-Zimdars, A. and Sabbagh, D. (2013). Fair access to higher education: A comparative perspective. *Comparative Education Review*, 57 (3), 359–368.

Organisation for Economic Cooperation and Development, OECD (2014a). *Education at a Glance 2014*. Paris: OECD.

Organisation for Economic Cooperation and Development, OECD (2014b). *United States: Tackling High Inequalities, Creating Opportunities for All*. Paris: OECD.

Organisation for Economic Cooperation and Development, OECD (2014c). *PISA 2012 Results in Focus: What 15 Year Olds Know and What They Can Do With What They Know*. Paris: OECD.

Organisation for Economic Cooperation and Development, OECD (2015). *Data on Income Distribution and Poverty*. http://stats.oecd.org/Index.aspx?DataSet Code=IDD

Oxfam (2014). *Even it Up: Time to End Extreme Inequality*. Oxford: Oxfam GB.

The PELL Institute (2015). Indicators of Higher Education Equity in the United States. http://www.pellinstitute.org/downloads/publications-Indicators_of_Higher_ Education_Equity_in_the_US_45_Year_Trend_Report.pdf

Piketty, T. (2014). *Capital in the Twenty-First Century*. Trans. A. Goldhammer. Cambridge, MA: Belknap Harvard University Press.

Rivera, l. (2011). Ivies, extracurriculars, and exclusion: Elite employers' use of educational credentials. *Research in Social Stratification and Mobility*, 29, 71–90.

Rivera, L. (2015). *Pedigree: How Elite Students get Elite Jobs*. Princeton, NJ: Princeton University Press.

Roksa, J., Grodsky, E., Arum, R., and Gamoran, A. (2007). United States: Changes in higher education and social stratification. In Y. Shavit, R. Arum and A. Gamoran (eds.), *Stratification in Higher Education: A Contemporary Study* (pp. 165–191). Stanford: Stanford University Press.

Roksa, J. and Levey, T. (2010). What can you do with that degree? College major and occupational status of college graduates over time. *Social Forces*, 89 (2), 389–416.

Saez, E. (2013). *Striking it Richer: The Evolution of Top Incomes in the United States*. Berkeley: University of California, Berkeley, Department of Economics. http:// eml.berkeley.edu//~saez/saez-UStopincomes-2012.pdf

Salmi, J. (2009). *The Challenge of Establishing World-Class Universities*. Washington: World Bank Publications.

Shavit, Y., Arum, R. and Gamoran, A. (eds.). (2007). *Stratification in Higher Education: A Comparative Study*. Stanford: Stanford University Press.

Smeeding, T. (2005). Public policy, economic inequality, and poverty: The United States in comparative perspective. *Social Science Quarterly*, 86, 955–983.

Soares, J. (2007). *The Power of Privilege: Yale and America's Elite Colleges*. Stanford: Stanford University Press.

Stiglitz, J. (2013). *The Price of Inequality*. London: Penguin.

Teichler, U. (2009). *Higher Education and the World of Work: Conceptual Frameworks, Comparative Perspectives, Empirical Findings*. Rotterdam: Sense Publishers.

Thomsen, P., Munk, M., Eiberg-Madsen, M. and Hansen, G. (2013). The educational strategies of Danish university students from professional and working class backgrounds. *Comparative Education Review*, 57 (3), 457–480.

Triventi, M. (2013a). Stratification in higher education and its relationship with social inequality: A comparative study of 11 European countries. *European Sociological Review*, 29 (3), 489–502.

Triventi, M. (2013b). The role of higher education stratification in the reproduction of social inequality in the labor market. *Research in Social Stratification and Mobility*, 32, 45–63.

Trow, M. (1973). *Problems in the Transition from Elite to Mass Higher Education*. Berkeley, CA: Carnegie Commission on Higher Education.

United Nations Educational, Social and Cultural Organization (UNESCO) (2015). *UNESCO Institute for Statistics Data on Education*. http://data.uis.unesco.org/

Wilkinson, R. and Pickett, K. (2010). *The Spirit Level: Why Equality is Better for Everyone*. London: Penguin.

Wolniak, G., Seifert, T., Reed, E. and Pascarella, E. (2008). College majors and social mobility. *Research in Social Stratification and Mobility*, 26, 123–139.

Section 2

Theoretical perspectives

This section provides an introduction to the theoretical work of six renowned international thinkers (or groups of thinkers) whose perspectives offer important insights into access issues in higher education, either at the macro level of whole societies (e.g. Boudon and Sen/Nussbaum) or the micro level of individual decision-making (e.g. Archer and Simon/Kahneman).

Chapter 3

Capitals and habitus

A Bourdieusian framework for understanding transitions into higher education and student experiences

Ciaran Burke

Introduction

The emergence of post-industrialisation and, with it, a knowledge economy, articulated by Daniel Bell (1973), introduced a supposed sea change in social stratification. Gone were positions based on birth right, and, instead, a social system was formed based on knowledge with the new elites earning their positions through hard work and diligence – creating an avenue for all, if hungry enough, to rise to these lofty heights. Through the meritocratic narratives of human capital theorists such as Theodore Schultz (1971), education became a cornerstone in the pursuit for social equality, and increased access to education became a simple yet elegant policy to foster social mobility. As Tight (2012) has discussed, while 'widening participation' has not always been in the public/policy vocabulary, it is a policy with its roots in post-war Britain, beginning with the 1944 Education Act and the Robbins Report (1963).

This chapter will encourage supporters/advocates of widening participation – in whose numbers I count myself – to pause and consider the structural and individual barriers still present within the UK higher education system,[1] characterised as being committed to widening participation, through a critical sociological lens: to be specific through Bourdieusian social theory. This chapter will provide an overview of Bourdieu's theoretical project and an introduction to these central thinking tools: habitus, capital and field. It will, then, turn to discuss his arguments concerning the education system – in particular, its socially reproductive role and the subjective barriers working-class students place over their educational trajectories – and illustrate the heuristic value of his thinking tools when critically examining widening participation.

The chapter will, then, turn to consider the critical reception Bourdieu has received from some corners within sociology – particularly, the work of Richard Jenkins and Margaret Archer – and, in light of these comments, discuss the limitations and merits of using this theoretical model. Moving on from critiques specifically focused on Bourdieu's work, the chapter will place Bourdieu within the wider context of contemporary social theory – late modernity. Bourdieu will be posited against the late modern tradition to provide space to critically consider the necessity and legitimacy of the continued application of Bourdieusian social theory in issues of widening participation and access. In order to strengthen the Bourdieusian position, the chapter will draw on a number of empirical studies which apply Bourdieusian social theory to illustrate these issues in practice.

Bourdieu: a generative theory of practice and the practice of reproduction

The starting point for Bourdieusian sociology is a commitment to provide a theory of practice which considers both structure and agency,[2] the two pillars which Mills (1959) reminds us are required to reflexively examine social space; however, for Bourdieu, theory is meant to be applied and used, and, as such, the theoretical concepts which he employs in his project should be understood as heuristic in nature. To that effect, Bourdieu refers to his theoretical concepts as 'thinking tools'. Bourdieu's toolbox expanded throughout his career, and, while it is beyond the focus of this chapter to itemise and apprise each in turn, there are a number of excellent sources which provide such a service (Grenfell, 2008; Webb, et al., 2002). Rather, the focus of this chapter will be on the three central thinking tools, fundamental to both Bourdieusian sociology and widening participation research: habitus, capital and field. It is these tools, according to Bourdieu, that allow us to examine the genesis of action. While it is necessary to apply a certain level of analytical dualism when discussing such terms, they are understood to work in partnership expressed in schematic form as '[(habitus) (capital)] + field = practice' (1979/1984: 101).[3]

Habitus, at a fundamental level, could be described as norms, values and dispositions that influence or direct action, often termed 'strategy' or 'practical mastery' (Bourdieu, 1972/1977). In keeping with Bourdieu's structural constructivist ontology, these dispositions are both structured and chosen. In an attempt to articulate what, on the surface, is a contradiction but which clearly alludes to the complicated and interpenetrative relationship between structure and agency, Bourdieu describes the habitus as 'socialised subjectivity' (1992: 126). In other words, habitus is an individual process involving choice but also influenced by structure. These structures, Bourdieu (1972/1977) argues, include the family, the educational system and the environment (including peer groups, (popular) culture and future life events). As the habitus is a thinking tool, it can be stretched and used in different contexts – to this effect, habitus can be appreciated both at individual but also group level. The group habitus is predicated on the argument that, while the structures which influence and form the habitus are unique to each individual, the environment (neighbourhood or school) is a shared space, so it is likely that members of the same group will have similar experiences/institutions influencing their habitus. In addition, the group habitus is more resilient, as a consensus is easier to reproduce and able to challenge dissent.

The second component within Bourdieu's theory of practice is capital. While it lies on equal footing within Bourdieu's schematic representation, it has often been seen as a secondary concept to habitus (Burke, 2015b). In an effort to move beyond a Marxist model of 'have and have-nots', Bourdieu's model contains three forms of capital: economic, social and cultural (1983/2004). Economic capital is concerned with access to financial resources, including money, investments and property. Social capital is measured by social contacts individuals have and the nature in which these contacts can be 'used'. Finally, cultural capital comprises cultural practices and cultural competencies. These forms of capital are relational and, as such, require a hierarchy to exist under or a centre from which to gain their buying power; the legitimate forms of these capitals are termed symbolic capital. For Bourdieu, capitals do two things: they can be exchanged, like any other form of capital, for goods and services, and they also act as reference points in which to locate an individual's (and, by extension, a group's) position within social space. It is the individual's position within social space that will influence levels of aspirations and expectations, which Bourdieu terms 'field of the possibles' (1979/1984: 110), creating a classed level of confidence – providing the context of Bourdieu's oft-referenced comment 'not for the likes of us' (1979/1984: 471).

The final concept within Bourdieu's theory of practice is field. The concept of field should be understood as the context in which habitus and capital interact; however, rather than providing an arena for this interaction, field is part of the interpenetrative relationship which directs practice. Particular fields are more amenable to a certain character of habitus and forms/levels of capital. An understanding of both the field's composition and particular requirements are needed for a Bourdieusian project. It is the combination of these three thinking tools that provides us with an opportunity to apply a structurally constructivist approach to practice.

Bourdieu: (higher) education and widening participation

A central feature from the above overview of Bourdieu's theoretical project is the tension between constraint and choice and how, essentially, neither works without the other. Within Bourdieu's substantial body of work, (higher) education plays a significant part. For the purposes of this chapter, I will focus on three pertinent themes throughout his work: the role of the sociology of education, *a priori* barriers to success and the role of the educational system in social reproduction.

For Bourdieu (1973), when examining power and privilege, the educational system is the central site of inheriting privilege; however, through the emergence of the knowledge economy, it is able to hide in plain sight, shrouded by a cloak of meritocracy, able to evade suspicion and criticism. The responsibility of sociology of education is to question the role of education in social reproduction. Our attention should be focused on dispositions and practices engendered by habitus and capital and the mechanisms in which structures can reproduce themselves.

In *The Inheritors*, Bourdieu and Passeron (1964/1979) examine the classed level of access to university, comparing the educational trajectories of the children of farmers, industrialists and professionals. Applying Bourdieu's range of capitals in a bid to move beyond a binary economic model of class, the authors advocate for a widening of the lens to consider the role of 'social origin'. The cumulative effect on the differing levels of participation – rather than a narrow explanation based on access to economic resources – alludes to the observation that the industrialist or professional's child will understand progression into higher education as natural, whereas entry into higher education for a farmer's child is a significant break in their 'expected' trajectory. The genesis of this disparity can be accounted for by habitus and capital.

For the sake of empirical discussion, with regrettable reduction in theoretical depth, these three groups can be divided into binary opposites of dominant and dominated groups (Bourdieu, 1979/1984). For Bourdieu, the habitus plays a central role in what he terms a 'self-denying ethos' (1966/1974: 34). Within a Bourdieusian model, our subjective expectations are directed/influenced by objective conditions. These objective conditions influencing working-class attitudes to education include previous educational trajectories, family/peer experiences and their general social environment. According to Bourdieu, these conditions are exacerbated by distrust and criticisms towards individuals' attempts to leave their place of social origin and, by extension, increased levels of aspiration. These influences will eventually formulate an attitude to education and constrained levels of aspirations, which can be extrapolated to a group attitude and level of aspiration.

In addition, the levels of capital which provide the dominant group (industrialists and professionals) their position in social space also form higher levels of aspirations. This, combined with the norms and dispositions of their habitus, formed in part by their family who would have also attended university, causes them to see entry into higher education as a normal trajectory. The opposite side of the coin can be understood for the dominated group (farmers) whose lower levels of capitals, as defined by symbolic forms of capital, produce a limit on aspirations and a habitus which, pre-reflexively, does not see higher education as a likely trajectory.[4] While, of course, access to financial resources will affect an individual's education decisions, there are social and cultural influences at work, too. Bourdieu demonstrates his structural constructivist ontology in line with education through his comments: 'in general, children and their families make their own choice by reference to the constraints which determine them' (1966/1974: 34). In the case of widening participation, the challenge is, then, to appreciate that increased access will not necessarily bring about increased participation.

In subsequent publications, Bourdieu provides an account of the external processes which reproduce social position and relations. In addition to the internalised levels of restraint, in the case of working-class students, the educational system was labelled an active mechanism in the reproduction of position within social space (Bourdieu and Passeron, 1970/1990). For Bourdieu and Passeron, the physical manifestation of the educational system – the school buildings – and the interactions within its walls, including the type of language teachers use and the focus of the curriculum (both academic and extracurricular), transmits and supports dominant practices and attitudes. Successful navigation of the educational system requires cultural competency and an understanding of unwritten rules, usually reserved for the dominant group. Bourdieu (1966/1974) suggests that middle-class/dominant students demonstrate their compatibility with the elite cultural values of the educational system through signifiers such as 'style, taste and wit' (1966/1974: 39), which are seen as natural and expected. The tacit fit and support between the educational system and the dominant group allows these students to flourish within its walls to the detriment of working-class/dominated students.

In effect, Bourdieu (1966/1974) contends that the school can reproduce social inequality through treating students equally. The dominant form of pedagogy at the time in France, Bourdieu writes, was concerned with unearthing students' potential and locating their predispositions towards particular subjects. A pedagogy promoting equality, Bourdieu argues, would, in contrast, be concerned with providing students an opportunity to gain knowledge and develop abilities other students were understood to have been 'gifted'. A form of pedagogy where knowledge is expected and lessons are implied rather than provided and explained is detrimental to working-class students who, in a bid to maintain their main form of symbolic capital (scholastic capital), will not risk devaluing it by asking a question (Sullivan, 2001). While this argument could be dismissed as out-dated, there are parallels with issues concerning the dominant form of pedagogy within UK higher education: constructive alignment (Biggs, 2003). The basic position that students are active learners and should be encouraged to construct knowledge has been heavily criticised by James (2013) on the grounds that it is unable/unwilling to take account of different levels of capitals and dispositions towards education. The issue for the widening participation agenda is that, while there is a focus on access to higher education, the dominant pedagogical approach within higher education does not take account of student background reducing the scope for equal opportunities for students.

In terms of language in the classroom or lecture theatre, the educational system can, again, operate on the claim that the language used is open to all. Bourdieu (1966/1974) suggests, however, that the classed disparities in language are quite significant and, therefore, limit the working-class students' ability to operationalise and 'acquire' the appropriate cultural practices required by the educational system for a successful trajectory. The detrimental consequences stemming from the classed style of language and the form in which information is transmitted can be exacerbated through the examination process. The more vague or open an examination question reads, Bourdieu argues, the greater the role of *a priori* capital and a habitus predisposed to the educational system, favouring the dominant class. During the examination process, students are effectively not only judged on technical knowledge and academic ability but also on more tacit qualities such as attitude and style – cumulatively termed 'cultural capital'.

The authority bestowed on the educational system translates into working-class students understanding their inability to move as easily as their middle-class counterparts through the education system as a personal failing, leading to a reinforcement of their limited aspirations. To paraphrase Mills (1959), working-class students understand the classed experience of education to be their trouble rather than the education system's issue. Bourdieu and Passeron (1970/1990) refer to this process as 'symbolic violence'. The violent act of simultaneously firmly capping aspirations and creating an environment where working-class students can opt out is also seen as legitimate because it comes from the educational system, itself.

Bourdieu and Passeron urge their readers to consider working-class access to middle-class institutions with caution, arguing that we must not misconstrue the progression of the few (working class) as the beginning of equality. They suggest that the reasons behind this 'ascension' are linked to 'exceptional abilities' and 'exceptional features of their family backgrounds' (1964/1979: 23). A further and more cynical account for the need for caution concerning working-class progression/mobility is that it serves to shield the apparatus of reproduction (Bourdieu and de Saint-Martin, 1970/1974). The education system earns and retains its authority through its meritocratic nature, admitting a limited number of students from the dominated social group provides the space in which to argue that access is based on ability and not background, preventing public backlash to the system.

When providing a systematic account of Bourdieu's contribution to higher education, Derek Robbins (1993) suggests that there are two stages or faces of Bourdieu in the context of education. Bourdieu's earlier work – in particular, *The Inheritors* (with Passeron, 1964/1979) – understood that, while there are deep-rooted problems in terms of access and experience of higher education on classed lines, the solution could be found through the educational system. In contrast, in work such as *Reproduction* (with Passeron, 1970/1990) and subsequent publications, Bourdieu accepts that social reproduction – what Robbins refers to as 'self-perpetuation' (1993: 154) – is a central facet of the educational system. Regardless of which 'face of Bourdieu' a researcher applies, the directive influence of habitus and capital within a field should be approached through the structural constructivist lens of Bourdieu's overall project. Habitus and capital are heuristic devices; through his own application of these thinking tools, Bourdieu has illustrated the power dynamics within the education system and challenged his readers to consider the structural and agentic facets of the educational system and the long-term effects and consequences of widening participation without such a critical examination.

Bourdieu: critique and the melting away of constraint

Bourdieu's theory of practice has been open to sustained critique. The central criticism of his work is the charge of structural determinism (Archer, 1996; Jenkins, 2002). The crux of this critique is that Bourdieu has not met the fundamental challenge of his theoretical project: to bridge structure and agency. Through a habitus largely based on inculcated norms and dispositions from family and school, there is only a limited role for the individual and no space to account/allow for social change. In defence of Bourdieu's position, his theoretical project provides a pragmatic and realistic account of relations between structure and agency beyond the abstract confines of social theory. As argued earlier in this chapter, concepts such as habitus are intended to contain both structural and agentic elements. In an effort to more clearly articulate this intention and to signpost the agentic dimension of Bourdieu's theory of practice, there have been extensions or developments of Bourdieu's thinking tools such as the 'permeable habitus' (Reay, 2004) and the reflective dimension of habitus (Burke, 2015a).

To describe the development of late modernity as a critique of Bourdieu would significantly diminish its purpose and scope; however, it can be read as the contradictory or alternative account of post-industrial society. While late modernity comprises three, at times competing, theorists – Bauman (2000, 2001), Beck (1992, 1997) and Giddens (1991, 1992) – the overarching focus is on the consequences of societal change. Atkinson (2010) provides a comprehensive account of the particular genesis of this societal change specific to each theorist, including reduction of social structures through welfare policies, increased and shared global risks, consumer culture, globalisation and the ubiquitous nature of advice and experts forcing us to choose. The shared consequences or knock-on effect from these developments in the structural composition of social space is increased reflexivity and individualisation when negotiating institutions in this late modern context, including higher education.

Bauman's (2001) liquid modernity thesis contends that contemporary society changes so fast there are no longer constant/solid structures for individuals to re-embed into after one of these changes and as a result an individual's identity is less structured to the point where the individual must create one themselves. Bauman compares this view of liquid modernity to 'heavy modernity' (2001: 22), which he characterises through long-term goals and the re-assurance of these long-term goals. It is the uncertainty of society and its temporal nature that prevents previous groups and collective trajectories from re-forming – 'the present-day uncertainty is a powerful *individualising* force' (2001: 24, emphasis in original).

It is the departure from the known and the increasingly de-structured and volatile social space that requires individuals to make choices for themselves.

As Giddens remarks, 'Modernity is a post-traditional order, in which the question "How shall I live?" has to be answered in day-to-day decisions' (1991: 14). Importantly, late modernity does not operate under the impression that structure has been replaced with a collection of individuals. On the contrary, they are sensitive to on-going social inequalities – for example access to resources. In line with the concept of a constantly shifting social structure, these inequalities are not fixed nor are they exclusive to one particular group. Stemming from this attitude of an 'opportunity for all' to be both dominant and dominated, social class is seen as an out-dated concept too reliant on traditional hierarchies to operate in the fast-paced liquid context of late modernity. Beck and Beck-Gernsheim (2002) declared class a 'zombie category' – essentially a dead concept kept alive by class researchers. There is a clear conflict between the composition and nature of social space as seen by late modern thinkers and Bourdieu. To briefly unpack Bourdieu's three central thinking tools, the main influences on the formation of the habitus and the empirically extrapolated group habitus (family, education and social environment) are no longer fixed, reducing the structural consistency of the habitus and allowing it to be increasingly flexible. In terms of capitals, the fast-paced nature of social space will create fluctuations in the buying power of capitals, as what are deemed legitimate/symbolic forms of capital will constantly be in motion. Additionally, a de-structured social space will provide individuals with opportunities to increase capitals previously seen to be fixed. Finally, the various fields within this new re-structured social space will be constantly shifting in terms of both rules of the game and parameters, providing increased scope for success and failure for *all* participants involved.

Late modernity has been open to a great deal of critique. Archer (1996, 2013) has, in a similar vein to her comments concerning Bourdieu, charged late modernity with providing too much focus and power to one side of the coin – in this case, agency. A key consequence of this trend to favour agency, despite recognising the on-going presence of inequality, is that it places the outcome of trajectories on the individual (Burke, 2015a; Reay, et al., 2005). In success, the individual may celebrate, but, in failure, the fault lies with them, reducing such pathways/experiences as individual problems without fully considering the societal issues. In an effort to further unpack the issues of late modernity's focus on agency – what Archer describes as 'upward conflation' (1996) – Atkinson (2010) questions the malleable and de-structuring nature of the genesis of late modernity. For Atkinson, access to education and health care (through welfare policies) or globalisation are tied to resources, which can be seen as classed, limiting the departure from a classed society. While Archer and Atkinson are convincing in their theoretical critiques of late modernity – with the latter in defence of Bourdieu – the lived experience of class and its continuing effect on higher educational trajectories and experience is perhaps the most practical form of critique of late modernity and promotion of Bourdieusian-inspired social theory.

Empirical studies: demonstrating inequality within the class(room) setting

A significant feature of UK higher education policy has been social justice through access. Framed in the context of the emergence of the knowledge economy and driven by a human capital ethos, widening participation was a central policy in addressing old inequalities and offering increased life chances for the population. In contradiction of some of the principles laid out by the Robbins Report (1963), the Higher Education: A New Framework (DfE, 1991) or, indeed, the primary role of education on social mobility discussed at length by then-Deputy Prime Minister Nick Clegg in *Opening Doors, Breaking Barriers* (Cabinet Office, 2011), a significant body of research has illustrated the continuing influence of class on access to higher education. Contemporary barriers and experiences of higher education have been thoroughly collected and well documented by Kate Purcell and her team at Warwick Institute for Employment Research through their longitudinal *Futuretrack* study, tracing students from the university application stage through to graduate life.

In their pre-university stage of research (Purcell, et al., 2008), the Future-track team reported a clear difference in terms of both attitudes and confidence towards progressing to higher education by social class background. Traditional students (often middle class and who, to continue with Bourdieusian terminology, could be described as members of the dominant group) often understood higher education as a natural progression, and, in many cases, it was the only accepted trajectory. This narrative of assured progression was contrasted by non-traditional students (often working-class students who could be termed members of the dominated group) who were quite hesitant and unsure towards university. Bourdieu's (1977) comments on the central role of family and school on the formation of habitus and dispositions towards education can unpack the genesis of this classed disparity between levels of confidence. Familial experience of higher education was reported to be a significant influence on student attitudes. A significantly higher proportion of student respondents with parents/guardians who had experience of higher education understood higher education as a normal progression. Complementary to this observation, a significantly higher level of students from a middle-class background were encouraged by their parents to apply for a university course compared to their working-class counterparts. While not as pronounced as family influence, a similar trend in levels of encouragement from teachers by class background of the student was also evident. In addition to the disparity of levels of encouragement by teaching staff, the quality of guidance concerning higher education pathways was understood to differ by the 'type' of school a student attended. Futuretrack found that more prestigious schools, with a tradition of students continuing their education into higher education, had greater connection to universities and were in a position to offer better advice. This experience was contrasted with the other end of the spectrum, identified as further education colleges. While the report's authors were careful to highlight that the type of school attended appeared to be more influential than socio-economic background, the type of school attended can and has been used as an empirical proxy for class background, therefore reinforcing the point of a classed disparity.

The initial findings of Futuretrack, at the stage of students applying to university, demonstrate the role of habitus (formed by family and school) on orientations towards higher education. While there is increased access to higher education, institutions with a history of higher education experience or connection to these institutions – 'inherited' from either familial or institutional habitus – played a significant role in the attitudes towards participating in higher education and the assumed ease in which this transition could be made. There are clear parallels between Futuretrack's findings and previous research on the role of family encouragement and disparity in advice by type of school (Reay, et al., 2001; Reay, et al., 2005). Further illustrating Bourdieu's reproduction thesis, subsequent stages of the larger Futuretrack project (Atfield, et al., 2010; Purcell, et al., 2009) reported a different type and quality of experience of higher education, both academically and socially, by dominant/dominated status. Working-class students were less likely to enjoy their time at university and displayed lower levels of confidence concerning their degree outcome as compared to their middle-class counterparts. In an extension of classed levels of confidence and ease of entering higher education, working-class students were less likely to attend an elite university. This capping of institutions where a working-class student feels confident to apply does carry long-term consequences. Through the process of expanding higher education in the UK, there are more graduates than graduate jobs (Brown, et al., 2003; Burke, 2015a). In a bid to 'stand out from the crowd', students are increasingly using the institutional status as a proxy for their own value (Smetherham, 2006; Tomlinson, 2008). If the classed disparity within types of universities continues, it will contribute to a classed gap post-graduation.

In addition to self-imposed limits, directed by a subjective interpretation of structurally imposed conditions, working-class students are also subject to the same cultural competencies – or feel for the game – expected and required to, at times literally, be accepted by elite institutions. A critique against habitus is that it reduces the agent to a passive state following a tautological path paved by their position in social space; however, from a Bourdieusian perspective, individuals are active, but their ability to manoeuvre within social space – or, as Bourdieu put it, their ability to 'play the game' – is influenced by habitus and capital. To conclude this section and to add a thick(er) description to some of the processes going on which Futuretrack observed, I want to look at a specific study (Jones, 2013) examining the process of access to university in the UK: the UCAS personal statement.[5]

According to Jones (2013), the UCAS personal statement, or college essay, is the central non-academic indicator for entry into higher education. It is the main opportunity for students to introduce themselves to selection committees and add to the objective measurement of academic qualifications. Through an examination of UCAS personal statements, controlled for academic qualifications, Jones demonstrates the classed disparities in the application by style and strategic content. In terms of the stylistic and linguistic quality of the personal statements, Jones found that personal statements from private and grammar school students were longer, contained longer sentences and used longer words. In addition to quantitative variations, Jones observed a classed difference in the quality of personal statements in terms of spelling and grammar based on the type of school the applicant attended. For Jones, the 'level of fluency with which applicants express themselves is constructed in terms of cultural capital' (2013: 404), illustrating the classed nature of playing the game. Students from the private and grammar schools would presumably have had access to facilities, such as specialist writing services, however this reinforced/reproduced their 'cultural competency' rather than formed it.

Cultural capital not only accounts for how something is said, but also what is said, demonstrating both the cultural fluency and competency it provides. The strategic content within these statements concerned passages alluding to both work-related experience and extra-curricular activities. According to Jones, comments concerning either of these types of activities from the middle-class applicants elicited an increased sense of prestige or status. Middle-class students' work-related experience often involved a greater level of responsibility, increasing the potential buying power of that experience; similarly, middle-class students would include the name of their school when discussing extra-curricular activities to demonstrate an increased level of 'institutional cultural capital' (Bourdieu, 1983/2004). Jones suggests that middle-class students employ social class to secure these work-related positions, reinforcing the classed gap in UCAS personal statements. In addition to Jones's comments, the focus on work-related activity points to a greater understanding of the need to supplement educational capital with additional resources (Reay, et al., 2009a, 2009b; Tomlinson, 2008), once again associated with a 'feel for the game'. To summarise his argument, Jones writes, 'applicants from different educational backgrounds are not equally prepared and predisposed to play the admissions game' (2013: 418). Jones's work is of particular significance not only because of his original application of linguistic research to unpack cultural capital but because the central non-academic indicator for admissions, which operates under the assumption of neutrality, appears to be 'rigged' in favour of the middle-class applicants due to contrasting levels of accepted/expected capital. In a similar vein to Bourdieu's argument on the socially culling effect of exams, operating through a narrative of equal opportunity but which rewards a particular type of student, UCAS personal statements serve as an under-researched cog in social reproduction. In the context of widening participation, this research is quite a significant addition to the literature pointing to a classed tension in the subjective admissions process.

Bourdieu's conceptual tools are thinking tools; they are to be used, refined and also challenged in the pursuit of research. It would be remiss of me to conclude this section without engaging in more critical comments. Beyond the often-referenced critiques of structuralism a thorough and compelling critique, especially on cultural capital and educational attainment, is offered by Sullivan (2001). Here Sullivan argues that, while cultural capital does play a role in educational attainment, it is only one piece of the puzzle. I agree with this statement; however, there are two points of contention with her argument. First, Sullivan is considering capital in its transactional model, rather than the multi-faceted tool it actually is – in particular, its effect on the field of the possibles. Second, she examines capital – in particular, cultural capital – in isolation. The above discussion of the body of literature which illustrates the effectiveness of Bourdieusian social theory when examining widening participation demonstrates the role of habitus, capital and field.

Conclusion

Malcom Tight (2012), in his widening participation 'score card', argues that, out of four central categories of under-representation – gender, class, mature and ethnic minority – social class has demonstrated the weakest progression in post-war UK higher education. While there are more individuals participating in higher education, the class gap has remained durable. Studies such as Futuretrack and many more like it argue that more work needs to be done to increase student confidence and consider the barriers/limits students place on themselves. Widening participation does not end with the offer of a university place; classed inequalities persist. A key argument stemming from Bourdieu's work on (higher) education and that of subsequent Bourdieusian researchers is that social inequality is reproduced through treating students equally. This assumption is what the greater widening participation agenda needs to address: that equal opportunity equals equality. The class habitus directing orientations towards higher education and the application/exchange of capital(s) before and during higher education provide the theoretical language and a point of departure to examine and address these assumptions and unresolved barriers.

The above discussion illustrating the classed nature of both attitudes concerning higher education and barriers to such participation demonstrate the continuing relevance of Bourdieusian social theory – in particular, in the context of widening participation. These studies and many more like them cast considerable doubt on the de-structured nature of society characterised by increased individualisation and choice proposed by late modernity theorists. While structures may have changed, reminiscent of Bauman's image of a liquid society, the foundations of such structures – built on classed inequality and social reproduction – run deep.

Despite the, at times, fatalistic arguments and findings discussed in this chapter, widening participation is not a lost cause – it does need to be approached critically and in the context of both structures and agency. To be quite plain, widening participation is important to get right. From a Bourdieusian perspective, society is an extension of the educational system (1967/1971), and the character of our social system can be set/directed by how we organise the educational system. In addition, from a more instrumentalist perspective: "it's the knowledge economy, stupid". In other words, while there are clear classed issues concerning the graduate labour market (Brown, et al., 2003; Burke, 2015a), credentials – in particular, university credentials – are required to stand a chance of successfully negotiating a post-industrial labour market.

At the centre of Bourdieusian sociology is a critical examination of the role of structures and agency in institutions and processes understood to be directed by individuals and choice. It is also the starting point for effective widening participation – a critical focus on the structural and agentic dimensions within this policy. Bourdieu argues quite clearly that social reproduction through the education system is facilitated by an under-theorised and uncritical lay understanding of the system:

> It is probably cultural inertia which still makes us see education in terms of the ideology of the school as a liberating force and as a means of increasing social mobility, even when the indications tend to be that it is in fact one of the most effective means of perpetuating the existing social pattern, as it both provides an apparent justification for social inequalities and gives recognition to the cultural heritage, that is, to a *social* gift treated as a *natural* one.
>
> (Bourdieu, 1966/1974: 32, emphasis in original)

Notes

1 Widening participation is of course an issue beyond the UK, for the purposes of this chapter the UK was used as an empirical case study to support the theoretical argument. Similar discussions can be found in the USA through the work of Mullen and Lehmann's contributions in Canada (Lehmann, 2009; Mullen, 2010).

2 Structure being understood as the objective and internalised rules and regulations of a particular social system spanning from large institutions such as the state to individual manifestations such as gender or class. In turn, agency is the action/attitudes of the individual or a collection or individuals.

3 To provide a sense of continuity and adjust for Bourdieu's work being translated out of order, I have included the French publication date or the date in which it was first published in English followed by the date of the publication I am referring to in this chapter.

4 It could be argued that this sort of position creates a "deficit model"; however, through the emergence of the knowledge economy, knowledge – in particular, knowledge acquired and accredited by a higher education institution – is seen to be crucial for life chances and the ability to be competitive within a shifting labour market.

5 In addition to the UCAS statement, some elite UK institutions conduct admissions interviews. Similar research examining the role of cultural capital – in particular, cultural knowledge – on successful admissions interviews was carried out by Zimdars, et al. (2009).

References

Archer, M.S. (1996) *Culture and Agency: Revised Edition*. Cambridge: Cambridge University Press.

Archer, M.S. (2013) "Social Morphogenesis and the Prospects for Morphogenic Society", In: Archer, M.S. (ed.) *Social Morphogenesis*. London: Springer. pp. 1–25.

Atfield, G., Purcell, K. and Artess, J. (2010) The Experience of UK Undergraduate education: how higher education courses and study contexts studies impacted on students' assessments, evaluations and predictions of educational outcomes Skills development and perceptions of skills required. *Futuretrack Working paper.*

Atkinson, W. (2010) *Class, Individualisation and Late Modernity: In Search of the Reflexive Worker.* Hampshire: Palgrave MacMillan.

Bauman, Z. (2000) *Liquid Modernity*. Cambridge: Polity Press.

Bauman, Z. (2001) *The Individualised Society*. Malden: Polity Press.

Beck, U. (1992) *Risk Society*. London: Sage Publications.

Beck, U. (1997) *The Reinvention of Politics: Rethinking Modernity in the Global Social Order.* Cambridge: Polity Press.

Beck, U. and Beck-Gernsheim, E. (2002) *Individualisation*. London: Sage Publications.

Bell, D. (1973) *The Coming of Post-industrial Society: A Venture in Social Forecasting.* New York: Basic Books.

Biggs, J. (2003) *Teaching for Quality Learning at University* (2nd ed.). Buckingham: Open University Press.

Bourdieu, P. (1966/1974) "The School as a Conservative Force: Scholastic and Cultural Inequalities", In: Eggleston, J. (ed.) *Contemporary Research in the Sociology of Education.* London: Methuen and Co. Ltd. pp. 32–47.

Bourdieu, P. (1967/1971) "Systems of Education and Systems of Thought", In: Young, M.F.D. (ed.) *Knowledge and Control: New Directions for the Sociology of Education.* London: Collier MacMillan. pp. 189–209.

Bourdieu, P. (1972/1977) *Outline of a Theory of Practice*. Cambridge: Cambridge University Press.

Bourdieu, P. (1973) "Cultural Reproduction and Social Reproduction", In: Brown, R. (ed.) *Knowledge, Education, and Cultural Change: Papers in the Sociology of Education.* Birkenhead: Tavistock Publications Limited. pp. 71–112.

Bourdieu, P. (1979/1984) *Distinction: A Social Critique of the Judgement of Taste.* London: Routledge and Kegan Paul.

Bourdieu, P. (1983/2004) "The Forms of Capital", In: Ball, S.J. (ed.) *The Routledge-Falmer Reader in Sociology of Education*. London: Routledge Falmer. pp. 15–29.

Bourdieu, P. (1992) "The Purpose of Reflexive Sociology (The Chicago Workshop)", In: Bourdieu, P. and Wacquant, L. (eds.) *An Invitation to Reflexive Sociology*. Cambridge: Polity Press. pp. 61–217.

Bourdieu, P. and de Saint-Martin, M. (1970/1974) "Scholastic Excellence and the Values of the Educational System", In: Eggleston, J. (ed.) *Contemporary Research in the Sociology of Education.* London: Methuen and Co. Ltd. pp. 338–371.

Bourdieu, P. and Passeron, J-C. (1964/1979) *The Inheritors: French Students and Their Relation to Culture.* Chicago: The University of Chicago Press.

Bourdieu, P. and Passeron, J-C. (1970/1990) *Reproduction in Education Society and Culture* (2nd ed.). London: Sage Publications.

Brown, P., Hesketh, A. and Williams, S. (2003) "Employability in a Knowledge-Driven Economy", *Journal of Education and Work, 16* (2), 107–126.

Burke, C. (2015a) *Culture, Capitals and Graduate Future: Degrees of Class*. London: Routledge.

Burke, C. (2015b) "Habitus and Graduate Employment: A Re/Structured Structure and the Role of Biographical Research", In: Costa, C. and Murphy, M. (eds.) *The Art of Application: Bourdieu, Habitus and Social Research*. London: Palgrave. pp. 55–73.

Cabinet Office (2011) "Opening Doors, Breaking Barriers: a Strategy for Social Mobility". Retrieved 25 September 2014 from: www.gov.uk/government/publications/opening-doors-breaking-barriers-a-strategy-for-social-mobility

Department for Education (DfE) (1991) *Higher Education: A New Framework (White Paper), Cm 1541*. London: HMSO.

Giddens, A. (1991) *Modernity and Self-Identity: Self and Society in the Late Modern Age*. Cambridge: Polity.

Giddens, A. (1992) *New Rules of Sociological Method* (2nd ed.). Cambridge: Polity Press.

Grenfell, M.J. (ed.) (2008) *Pierre Bourdieu: Key Concepts*. Acumen: Durham.

James, D. (2013) "Investigating the Curriculum through Assessment Practice in Higher Education: The Value of a 'Learning Cultures' Approach", *Higher Education, 67* (2): 155–169.

Jenkins, R. (2002) *Pierre Bourdieu: Revised Edition*. London: Routledge.

Jones, S. (2013) "'Ensure that You Stand Out from the Crowd': A Corpus-Based Analysis of Personal Statements according to Applicants' School Type", *Comparative Education Review, 57* (3): 397–423.

Lehmann, W. (2009) "Becoming Middle Class: How Working Class University Students Draw and Transgress Moral Class Boundaries", *Sociology, 43* (4), 631–648.

Mullen, A.L. (2010) *Degrees of Inequality: Culture, Class and Gender in American Higher Education*. Baltimore, MD: The Johns Hopkins University Press.

Mills, C. Wright (1959) *The Sociological Imagination*. Oxford: Oxford University Press.

Purcell, K., Elias, P., Atfield, G., Behle, H., Ellison, R., Hughes, C., Livanos, L. and Tzanakou, C. (2009) "Plans, Aspirations and Realities: Taking Stock in Higher Education and Career Choices One Year On". The Higher Education Careers Service Unit.

Purcell, K., Elias, P., Ellison, R., Atfield, G., Adam, D. and Livanos, L. (2008) "Applying for Higher Education – The Diversity of Careers Choices, Plans and Expectations – Findings from the First Futuretrack Survey of the 'Class of 2006' Applicants for Higher Education". The Higher Education Careers Service Unit.

Reay, D. (2004) "It's All Becoming a Habitus: Beyond the Habitual Use of Habitus in Educational Research", *British Journal of Sociology of Education, 25* (4), 431–444.

Reay, D., Crozier, G. and Clayton, J. (2009a) "'Fitting In' or 'Standing Out': Working-Class Students in UK Higher Education", *British Educational Research Journal, 32* (1), 1–19.

Reay, D., Crozier, G. and Clayton, J. (2009b) "'Strangers in Paradise'? Working-Class Students in Elite Universities", *Sociology, 43* (6), 1103–1121.

Reay, D., David, M.E. and Ball, S. (2005) *Degrees of Choice: Social Class, Race and Gender in Higher Education*. Stoke on Trent: Trentham Books.

Reay, D., David, M. and Ball, S. (2001) "Making a Difference? Institutional Habituses and Higher Educational Choice", *Sociological Research Online, 4* (5). Retrieved 5 June 2014 from: www.socresonline.org.uk/5/4/Reay.html

Robbins, D. (1993) "The Practical Importance of Bourdieu's Analysis of Higher Education", *Studies in Higher Education, 18* (2), 151–163.

Robbins, L. (1963) *Higher Education: Report of a Committee (The Robbins Report).* London: HMSO.

Schultz, T.W. (1971) *Investment in Human Capital: The Role of Education and of Research.* New York: The Free Press.

Smetherham, C. (2006) "Firsts Among Equals? Evidence on the Contemporary Relationship between Educational Credentials and the Occupational Structure", *Journal of Education and Work, 19* (1), 29–45.

Sullivan, A. (2001) "Cultural Capital and Educational Attainment", *Sociology, 35* (4): 893–912.

Tight, M. (2012) "Widening Participation: A Post-War Scorecard", *British Journal of Educational Studies, 60* (3): 211–226.

Tomlinson, M. (2008) " 'The Degree Is Not Enough': Students' Perceptions of the Role of Higher Education Credentials for Graduate Work and Employability", *British Journal of Sociology of Education, 29* (1), 49–61.

Webb, J., Schirato, T. and Danaher, G. (2002) *Understanding Bourdieu.* London: Sage Publications.

Zimdars, A., Sullivan, A. and Heath, A. (2009) "Elite Higher Education Admissions in the Arts and Sciences: Is Cultural Capital the Key?", *Sociology, 43* (4): 648–666.

Chapter 4

Explaining inequality? Rational action theories of educational decision making

Ron Thompson

Introduction

This chapter addresses a number of important questions. First, how are inequalities in educational opportunity created, and why should they remain significant in spite of social and technological progress, and the increasing meritocracy claimed by many politicians? Second, although stratification research shows that patterns of inequality in Western countries are more similar than dissimilar, why do countries differ in levels of inequality and the extent of change? The chapter discusses the rational action approach to social class differences in educational attainment, a perspective designed specifically to answer such questions and to explain observed patterns of stability and change. Unlike the cultural reproduction perspective associated particularly with the work of Pierre Bourdieu, rational action theory seeks micro-level explanations based on the decisions made by individual actors and their subjective evaluations of the costs, benefits and chances of successful completion associated with different educational routes.

Although greatly developed by later authors, the rational action approach derives from the methodological individualism utilised by Raymond Boudon in his *Education, Opportunity and Social Inequality* (1974). Writing some time later, Boudon describes the centrality of individual behaviour to this work:

> [I]n order to analyse the system of macroscopic data which social mobility represents, it was vital to take it for what it in fact *is* – the statistical imprint of the juxtaposition of a host of individual acts . . . [by] individuals who are socially *situated*, in other words people who are part of a family and other social groups, and who have resources which are cultural as well as economic. Moreover, the choices which these individuals face are not abstract, but are choices the terms of which are fixed by specific institutions – for example, in the field of education; or by constraints – for example, the supply of and demand for skills in the context of career choices.
>
> (Boudon 1989, pp.6–7)

Whilst the degree to which its theoretical constructs are supported by empirical evidence is contested, rational action theory has the potential to offer an elegant and parsimonious explanation for many of the observed features of persistent – and nonpersistent – inequality.

Inequality of educational opportunity in comparative perspective

Educational attainment differs between groups of people defined in many different ways; for example according to 'race', gender, disability or looked-after status. However, in the literature discussed in this chapter, inequality of educational opportunity (IEO) refers specifically to "differences in level of educational attainment according to social background" (Boudon 1974, p.xi). In the theoretical literature, social background is usually understood in terms of class, enabling a focus on patterns of difference between categories with specific social meanings, but in empirical studies background variables such as parental education, occupational status or family income may be used in place of or in addition to social class.

Two further methodological questions arise: what measure of educational attainment to adopt, and how best to represent the differences in attainment that emerge from the analysis. Attainment may be thought of in various ways, for example highest level of education reached or qualifications achieved. For many years, statistical models of completed years of schooling, or the transition probabilities between one level of education and the next, were used to analyse social inequalities in education. However, as Mare (1980, 1981) has shown, these approaches are deficient in periods of educational expansion. The way in which years of schooling or transition probabilities change with social background depends on both the 'pure' relationship between educational attainment and social background and the average length of schooling (or transition probability) in society. To allow for educational expansion, it is necessary to develop models which are unaffected by overall increases in participation rates. This requirement is satisfied by statistical models of transition propensities at successive levels of education which take the so-called log-odds of making a transition[1] as the dependent variable.

Following Mare's work, this approach and its variants came to dominate research on IEO (Breen & Jonsson 2005), and odds ratios at specified transition points[2] became the standard way of representing differences in attainment between classes. The transition points typically studied include entry to lower secondary, upper secondary and tertiary education levels. Although lower secondary education became almost universal as the twentieth century progressed, in countries such as Germany where early selection into different educational tracks takes place, the transition to lower secondary education remains of great interest, not least for its impact on access to higher education (Neugebauer & Schindler 2012).

The first major comparative study to use the Mare model was aptly titled *Persistent Inequality* (Shavit & Blossfeld 1993). Based on analyses of thirteen industrial countries, the effects of social origin on educational attainment appeared stable, with only two countries – Sweden and the Netherlands – showing a reduction in the strength of association between origin and attainment. However, subsequent analyses show that some equalisation occurred in several countries, particularly in the years between 1930 and 1970 and typically at lower transition points (Breen & Jonsson 2005, pp.226–7). More recent studies provide an increasingly detailed picture of continuity and change. A study of cohorts born in the first two-thirds of the twentieth century in eight European countries found notable decreases in educational inequality, largely for children born in a period of around thirty years in the middle of the century (Breen et al. 2009). Again, equalisation tended mainly to affect earlier transitions, with a substantial reduction in class origin effects at the transition to lower secondary education whilst inequalities in the transition to tertiary education remained unchanged.

Comparisons of the magnitude of IEO across countries and over time, particularly between different studies, are often difficult to make because of variations in the sample sizes and data collection methods used, together with differences in how social background and educational attainment are captured. For this reason, the work of Breen et al. (2009) is helpful in providing a relatively uniform analysis across the countries studied. Log odds ratios[3] between highest and lowest social classes in countries with relatively high levels of IEO, such as Germany, France and Italy, have reduced from around 3·0 (greater in the case of Italy) for children born in the period 1925–34, to around 2·5 for children born in the period 1955–64. In Great Britain, Sweden and the Netherlands, these ratios were around 2·0–2·5 for the earlier cohort, reducing to around 1·5 for Great Britain and 2·0 for Sweden and the Netherlands (Breen et al. 2009, p.1510). A systematic comparison across eight countries for more recent birth cohorts is provided by Jackson and Jonsson (2013, p.319), indicating a sharp decline in class origin effects between early transitions and the transition to higher education. For example, in England log odds ratios fall from around 1·25 for the transition to A-level courses to 0·4 for the transition to a university degree course, whilst in France the fall is even greater: from around 1·85 to 0·25. By contrast, in the United States the log odds increase, from approximately 1·3 to 1·6.

The relationship between stratified educational systems and IEO is well documented. In particular, systems with 'dead-end' pathways, curriculum differentiation and a lack of mobility between educational tracks are likely to result in persistent inequality, especially when allocation to different pathways occurs early in the educational career (Pfeffer 2008; van de Werfhorst & Mijs 2010; Burger 2016). There is also evidence that higher levels of parental choice, allowing working-class children to be diverted into less-prestigious vocational pathways, tend to increase IEO (Becker & Hecken 2009a; Dollmann 2016). In higher education, stratification also tends to maintain or increase IEO, as working-class candidates are more likely to avoid prestigious institutions and courses (Ianelli 2007; Boliver 2011; Blossfeld et al. 2015; Thomsen 2015).

Inequalities in access to higher education have shown considerable resistance to change. For example, Halsey, Heath and Ridge (1980) found that, whilst working-class participation in England and Wales more than tripled across four cohorts born between 1913 and 1952, the actual growth – from 0·9 per cent to 3·1 per cent – was dwarfed by the increase in participation of young people from the highest social classes – from 7·2 per cent to 26·4 per cent. Over this period, the odds ratio between middle-class and working-class young people actually increased in favour of the middle class. Ianelli (2007) finds little change for later cohorts in England and Wales, with odds ratios roughly constant for entry to higher education in both 1987 and 1993, albeit reducing to some extent by 2000. Boliver (2011) finds that during two periods of expansion, in the 1960s and the 1990s, class differentials between working- and service-class[4] positions decreased only in the first expansion period. Although measures vary, similar inequalities by social origin exist across OECD countries in spite of the expansion that has taken place.

The persistence of inequalities in access to higher levels of education is often discussed in terms of *maximally maintained inequality* (Raftery & Hout 1993). This term describes a situation in which the less advantaged lose out in the process of educational expansion because their more advantaged peers are better placed to take up new educational opportunities. Relative transition rates or odds ratios therefore remain constant, even during periods of educational expansion, unless enrolments increase so much that demand for more education from higher social classes is saturated. More specifically, maximally maintained inequality would be an appropriate description in any of three cases: (a) expansion keeps pace with increased demand due to population growth generally or a growing middle class – in this case there is no trend towards universality of the educational level in question and transition rates show little change; (b) expansion exceeds this basic level of demand – transition rates increase across all social classes, but odds ratios are preserved or even increased because educational demand grows more rapidly in higher classes; (c) demand is saturated (approaching full participation) for higher social classes – in this case transition rates for lower social classes increase more rapidly than those for higher classes, and odds ratios decrease.

If a particular level of education becomes accessible to the majority of people, the social meaning of education at this level changes and it no longer offers positional advantage to its recipients. However, this does not imply that the contest for advantage moves elsewhere. The thesis of *effectively maintained inequality* (Lucas 2001) states that "socioeconomically advantaged actors secure for themselves and their children some degree of advantage wherever advantages are commonly possible" (p.1652). Thus, as universality is approached, higher social classes will exploit qualitative differences in education to maintain their advantage. For example, stratified curricular or institutional structures offer strategic opportunities to these classes, who will seek to appropriate the more prestigious strata. Even though universality is some way off, effectively maintained inequality (EMI) has obvious implications for informally stratified systems of higher education such as in the UK. Several studies offer support to the EMI thesis (Boliver 2011; Thomsen 2015), although it is unclear whether the exploitation of qualitative differences is intensifying, as EMI would predict (Reimer & Pollack 2010; Ianelli et al. 2015).

Primary and secondary effects of social stratification

The distinction between primary and secondary effects has a relatively long history (Jackson 2013, pp.5–8), originating in studies showing that the impact of social class on academic performance could not fully explain class differences in the transition to secondary education (Boalt & Jansen 1953; Girard & Bastide 1963). However, Boudon (1974) was the first to integrate the distinction within a systematic sociological explanation of inequalities in educational attainment. In his formulation, the *primary effects* of social stratification are class differences in academic performance generated by cultural inequalities; *secondary effects* are the impact of social class on educational attainment, after taking into account differences in performance.[5] Here, the term 'cultural inequalities' is to be taken as referring to theoretical explanations for class differences in school performance which attribute these differences to the cultural advantages possessed by those from higher class backgrounds. Boudon accepts that these advantages will be responsible for producing class differences in the ability to thrive in educational settings. However, he does not regard cultural advantage as being the full story. Boudon proposed that secondary effects take place through social class differences in the educational decisions made by children with similar levels of performance, and that these decisions are influenced by differences in objective conditions, not cultural differences between classes.

Unlike Bourdieu, for whom IEO results from a unitary cultural process in which the interaction between habitus and field conditions one's whole experience of education, Boudon regards the processes responsible for primary and secondary effects as being essentially different in nature:

> IEO is generated by a two-component process. One component is related mainly to the cultural effects of the stratification system. The other introduces the assumption that even with other factors being equal, people will make different choices according to their position in the stratification system. In other words, it is assumed (1) that people behave rationally in the economic sense . . . but that (2) they also behave within decision fields whose parameters are a function of their position in the stratification system.
>
> (Boudon 1974, p.36)

For Boudon, distinguishing between primary and secondary effects was intended to show that, whilst cultural inequalities are of great consequence in producing IEO, they are not the only factor involved, or even necessarily the most significant: he argues that, whilst primary effects tend to die away for those surviving to higher levels of education, secondary effects "assert themselves repeatedly throughout the life of a cohort" (1974, p.86). The relative contribution of primary and secondary effects to overall levels of IEO is therefore an important subject of empirical research.

The standard approach to estimating the magnitude of secondary effects is based on so-called counterfactual reasoning, in which observed data is used to construct distributions, specific to each social class, of (a) academic performance, and (b) transition propensities conditional on performance. These distributions are then interchanged in various ways to produce synthesised transition probabilities combining the performance and choice characteristics of paired social classes. For example, if we are interested in the proportion of IEO between social classes S_1 (higher) and S_2 (lower) that can be attributed to secondary effects, we replace the performance distribution for S_2 by the performance distribution for the higher-performing class S_1, while keeping the transition distribution the same. Combining the two distributions allows us to predict the proportion of children from S_2 who would have made the transition *if* there were no class difference in performance but the class difference in transition propensity remained.

One problem with decomposing primary and secondary effects in this way is that, when interpreted as a distinction between performance and choice, it assumes a causal model in which pathways between class, performance and attainment are not compromised by intervening unobserved variables. Following Erikson et al. (2005), the contribution of primary and secondary effects to IEO may be represented by the diagram in Figure 4.1a. In this diagram, S stands for social class, P for academic performance and A for educational attainment. As the diagram shows, social class affects achievement in two ways: indirectly, through its effects on performance, which in turn affects attainment; and directly, through processes unrelated to performance. Thus (perhaps slightly confusingly) primary effects are the *indirect* effects of social stratification on educational attainment, and secondary effects are the *direct* effects.

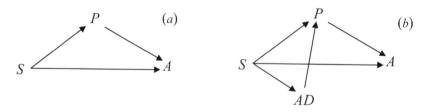

Figure 4.1 Causal pathways implied by models of primary and secondary effects
Source: Adapted from Erikson et al. 2005; Morgan 2012.

Unobserved variables may lead to estimates of secondary effects that are too high or too low. Erikson et al. (2005) point out that anticipatory decisions, where students reduce their efforts some time before a transition point because they have already decided not to prolong their educational careers, may lead to underestimates of secondary effects. This is because the resulting lower performance would be absorbed into estimates of the primary effect, even though it arose from an educational decision (see Figure 4.1b), in which AD represents anticipatory decisions.

However, Morgan (2012) argues that a more complex causal model is required to understand how incorrect estimates of secondary effects may emerge. In Figure 4.2, U is one or more unobserved variables which may affect attainment indirectly through performance or directly, where U is determined by the exogenous variable X, which also directly influences the social background variable S, performance P and educational attainment A.

This kind of causal structure could also lead to erroneous estimates of secondary effects. Race would perhaps be the most obvious candidate for an exogenous variable, but other possibilities may include place of residence (Morgan 2012, p.33). Either way, the argument suggests that unobserved variables could have more complex effects than the anticipatory decision in Figure 4.1b.

> These variables in U then must have effects on both prior performance . . . as well as direct effects on college entry . . . Such causal pathways cannot be considered mechanistic elaborations of Boudon's choice-theoretic conception of the secondary effects of stratification. They are instead a separate component of the net association between class and college entry that is best attributed to a broad structural interpretation.
>
> (Morgan 2012, p.33)

More general criticisms of the distinction between primary and secondary effects have been made, largely aimed at the characterisation of secondary effects as

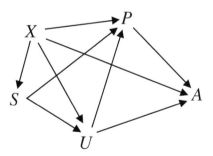

Figure 4.2 Causal network for primary and secondary effects involving an exogenous variable X

Source: Adapted from Morgan 2012, p.35.

mainly due to a separate set of processes structuring educational choice and the theoretical adequacy of rational action frameworks stemming from Boudon's distinction (Hatcher 1998; Nash 2005, 2006). These criticisms will be discussed later, in the context of critiques of rational action itself.

Rational action theories and educational decision making

The rational action theory of educational decisions is part of the broader enterprise of rational action (or rational choice) sociology. This tradition, stemming from the work of Hayek and Popper, is an often-controversial project whose critics regard it as at best reductionist, at worst simply wrong. For its advocates, rational choice sociology provides analytical precision, high empirical content and testable hypotheses. In general, rational action theories assume that actors consider the costs and benefits of alternative courses of action, selecting the one which maximises utility, where utility is defined in relation to specified preferences and goals. Although terms such as 'maximisation' suggest the quantitative-economic approach with which some critics equate rational choice sociology, in recent decades a wider conception has emerged in which preferences can derive from softer motivations including identity and values. Moreover, 'rationality' does not imply that actors have perfect knowledge of their situation:

> I would recognize that departures from the standard of 'perfect' rationality are very frequent. I make no assumption that actors are always entirely clear about their goals, are always aware of the optimal means of pursuing them, or in the end do always follow the course of action that they know to be rational.
>
> (Goldthorpe 1996, p.485)

The introduction of rational choice sociology to the study of educational opportunity is closely associated with the work of Raymond Boudon, and his explanation of secondary effects (Boudon 1974, pp.29–31) contains a number of features evident in later work. First, educational systems are conceptualised as a sequence of branching points where students choose between alternatives with different costs and benefits (social as well as economic), which vary according to social origin. Second, social classes are regarded as essentially similar in the way that they think about educational decisions. For all classes, the probability of choosing a particular alternative increases with its utility, which in turn increases with the benefit-cost difference. Rejecting the 'value' theory that working-class families desire less education, Boudon adopted a counter-argument proposed by Keller and Zavalloni (1964, p.60): the problem is not that working-class families have lower levels of aspiration, but that the social distance they must traverse to reach higher educational levels is greater. Indeed, for a working-class child to reach university requires *greater* aspiration than for a middle-class child. Downward mobility is feared by all classes, but to avoid it children from higher social classes require more education: this is why class similarities in aspiration give rise to class differences in behaviour. Based on these assumptions, Boudon develops a simulation model of an ideal-typical society which, he claims, reproduces observed patterns of IEO.

Although an impressive achievement, Boudon's model was less influential than might be thought, particularly in the sociology of education where Pierre Bourdieu and Basil Bernstein are better known as theorists of IEO. This was in part due to a review of *Education, Opportunity and Social Inequality* that was entirely unsympathetic to Boudon's arithmetical simulation approach (Hauser 1976). Nevertheless, the distinction between primary and secondary effects received serious attention from some researchers. Halsey, Heath and Ridge (1980) noted its potential for understanding IEO, although they concluded that a 'primary effects only' model appeared closer to reality than one with only secondary effects (p.134). These authors also constructed a model of school choice in some respects similar to the rational action models developed in the mid-1990s by Erikson and Jonsson (1996), Goldthorpe (1996) and Breen and Goldthorpe (1997). In the remainder of this section, the Breen-Goldthorpe model, which has since been the focus of extensive empirical testing, will be discussed in detail.

The Breen-Goldthorpe model was developed as a formalisation of the rational action framework proposed by Goldthorpe (1996) to explain stability or change in IEO, as well as between-country variation. Like Boudon, Breen and Goldthorpe (1997) construct a model of educational decision making in which individuals must choose between various options at certain branching points. Assume that the options are to stay in education and aim for the next level, or to leave education and enter the labour market. For those who remain, the next level may be successfully completed, or not. A more complex model could involve a differentiated educational level, in which one pathway gives high rewards but carries high risk of failure, whilst another is less risky but leads to smaller rewards (Erikson & Jonsson 1996, p.15). Three factors are taken to be significant in making a decision: the cost of remaining in education, including opportunity costs such as lost income; the (subjective) likelihood of success at the next level; and the benefits attached by the individual and their family to each of the three possible outcomes of the decision. These benefits are expressed through the subjective probabilities of gaining access to one of three ordered social classes – a service class, a working class and an underclass of precarious workers and the unemployed. Classes of origin are assumed to differ in only two ways: through average academic ability, that is, through the primary effects of social stratification; and through the different levels of resources they can draw on to meet the costs of remaining in education.

Three mechanisms through which class differentials in educational decisions may arise are proposed. First, *relative risk aversion* postulates that families from all social classes wish to avoid downward mobility for their children; families from higher social classes desire more education because in a (partly, at least) meritocratic society this is a pre-requisite of maintaining their higher social position. By contrast, children from working-class families need less education to be reasonably confident of maintaining their position. Middle-class children settling for modest educational qualifications run a higher risk of downward mobility than working-class children gaining the same qualifications, hence the term *relative* risk aversion. Second, class differences in the subjective probability of success at higher levels of education will exist, partly because they correspond to objective differences and partly because a higher subjective probability of success may be required for working-class children to commit to the next stage. Finally, differences in economic resources are likely to mean that the cost burden of education – even when confined to foregone earnings – will weigh relatively more heavily on working-class families. The cultural resources of parents may also be important, in terms of differences in strategic knowledge about the educational system and the ability to offer help with schooling (Erikson & Jonsson 1996, p.26).

Constructing a formal mathematical model from their assumptions, Breen and Goldthorpe (1997, pp.294–5) show that as costs at a particular level of education decrease and participation expands, IEO as measured by odds ratios remains roughly constant, as observed for most countries in Shavit and Blossfeld (1993). Between-country variations are explained through variations in the class distribution of resources and the balance between costs and benefits. Note that costs may decrease not just because certain levels of education are made free or grants/loans are provided; opportunity costs may decrease because labour market entry may not be an effective option, due to high youth unemployment or increases in the school-leaving age. Breen and Goldthorpe also claim that the model helps to explain maximally maintained inequality: once costs have reduced to the level at which all children from higher-class backgrounds may continue in education should they wish – the saturation condition – further cost reductions will have no impact on this class, but participation rates for lower social classes will continue to increase and odds ratios will decrease. Effectively maintained inequality can also be explained, provided that qualitative differences within an educational level are associated with an element of risk, for example through variations in academic challenge or social selectivity, or entail different cost burdens.

The Breen-Goldthorpe model claims to account not only for persistent inequality in educational attainment but also for the decline in gender-based differentials which has occurred in virtually all Western nations. Because formerly the returns to education for women were structured differently, including flatter gradients in returns for higher levels of attainment, the proportion of women remaining in education at each transition point would be expected to be smaller than for men, as would class differentials in educational attainment between women. More recently, the pattern of returns to education for women has changed as labour market participation rates, especially for married women, have increased and as the financial contribution of a woman's own employment has acquired greater significance to her family (Breen & Goldthorpe 1997, p.297). In the Breen-Goldthorpe model, therefore, gender differentials in education should decrease. Class differences among women should increase, or at least diminish less, unless other factors intervene. This argument is partly, although not wholly, supported by empirical evidence; certainly, gender differentials in educational attainment have declined, but across countries there appears to be no pattern of higher or lower class differences between men and women, and amongst women class differentials have decreased over time in the same way as men (Breen et al. 2010, pp.44–5).

Breen and Goldthorpe (1997, p.293) identify relative risk aversion as the key feature of their model: its ability to generate observed empirical patterns comes largely from the element of risk, in terms of destination class, attached to making more ambitious educational decisions, and its unequal distribution across origin classes. However, the relationship between individual attitudes to risk and relative risk aversion is not fully explored. More recently, Breen et al. (2014) have developed a rational action model in which, as well as costs and benefits, the utility of educational choices is made to depend on students' individual level of risk aversion and the weight they assign to future rather than immediate returns (time discounting) in an uncertain world. They distinguish two possible mechanisms through which social background may produce class differentiation in educational choices: *socioeconomic mediation*, in which students from different class backgrounds actually differ on average in terms of risk aversion and time discounting, and *socioeconomic heterogeneity*, in which the distribution of risk aversion and time discounting is the same for all class backgrounds but their impact on educational decisions differs. For example, individual students from advantaged backgrounds may be highly risk averse but still pursue high-stakes educational tracks because in the event of failure they can draw on parental resources for support. Socioeconomic heterogeneity can therefore produce the class phenomenon of relative risk aversion, because irrespective of risk tolerance more advantaged students disproportionately choose the forms of education most likely to result in reproducing their class position (Breen et al. 2014).

Empirical tests of the Breen-Goldthorpe model

The empirical testing of rational action theories in sociology has centred around two strategies (Jaeger 2007; Kroneberg & Kalter 2012). The first involves direct measurement of the subjective preferences motivating individual behaviour, usually by means of rating scales. In the case of the Breen-Goldthorpe model, these variables would include the desire to avoid downward mobility, alongside subjective evaluations of costs, benefits and success probabilities. Hypotheses involving these subjective preferences, for example that the desire for status maintenance should be independent of social class, are then tested. This strategy has been the subject of various criticisms, including the validity of capturing subjective preferences through rating scales, the practicalities of gathering the relevant data, and – perhaps most telling – that the direct method distracts attention from an actor's objective situation (Goldthorpe 1998).

The second strategy, revealed preference analysis (Jaeger 2007), tests theory indirectly by using it to make behavioural predictions relating to more easily observed data, for example in the present context the actual educational choices made by students (Breen & Yaish 2006). The main difficulty with this approach is its theoretical ambiguity – that is, it is difficult to construct hypotheses that are so specific to rational action theory that they are not consistent with other, competing theories. An example of this problem appears in Davies et al. (2002), who argue that relative risk aversion implies a relationship between social background, transition probability and educational level that is inconsistent with standard human capital theory. However, although their data supports relative risk aversion on this basis, they note that other variants of human capital theory could still explain their findings.

A further difficulty in testing the Breen-Goldthorpe model is its complexity. Lucas (2009) identifies three separable components, each containing a number of subordinate propositions: a relational model of opportunity structures in education and the labour market; a model of how student beliefs about these opportunity structures are produced, both subjectively and inter-subjectively; and mechanisms generating patterns of class-differentiated behaviour that produce an association between class and educational attainment. Along with class differences in average ability and economic resources, relative risk aversion, the model's key principle, is just one element of this third component.

Given these challenges, it is not surprising that the status of the Breen-Goldthorpe model is still uncertain. Nevertheless, qualified support from a range of studies, involving both direct and indirect measures, has emerged. Relative risk aversion has been tested a number of times, across different countries and contexts, leading to quite a complex picture. Holm and Jaeger (2005) find strong support for the principle, and more recently Jaeger and Holm (2012) find that it explains part of the social class gradient in educational outcomes. By contrast, Gabay-Egozi et al. (2010) in Israel find that class maintenance motivations do not affect educational choice. For the Netherlands, using a direct measure of the desire to avoid downward mobility, van de Werfhorst and Hofstede (2007) found near-constancy of relative risk aversion across social classes. However, German data analysed by Stocké (2007), which involved a comprehensive set of direct measures as well as revealed preferences, indicated that parents from lower social classes attached greater importance to avoiding downward mobility than did parents in service-class positions.

Breen and Yaish (2006) find that the unskilled working class showed the greatest propensity to early school-leaving, despite the impossibility of downward mobility for this class. Jaeger and Holm (2012) modify relative risk aversion to allow for some heterogeneity in the desire to avoid downward mobility, finding that although the majority of young people wish to reach at least the class position of their parents, a minority reject this aspiration. In a study of transitions in Denmark, Breen et al. (2014) found that higher individual risk aversion did not reduce the probability of choosing the academic route for the most privileged students, whereas such a relationship did exist for students from disadvantaged and middle socioeconomic backgrounds. Higher risk aversion in lower classes is also reported by Obermeier and Schneider (2015) in Denmark.

Beliefs about opportunity structures have also been tested, and class differences in subjective evaluations of costs, benefits and success probabilities are reported by Stocké (2007), Becker and Hecken (2009b) and Gabay-Egozi et al. (2010). Hansen (2008) reports a significant impact of parental economic resources on educational attainment, after controlling for parental education and other independent variables. However, although several key aspects of the Breen-Goldthorpe model are supported by these studies, their analyses differ in their evaluation of the model as an explanation for social class differences in educational attainment. Becker and Hecken (2009b) conclude that their results support the Breen-Goldthorpe model; however, they also support the subjectively expected utility model of Esser (1999), and Stocké (2007, p.515) found that the Breen-Goldthorpe model did not fully explain the secondary effects of class on educational decisions.

In summary, then, it appears that several individual features of the Breen-Goldthorpe model are supported by studies across a range of national and institutional contexts. These include the key principle of relative risk aversion, although it is likely that some variation between social classes must be allowed in the desire to avoid downward mobility. The anomalous position of the unskilled working class (Breen & Yaish 2006) also requires explanation. It also appears that the Breen-Goldthorpe model, and by implication other forms of rational action theory, can explain at least part of the secondary effects of social stratification on educational attainment. However, as the careful analysis by Stocké (2007) makes clear, not all of these effects are accounted for by this model. Finally, the theoretical ambiguity associated with indirect tests based on student behaviours is a continuing obstacle to drawing conclusions about the superiority of rational action theory over competing accounts of IEO.

Conclusion

The explanations of IEO which have hitherto been most influential in the sociology of education, notably Bourdieu's cultural reproduction, find it difficult to escape accusations of determinism, essentialising working-class deficiency, or both. Rational action theories, which place agency at the centre of their account and emphasise that class differences in behaviour arise from the socially situated nature of the decisions behind them, offer significant advantages in all phases of education and perhaps most particularly in the context of higher education. Not only does university entry lie at the end of a sequence of educational transition points, highlighting the cumulative impact of secondary effects; in addition, the estimation of costs and benefits in relation to family resources surely has critical weight at the transition to the various strata of higher education encountered in Western industrial nations.

As we have seen, rational action theory – particularly in the form given to it by Breen and Goldthorpe (1997) and later Breen et al. (2014) – can successfully account for observed trends in IEO such as the relatively persistent inequality seen in numerous countries, the behaviour of IEO as participation by higher social classes approaches saturation, and the decline in IEO as economic inequality or the costs of education are reduced. It can also explain some features of *decreasing* gender inequality in education. However, rational action theories in general suffer from the serious problem of theoretical ambiguity: where they rely on macro-level behaviour for verification, it is impossible to exclude other explanations, and even when the individual motivations underlying behaviour are made empirically accessible, it can still be difficult to differentiate rational action explanations from other theories. Although an impressive body of evidence has been accumulated in favour of the Breen-Goldthorpe model in particular, it is by no means conclusive and more empirical research is needed.

These challenges are particularly important in view of certain criticisms made largely from within the Bourdieusian tradition. This critique accepts that the distinction between primary and secondary effects may be useful methodologically, in highlighting the fact that class differences in educational attainment remain after controlling for performance (Nash 2005, 2006). However, it disputes the proposition that primary and secondary effects arise from distinct processes, or that 'choice' can be conceptualised apart from the field relations of dominance and subordination that produce primary effects. Furthermore, separating primary effects from a unitary theory of schooling in class society allows a deficit account to re-emerge. To interpret the distinction between primary and secondary effects as anything more than an analytical device would therefore have little meaning, and perhaps be ill-considered.

Turning to the micro-processes of rational action theory, Hatcher (1998, p.20) argues that "real-life choices . . . cannot be reduced to utilitarian calculations of costs, benefits and probabilities". Drawing on studies which highlight diverse individual responses to educational opportunities, he sees rational action theories as applying a reductionist economic model of the individual and counterposing rational choice to culture rather than uniting them. This is, perhaps, to misrepresent rational action, which does not claim to be a model of social behaviour in its full complexity, but in its average effects: "We . . . assume that, *in their central tendencies*, these patterns of educational choice reflect action on the part of children and their parents that can be understood as rational" (Breen & Goldthorpe 1997, p.277, original emphasis). However, such disputes do not imply that cultural reproduction and rational action theory are necessarily incompatible. Hatcher (1998) points out that Bourdieu has acknowledged that rational action may supersede the operation of habitus in certain circumstances. More recently, van de Werfhorst and Hofstede (2007) have used both cultural capital and relative risk aversion to investigate educational choices, whilst Glaesser and Cooper (2013) argue that habitus and relative risk aversion can be complementary, with habitus providing boundaries for an essentially subjective rationality.

Rational action theory should, in any case, be judged in terms of explanatory power, and from this point of view, its potential for informing policy is considerable. The decomposition of IEO into primary and secondary effects indicates different kinds of policy intervention that would be relevant, and their possible impact on equality (Jackson 2013, p.5). For example Neugebauer and Schindler (2012) find that neutralising secondary effects at the transition to upper second-ary school would be the single most effective means to increase participation rates in tertiary education among working-class students. However, rational action theory warns that initiatives to raise working-class aspirations in pursuit of this aim need to be interpreted carefully in the light of objective barriers such as opportunity costs, together with positional competition from more advantaged families who can draw on greater resources to ensure that their children maxim-ise their academic potential. Finally, it underlines the point that slogans such as choice and excellence come at a cost, providing further opportunities for higher social classes to consolidate their advantage.

Notes

1 Odds and odds ratios between social classes (or other social background catego-ries) for an educational transition are calculated from the observed proportions in each class making the transition. If p_1 is the probability of making the transition for children in class S_1, and p_2 the corresponding probability for class S_2, the odds for class S_1 are $p_1/(1 - p_1)$. The log-odds for the transition are obtained by taking the natural logarithm of this quantity, that is $\ln [p_1/(1 - p_1)]$. The odds ratio between the two classes, taking S_1 as the reference class, is the ratio between the odds for S_1 and the odds for S_2, that is $[p_1(1 - p_2)/p_2(1 - p_1)]$.

2 Some studies use as their measure of attainment the completion of specified stages of education rather than having made the transition from one stage to the next; see Breen et al. (2009).

3 Table 4.1 may be helpful in illustrating the relationship between odds ratios and participation rates. Because odds ratios are independent of overall participation rates there is no unique correspondence, but the table gives three illustrations of educational systems with 'low', 'medium' and 'high' participation.

Table 4.1 Odds ratios and corresponding 'working-class' participation rates W when compared with 'service-class' participation rates S of 20, 50 and 90 per cent (see note 4 below).

Log odds	Odds ratio	W (%) Low participation system (S = 20%)	W (%) Medium participation system (S = 50%)	W (%) High participation system (S = 90%)
0	1.0	20.0	50.0	90.0
0.5	1.6	13.2	37.8	84.5
1.0	2.7	8.4	26.9	76.8
1.5	4.5	5.3	18.2	66.8
2.0	7.4	3.3	11.9	54.9
2.5	12.2	2.0	7.6	42.5
3.0	20.1	1.2	4.7	30.9

4 The ill-defined nature of the term 'middle class' leads some authors to specify class in terms of the labour process. In this context, 'service class' or 'salariat' refers to individuals with a service-contract relationship implying greater autonomy and security, and more flexible working conditions, as opposed to a labour-contract relationship associated with working-class employment.
5 Some authors consider also the tertiary effects of social stratification; that is, the effect of social background on the evaluations of students' performance by teachers and educational institutions. See Blossfeld et al. (2015).

References

Becker, R. & Hecken, A. (2009a) Why are working-class children diverted from universities? An empirical assessment of the diversion thesis. *European Sociological Review*, 25(2), 233–250.

Becker, R. & Hecken, A. (2009b) Higher education or vocational training? An empirical test of the rational action model of educational choices suggested by Breen and Goldthorpe and Esser. *Acta Sociologica*, 52(1), 25–45.

Blossfeld, P., Blossfeld, G. & Blossfeld, H.-P. (2015) Educational expansion and inequalities in educational opportunity: Long-term changes for East and West Germany. *European Sociological Review*, 31(2), 144–160.

Boalt, G. & Jansen, C.-G. (1953) A selected bibliography of the literature on social stratification and social mobility in Sweden. *Current Sociology*, 2, 306–327.

Boliver, V. (2011) Expansion, differentiation and the persistence of social class inequalities in British higher education. *Higher Education*, 61, 229–242.

Boudon, R. (1974) *Education, Opportunity and Social Inequality: Changing Prospects in Western Society*. London: John Wiley.

Boudon, R. (1989) *The Analysis of Ideology*. Cambridge: Polity Press.

Breen, R. & Goldthorpe, J. (1997) Explaining educational differentials: Towards a formal rational action theory. *Rationality and Society*, 9(3), 275–305.

Breen, R. & Jonsson, J. (2005) Inequality of opportunity in comparative perspective: Recent research on educational attainment and mobility. *Annual Reviews of Sociology*, 31, 223–243.

Breen, R., Luijkx, R., Müller, W. & Pollak, R. (2009) Nonpersistent inequality in educational attainment: Evidence from eight European countries. *American Journal of Sociology*, 114(5), 1475–1521.

Breen, R., Luijkx, R., Müller, W. & Pollak, R. (2010) Long-term trends in educational inequality in Europe: Class inequalities and gender differences. *European Sociological Review*, 26(1), 31–48.

Breen, R., van de Werfhorst, H. & Jaeger, M. (2014) Deciding under doubt: A theory of risk aversion, time discounting preferences, and educational decision-making. *European Sociological Review*, 30(2), 258–270.

Breen, R. & Yaish, M. (2006) Testing the Breen-Goldthorpe model of educational decision making. In S. L. Morgan, D. B. Grusky & G. S. Fields (eds.) *Mobility and Inequality*. Stanford, CA: Stanford University Press, 232–258.

Burger, K. (2016) Intergenerational transmission of education in Europe: Do more comprehensive education systems reduce social gradients in student achievement? *Research in Social Stratification and Mobility*, 44, 54–67.

Davies, R., Heinesen, E. & Holm, A. (2002) The relative risk aversion hypothesis of educational choice. *Journal of Population Economics*, 15, 683–713.

Dollmann, J. (2016) Less choice, less inequality? A natural experiment on social and ethnic differences in educational decision-making. *European Sociological Review*, 32(2), 203–215.

Erikson, R. & Jonsson, J. (1996) Explaining class inequality in education: The Swedish test case. In R. Erikson & J. Jonsson (eds.) *Can Education Be Equalised? The Swedish Case in Comparative Perspective*. Boulder, CO: Westview Press, 1–64.

Erikson, R., Goldthorpe, J., Jackson, M., Yaish, M. & Cox, D. (2005) On class differentials in educational attainment. *Proceedings of the National Academy of Sciences of the United States of America*, 102(27), 9730–9733.

Esser, H. (1999) *Soziologie. Spezielle Grundlagan. Band 1: Situationslogik und Handeln*. Frankfurt am Main: Campus.

Gabay-Egozi, L., Shavit, S. & Yaish, M. (2010) Curricular choice: A test of a rational choice model of education. *European Sociological Review*, 26(4), 447–463.

Girard, A. & Bastide, H. (1963) La stratification sociale et la démocratisation de l'enseignement. *Population*, 18, 435–72.

Glaesser, J. & Cooper, B. (2013) Using rational action theory and Bourdieu's habitus theory together to account for educational decision-making in England and Germany. *Sociology*, 48(3), 463–481.

Goldthorpe, J. (1996) Class analysis and the reorientation of class theory: The case of persisting differentials in educational attainment. *British Journal of Sociology*, 47(3), 481–505.

Goldthorpe, J. (1998) Rational action theory for sociology. *British Journal of Sociology*, 49(2), 167–192.

Halsey, A.H., Heath, A.F. & Ridge, J.M. (1980) *Origins and Destinations: Family, Class and Education in Modern Britain*. Oxford: Clarendon Press.

Hansen, M. (2008) Rational action theory and educational attainment: Changes in the impact of economic resources. *European Sociological Review*, 24(1), 1–17.

Hatcher, R. (1998) Class differentiation in education: Rational choices? *British Journal of Sociology of Education*, 19(1), 5–24.

Hauser, T. (1976) On Boudon's model of social mobility. *American Journal of Sociology*, 81(4), 911–928.

Holm, A. & Jaeger, M. (2005) Relative risk aversion and social reproduction in intergenerational educational attainment: Application of a dynamic discrete choice model. Paper presented at the RC28 Conference *Inequality and Mobility in Family, School, and Work*, August 18–21, University of California, Los Angeles.

Ianelli, C. (2007) Inequalities in entry to higher education: A comparison over time between Scotland and England and Wales. *Higher Education Quarterly*, 61(3), 306–333.

Ianelli, C., Smyth, E. & Klein, M. (2015) Curriculum differentiation and social inequality in higher education entry in Scotland and Ireland. *British Educational Research Journal*, doi: 10.1002/berj.3217.

Jackson, M. (ed.) (2013) *Determined to Succeed? Performance versus Choice in Educational Attainment*. Stanford, CA: Stanford University Press.

Jackson, M. & Jonsson, J. (2013) Why does inequality of educational opportunity vary across countries? Primary and secondary effects in comparative perspective. In M. Jackson (ed.) *Determined to Succeed? Performance versus Choice in Educational Attainment*. Stanford, CA: Stanford University Press, 306–337.

Jaeger, M. (2007) Economic and social returns to educational choices: Extending the utility function. *Rationality and Society*, 19(4), 451–483.

Jaeger, M. & Holm, A. (2012) Conformists or rebels? Relative risk aversion, educational decisions and social class reproduction. *Rationality and Society*, 24(2), 221–253.

Keller, S. & Zavalloni, M. (1964) Ambition and social class: A respecification. *Social Forces*, 43(1), 58–70.

Kroneberg, C. & Kalter, F. (2012) Rational choice theory and empirical research: Methodological and theoretical contributions from Europe. *Annual Reviews of Sociology*, 38, 73–92.

Lucas, S. (2001) Effectively maintained inequality: Education transitions, track mobility, and social background effects. *American Journal of Sociology*, 106(6), 1642–1690.

Lucas, S. (2009) Stratification theory, socioeconomic background, and educational attainment: A formal analysis. *Rationality and Society*, 21(4), 459–511.

Mare, R. (1980) Social background and school continuation decisions. *Journal of the American Statistical Association*, 75(370), 295–305.

Mare, R. (1981) Change and stability in educational stratification. *American Sociological Review*, 46, 72–97.

Morgan, S. (2012) Models of college entry in the United States and the challenges of estimating primary and secondary effects. *Sociological Methods & Research*, 41(1), 17–56.

Nash, R. (2005) Boudon, realism and the cognitive habitus: Why an explanation of inequality/difference cannot be limited to a model of secondary effects. *Interchange*, 36(3), 275–293.

Nash, R. (2006) Controlling for 'ability': A conceptual and empirical study of primary and secondary effects. *British Journal of Sociology of Education*, 27(2), 157–172.

Neugebauer, M. & Schindler, S. (2012) Early transitions and tertiary enrolment: The cumulative impact of primary and secondary effects on entering university in Germany. *Acta Sociologica*, 55(1), 19–36.

Obermeier, V. & Schneider, T. (2015) Educational choice and risk preferences: How important is relative vs. individual risk preference? *Journal for Educational Research Online*, 7(2), 99–128.

Pfeffer, F. (2008) Persistent inequality in educational attainment and its institutional context. *European Sociological Review*, 24(5), 543–565.

Raftery, A. & Hout, M. (1993) Maximally maintained inequality: Expansion, reform and opportunity in Irish education, 1921–75. *Sociology of Education*, 66, 41–62.

Reimer, D. & Pollack, R. (2010) Educational expansion and its consequences for vertical and horizontal inequalities in access to higher education in West Germany. *European Sociological Review*, 26(4), 415–430.

Shavit, Y. & Blossfeld, H. P. (1993) *Persistent Inequality: Changing Educational Attainment in Thirteen Countries*. Boulder, CO: Westview Press.

Stocké, V. (2007) Explaining educational decision and effects of families' social class position: an empirical test of the Breen-Goldthorpe model of educational attainment. *European Sociological Review*, 23(4), 505–519.

Thomsen, J. (2015) Maintaining inequality effectively? Access to higher education programmes in a universalist welfare state in periods of educational expansion 1984–2010. *European Sociological Review*, 31(6), 683–696.

Van de Werfhorst, H. & Hofstede, S. (2007) Cultural capital or relative risk aversion? Two mechanisms for educational inequality compared. *British Journal of Sociology*, 58(3), 391–415.

Van de Werfhorst, H. & Mijs, J. (2010) Achievement inequality and the institutional structure of educational systems: A comparative perspective. *Annual Reviews of Sociology*, 36, 407–428.

Chapter 5

Student choices under uncertainty

Bounded rationality and behavioural economics

Neil Harrison

Encouraging prospective students to make 'better' decisions about higher education has been a concern of the government in England since at least the early 2000s, but it has gathered pace with the increasing marketisation of the sector. There is a barely voiced assumption that students are poor consumers within the marketplace and that this needs policy intervention. In particular, there is often considered to be a problem with high achievers not selecting elite universities (Sutton Trust, 2004). Meanwhile, political, academic and journalistic assessments have been repeatedly confounded in their attempts to predict student behaviour. This is, in part, due to the simplistic application of economics to a complex social field, where, for example financial (dis)incentives have proved largely ineffective at influencing demand, despite students' assumed sensitivity around the cost of higher education.

This chapter explores theoretical perspectives drawn from the work of Herbert Simon and Daniel Kahneman. Both won the Nobel Prize (1978 and 2002, respectively), despite not ostensibly being economists, for their work on human decision-making under uncertainty. Their insights, drawn from an interdisciplinary space between economics, psychology and sociology, have subsequently been applied to dozens of real-world and experimental scenarios, with a consistency of empirical support for the basic tenets. However, these insights have not generally been extended to educational decision-making contexts.

This chapter therefore aims to open up this space in the context of the decisions that prospective students make about higher education. It begins with an overview of key theoretical concepts before tentatively applying these to real-life decisions facing prospective students when making the decision to enter higher education.

From bounded rationality to behavioural economics

Simon's formative work focused on decision-making within organisations. He argued that neoclassical economic theory was critically flawed in assuming that human actors were mechanically rational in their decisions, seeking to maximise the 'expected utility' (generally financial) that could to be derived from the various possible outcomes. This became the basis for his theory of 'bounded rationality', developed and applied over the next fifty years across business and organisational psychology, but with later attempts to integrate it into general social science (Simon, 2000).

Bounded rationality as an idea is deceptively simple and intuitively compelling, in comparison to the 'psychologically unrealistic' (Kahneman, 2003, p. 1449) expected utility model that had previously dominated:

> Global rationality, the rationality of neoclassical theory, assumes that the decision maker has a comprehensive, consistent utility function, knows all the alternatives that are available for choice, can compute the expected value of utility associated with each alternative, and chooses the alternative that maximizes expected utility.
>
> (Simon, 1997, p. 17)

Instead, bounded rationality asserts that

> the choices people make are determined not only by some consistent overall goal and the properties of the external world, but also by the knowledge that decision makers do and don't have of the world, their ability or inability to evoke that knowledge when it is relevant, to work out the consequences of their actions, to conjure up possible courses of action, to cope with uncertainty [. . .] and to adjudicate among their many competing wants.
>
> (Simon, 2000, p. 25)

Simon argued that humans are not generally able to exercise full rationality and that there are constraints impacting on all decisions:

> Rationality is bounded when it falls short of omniscience. And the failures of omniscience are largely failures of knowing all the alternatives, uncertainty about relevant exogenous events, and inability to calculate consequences.
>
> (Simon, 1979, p. 502)

Bounded rationality does not, therefore, argue that decisions and the people taking them are inherently *irrational*, but that there are realistic limits on the ability of people to weigh complex options in a fully logical and objective way; it is often placed in opposition to 'rational choice' theory. In describing bounded rationality, Simon (1986) railed against the 'armchair economics' of neoclassical thinkers, which he felt sought to reduce decision-making to a simplistic model of human behaviour without engagement with empirical data. Bounded rationality therefore concerns itself with the interaction between the human mind (with its prior knowledge, competing value systems and finite cognitive resources) and the social environment. It does not primarily concern itself with the outcome of decisions, but the processes by which they are made and how these processes are shaped by the individual and their wider circumstances (Simon, 1955).

Some bounds derive from the prevailing environment, particularly with respect to the availability of information and the 'cost' of that information in terms of time seeking it. Individuals are unlikely to be 'able to foresee what additional information further search would bring, what it would cost, and what opportunities one would forgo during that search' (Todd and Gigerenzer, 2003, p. 146), leaving them uncertain whether they have enough; this challenge has only increased with the arrival of the Internet, with the information available spiralling into overload and making its collection and evaluation more problematic rather than less (Agosto, 2002; Benselin and Ragsdell, 2016).

Other environmental bounds include the number of possible options for action and the number of potential criteria (or 'cues') for distinguishing between them. The complexity of decisions increases exponentially with increases in either feature, leading to problems with evaluating the expected utility of each; a decision with two options and one cue is simple to resolve, but one with twenty options and five cues is considerably more problematic. Furthermore, decisions taken under risk (i.e. with various possible outcomes for each option) add further to this complexity, especially where the probabilities of these outcomes occurring are unknown (requiring estimation) or unknowable due to the novelty of the situation; fundamentally, the decision-maker 'has egregiously incomplete and inaccurate knowledge about the consequences of actions' (Simon, 1997, p. 17).

The individual decision-maker is the source of other bounds. Estimates of probability and utility of outcomes are shaped by different levels of pre-existing knowledge and experience. This defines a starting point of which information is readily accessible at the outset of the decision-making process, as well as influencing the unfolding of the process itself; this is further influenced by the circle of advisers on which they are able to draw. Individuals will also have conflicting priorities that extend beyond the purely financial, touching perhaps on personal wellbeing or the need to maintain social relations, with different cues having different levels of salience for each person. Finally, cognitive resources are limited and mediated through a range of systematic biases, particularly under time pressure and emotional stress (Simon, 1987).

A key tenet of bounded rationality is the concept of 'satisficing', which Simon (1955) used to explain decisions he witnessed in field studies. Satisficed decisions are not intended to be optimal, but to provide an intuitive balance between outcomes and the costs (in time, mental effort and things forgone) of the decision itself, while meeting a threshold criterion of expected utility. These 'fast and frugal' (Gigerenzer and Goldstein, 1996) heuristic approaches were not only commonly used, but often provided good decisions which were comparable to an exhaustive 'rational' analysis. Indeed, subsequent work by followers of Simon (e.g. Todd and Gigerenzer, 2003) has shown that heuristic approaches can even be preferable to rational ones when they eliminate unnecessary and confounding information or cues.

Kahneman's work draws heavily on bounded rationality and focuses on the role of intuitive processes as a means of navigating complexity. It primarily concerns the cognitive biases that impede rational decision-making and the heuristics used by individuals when operating with unknown outcomes under risk. The list of these biases and heuristics is legion (Kahneman, Slovic and Tversky, 1982; Kahneman and Tversky, 2000; Kahneman, 2011).

While Simon drew his theoretical insights mainly from fieldwork, Kahneman and colleagues within what has become known as 'behavioural economics' have worked mainly through experimental psychology, presenting people with a range of carefully designed tasks to examine underpinning decision processes. This initially culminated in 'prospect theory' (Kahneman and Tversky, 1979) derived from simple gambles concerning different probabilities and financial outcomes – positive and negative. They were able to demonstrate the use of intuition in decision-making under risk rather than 'rational' reasoning, and like Simon, demonstrated the fallacy of a simple calculation of expected utility:

> The central characteristic of agents is not that they reason poorly but that they often act intuitively. And the behaviour of these agents is not guided by what they are able to compute, but by what they happen to see at a given moment.
> (Kahneman, 2003, p. 1469)

Behavioural economics views people as inherently intuitive and emotional decision-makers (Kahneman, Wakker and Sarin, 1997), with the use of intuition over reason as an obstacle to rational decisions, although the result of intuitive processes is not necessarily significantly poorer, especially given the lower informational and cognitive needs (Kahneman, 2003). This holds even where the decision is complex and the outcomes are expressed over long time periods. Indeed, studies that have focused on real-world, long-term decision-making such as investments or house purchases have found results that are consistent with prospect theory (Barberis, 2012). List (2003) demonstrates that substantial professional experience involving repeated decisions is needed to overcome intuitive biases to maximise long-term financial returns.

Kahneman's experiments have generated a number of specific insights that are relevant here. First, people prefer to risk a larger loss over a certain small loss, in contrast to gains, where preferences are generally for a certain gain over riskier gambles; in other words, individuals tend to be loss-averse rather than risk-averse. Importantly, the individual's current situation (e.g. level of wealth) is vital in determining the choices made, with the potential change in circumstances influencing the decision, rather than the absolute value of the outcome.

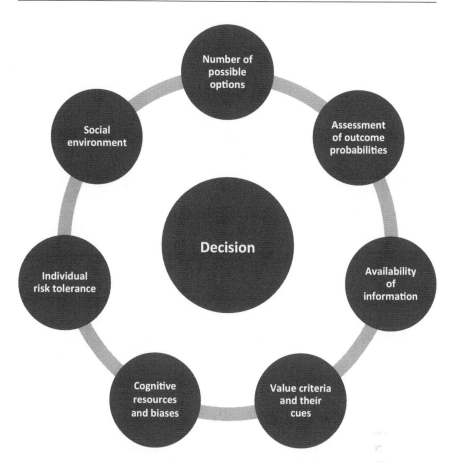

Figure 5.1 Visualisation of factors impacting on decision-making under risk

In concrete terms, a £1,000 gain has more utility to someone with £10,000 than someone with £100,000, and the two individuals make decisions accordingly: 'Utility cannot be divorced from emotion, and emotions are triggered by changes' (Kahneman, 2003, p. 1457). This 'reference-dependency' (Koszegi and Rabin, 2007) is considerably more nuanced than a simple scale of risk aversion as is often used in studies of decision-making (e.g. Breen, van de Werfhorst and Jaegar, 2014).

Kahneman has also identified a 'framing effect', whereby decisions are strongly influenced by the wording and explanation of the possible outcomes, even where the inherent information is identical. There is often a 'passive acceptance of the formulation given' (Kahneman, 2003, p. 1459), as well as a process of editing to simplify options into more recognisable categories (Kahneman and Tversky,

1979). Two related heuristics are particularly relevant to this chapter. The first is 'accessibility', where the brain uses information from memory that is most readily brought to mind. This is built on the individual's past experiences, as well as a general privileging of the familiar. The second is 'representativeness', where the specifics of a decision are intuitively linked to known archetypes – e.g. with people in certain occupations being substituted with personality types associated with those occupations.

This brief introduction to bounded rationality and behavioural economics for those unfamiliar with the theoretical foundations and empirical results is necessarily partial in its treatment, but, it is hoped, clear in its basic premise: that individual decision-makers have marked constraints on their ability to distinguish between options, especially where (a) these options are numerous, (b) the outcomes are probabilistic and 'risky', (c) there are multiple (and conflicting) measures of utility and (d) their ability to draw on experience or advisers with experience is limited. Furthermore, finite cognitive resources are compromised by involuntary systematic biases, especially where there is an emotional component to the decision or where it is taken under pressure. This is summarised diagrammatically in Figure 5.1.

Applying bounded rationality and behavioural economics

While bounded rationality and behavioural economics have been applied to numerous environments, they have not yet enjoyed wide use within education. This is perhaps due to a discomfort in viewing educational decisions as economic ones, but there is good evidence that this is how they are increasingly viewed by prospective students (Purcell et al., 2008). Indeed, one of the advantages of bounded rationality as a theoretical lens is that it draws focus to the social and individual elements of financial decisions, while acknowledging the economic imperatives behind the decision.

A number of useful conceptual insights can be summarised from the theory and empirical findings introduced above; these are not intended to be exhaustive.

1   **More information is not always useful.**

Neoclassical economic theory is predicated on perfect information as the basis of rational decision-making. Conversely, bounded rationality posits that the acquisition of information is not a costless exercise, in terms of time needed for collection and analysis. This is further complicated if the size of the information set is unknown and if the relative value of full information compared to partial information is not known – i.e. how much is enough? Even if full information is achieved, it can actually have an adverse impact on decisions by clouding or adding unnecessary cues.

2   Decision complexity increases exponentially.

Laboratory experiments are generally based around relatively simple decisions between a small number of options with known outcome probabilities
and clear distinguishing cues (e.g. financial gain/loss). However, real-life
decisions tend to be significantly more complex than this, with numerous
options, unknown probabilities and multiple criteria. Weighing these cues
quickly becomes challenging and overall complexity of the analytical task
grows exponentially. Behavioural economics predicts that people will take
intuitive, rather than rational, opportunities to reduce this complexity using
heuristics drawing on familiar memories or archetypes.

3   Money is not the only source of utility.

While neoclassical economics does allow for non-financial forms of utility,
these are generally underplayed. Conversely, bounded rationality expects
decisions to be exercised across multiple concepts of utility. Relevant other
forms of utility for educational decisions might include happiness/wellbeing,
the desire for academic success, the maintenance of positive social relationships or the non-transgression of societal expectations. In particular, both
Simon and Kahneman view humans as emotional decision-makers who seek
to maximise their positive affect, especially in the short-term.

4   Responses to cues are highly individual, but socially embedded.

Bounded rationality predicts that individuals will react differently to the
same options. Specifically, people react primarily to changes in their financial
situation rather than the absolute endpoint; as all financial situations differ,
so do the decisions. In particular, relative gains are more likely to be valued
by those with lower wealth. Furthermore, prior experiences and the wider
social environment will impact on their concepts of value and the criteria
used to estimate it, as well as shaping expectations – which, in turn, shape
the framing of decisions in ways that are redolent of Bourdieu's concept of
'habitus' (Collet, 2009).

5   Risk is contextualised and attitudes are non-linear.

Experimental studies suggest that people are risk-averse when considering
losses, but more risk-tolerant when considering gains. Furthermore, tolerance is higher when the probabilities and outcomes are known rather than
unknown or unknowable. People are not generally good estimators of the
likelihoods of particular events occurring, especially over a lengthy passage
of time and with an emotional component: 'the long term is not where life
is lived' (Kahneman, 2003, p. 1457).

Higher education choices

This section explores how these theoretical principles might be applied to higher education decisions. No specific claims to knowledge are made here; the discussion is speculative and illustrative in nature. It uses a bounded rationality lens to examine three key decisions where empirical evidence suggests that many students, especially from disadvantaged backgrounds, are making non-rational decisions; for simplicity, it will focus on young applicants, although the principles are likely to relate to mature students too. The decision-making process surrounding entry to higher education starts early in the teenage years for most and is undoubtedly complex, with a wide variety of higher education forms on offer, including thousands of degree programmes across around 150 universities in England.

For the purposes of this chapter, three principal decisions with the most obvious economic component are examined, although these will be supplemented by issues of personal preference (e.g. which specific university) and myriad micro-decisions (e.g. whether to live in halls of residence).

Should I enter higher education?

This is obviously the most fundamental decision and the one that contributes to national performance indicators on higher education access. It is predicated on the possession of qualifications that permit higher education entry and the majority of individuals who possess these do choose to progress, almost regardless of their socio-economic status (Coleman and Bekhradnia, 2011; Crawford, 2014). This imperative is strongest among those with the most and the highest status qualifications. Nevertheless, some do choose not to seek entry to higher education, particularly those with fewer or lower status qualifications.

Regardless of the reality, for most students the decision is driven in large part by a general belief in 'human capital' (Becker, 1994) – that the accumulation of qualifications will have a positive impact on their long-term finances and well-being (Purcell et al., 2008). This is juxtaposed against the short-term costs of higher education in terms of loan accumulated for tuition fees and living costs, as well as forgone earnings and career progression over the period of study.

There is, therefore, an economic decision to be made. On the one hand, basic information about direct costs is readily available through a host of official websites. The opportunity costs of participation are harder to estimate: what job could have been secured outside higher education, what might it pay and with what chances for progression? These estimates are assembled in a congested graduate employment market where work previously available to eighteen-year-olds now requires a degree as a minimum (Brown, 2013). Those with strong or vocationally focused qualifications (or useful family networks) might have realistic expectations of securing a traineeship or apprenticeship with on-the-job training and progression routes. However, for most, the alternative to higher education would be low wage and low prospect employment or unemployment.

Conversely, information on possible financial outcomes from higher education is harder to obtain (and inherently out-of-date). Partly due to the congested market, the likelihood of securing graduate-level work is uncertain (Scurry and Blenkinsopp, 2011; Purcell et al., 2012), while graduate salaries are heavily dependent on degree subject, university status and degree result (Chevalier, 2011; Walker and Zhu, 2011; Naylor, Smith and Telhaj, 2016). Even given figures for typical graduate pathways or average salaries, the prospective student is far from in possession of perfect information, especially given increasing dispersion in salaries (Green and Zhu, 2010), with their own estimates tending to be too high (Jerrim, 2011).

It is often assumed that young people from low income backgrounds will be disproportionately deterred by the cost of higher education due to higher risk aversion and lower family resources (Callender and Jackson, 2005), but this has been increasingly challenged by evidence. First, Crawford (2014) has shown that qualifications accrued at sixteen account for around 95 per cent of the variation in university participation rates, such that the social differences are created much earlier in the lifecourse, with little 'space' for debt aversion to play a major role. Second, official data (e.g. Universities and Colleges Admissions Service [UCAS], 2015) shows that major increases in costs in 2006 and 2012 were met with rising demand from lower socio-economic groups, rather than falling. Finally, interviews with students finds them mainly reporting tolerant attitudes to the costs of higher education (Harrison et al., 2015; Esson and Ertl, 2016).

Using a bounded rationality lens, this potentially counterintuitive situation can be more readily understood. First, the long-term financial returns from higher education are unpredictable and becoming more so. There is no reliable source of information available to prospective students; reliable data are always necessarily out-of-date. Government, universities and schools therefore rely on a general exhortation towards higher education with a tacit 'promise' of an improved future. Second, for young people from low income backgrounds, their ability to lose through the higher education 'gamble' is lower. While the precise outcome is unpredictable, there is confidence it will be higher than the likely alternative: unemployment or low prospect work, especially in periods of recession and in deprived areas. This is consistent with the loss-aversion (as opposed to risk-aversion) predicted by behavioural economics.

Furthermore, the anticipated gains from higher education *feel* more significant due to the low income context of the family. Conversely, the full costs of higher education are counterintuitively higher for those from more advantaged backgrounds as their alternatives are likely to be more lucrative, while the potential gains are more muted when pitched against higher family wealth. This may explain why this group has been more sensitive to increases in tuition fees (UCAS, 2015; Harrison, in press).

Which subject should I study?

This is often a vexed decision for prospective students, with contradictory influences and conflicting priorities. As noted above, the imperative to make decisions that lead to improved long-term life chances looms large, but students often also value subjects where they have been academically successful or that hold an intrinsic interest for them (Purcell et al., 2008).

As a result, students will need to trade off utility from future salary expectations with the need to enjoy (at least in part) their years of study and to choose a subject with a good prospect of academic success. They are likely to be significant social factors impacting on this utility equation – family expectations, classed and gendered concepts of 'respectable' work, local labour market opportunities and so on (e.g. Skeggs, 1997; Croll, 2008; Shah, Dwyer and Modood, 2010; Archer, DeWitt and Wong, 2014).

However, this decision will have important ramifications for the outcome of their initial decision to enter higher education. Walker and Zhu (2011) demonstrate that the financial returns across different academic subjects are widely distributed; indeed, students expect differential salaries depending on the degree chosen, while the confidence in (Davies, Qiu and Davies, 2014) and accuracy of (Jerrim, 2011) these estimates varies between social groups. There are also differences in the variance within subject choices (Chevalier, 2011), with some pathways having a relatively predictable salary while others have a high variance around the mean.

This primary effect of subject choice in terms of future salary potential is then mediated through the degree classification that the individual achieves (Naylor, Smith and Telhaj, 2016), which is, in turn, a partial function of their aptitude for and engagement with the subject. Indeed, Purcell et al. (2008) found that students rated future enjoyment as the most important factor in their subject choice, highlighting the emotionally grounded nature of the decision. Employment-related factors (either general or specific to a profession) were somewhat less important, while a record of academic success played some role for around 40 per cent of their sample. Many students are trading off between subjects with a lower predicted return which they enjoy and in which they might achieve highly against subjects with a higher predicted return in which they have little interest or record of success. In other words, even a seemingly rationally 'optimal' choice of subject can be undermined if the fit for the individual transpires to be poor, causing them to underperform. Of course, students may have a strongly preferred career where high financial returns coincide with enjoyment and aptitude – provided they meet the entry requirements.

The complexity of this decision is staggering when considered in the round and from an expected utility perspective. Rather, bounded rationality predicts that complex decisions like this will be simplified by the individual with intuitive recourse to the familiar to eliminate options and ignore cues. The individual's decision will inevitably be a satisficed one, attempting to square off multiple criteria (financial, social and individual) across a manageable quantity of information in a reasonable timeframe – in a period where they are working towards the examinations that will determine the success of their university applications. A bounded rationality approach does not see this as flawed, but an unavoidable consequence of complexity and finite resources.

A major initiative in recent years has been to increase the information provided about courses through the National Student Survey, as well as the 'Key Information Sets' which, *inter alia*, describe graduate outcomes. This is intended as an aid to decision-making, but a bounded rationality lens would question this if it adds new (and possibly spurious) cues to the existing decision. Indeed, Davies (2012) questions whether publishing mean starting salaries is useful without measures of dispersion, while 'student satisfaction' has a questionable relationship with outcomes. A more useful approach might be to help prospective students to identify the most important cues in determining their long-term outcome, as well as broadening the satisficing options out beyond the familiar – for example by stressing the need for enjoyment and illuminating the wider career paths associated with particular subjects, while downplaying simplistic representations of financial returns.

Undoubtedly satisficing is sometimes unsuccessful, with a relatively high proportion of students changing their degree programmes within or after their first year (Harrison, 2006), which has led to a focus on student retention (Thomas, 2012). This work is clearly valuable in promoting high-quality teaching and support, but there is a danger that it is predicated on students making the 'right choice' first time; indeed, financial support changes have made it increasingly difficult and costly for students to change their decision, even where they are shifting their position within higher education to increase their long-term utility from it. Under bounded rationality, government and universities should make it easier for students to change subject on the basis of their early experiences; this is likely to particularly benefit students from disadvantaged backgrounds who are more likely to make familiar (and low return) choices based on their limited knowledge of higher education (Davies, Qiu and Davies, 2014).

Should I maximise university status?

It would appear outwardly 'rational' that all students would seek to go to the 'best' university possible given their qualifications, especially in a hierarchical pseudo-meritocratic system like the UK (Croxford and Raffe, 2015), where elite institutions have their 'quality' legitimised and reinforced through media-generated and government-endorsed league tables. Indeed, there is substantial evidence that the status of the university is the strongest predictor of long-term outcomes, with many high-status employers choosing only to recruit from these (Milburn, 2009). However, it is moot whether these league tables measure anything more tangible than historical over-subscription for places.

Nevertheless, many students, and particularly those from lower socio-economic groups and minority ethnic communities, do choose not to maximise university status (Mangan et al., 2010; Modood, 2012; Boliver, 2013; Shiner and Noden, 2014). This phenomenon has had significant attention from sociologists, who find evidence of fears about 'social fit' and dissonance with the 'institutional habitus' of elite universities (Whitty, Hayton and Tang, 2015). Such universities are 'not for people like them', with assumptions about the socio-economic or ethnic mix, as well as the academic standards required. Behavioural economists might view this in terms of the representativeness heuristic, with elite universities being understood through an archetype (hyper-academic and for the social elite), perpetuated through media depictions and teacher expectations (Oliver and Kettley, 2010).

Decisions may also be influenced by a desire to remain in the family home for financial or cultural reasons (Holdsworth, 2006), potentially limiting university choices to the local. Mangan et al. (2010) find that where there is a nearby elite university, students from disadvantaged groups are as likely to choose it as other students, but where there is not, they are more likely to seek a local lower status option. In this instance, a familiarity heuristic would appear to be in play; that elite universities are accepted into the choice envelope if the individual has personal experience that overcomes the archetype.

Under the auspices of attempting to improve social mobility for 'talented' young people (e.g. Department for Education and Employment, 2000; Milburn, 2009; Department for Business, Information and Skills, 2016), successive governments have attempted to manipulate decisions from individuals who it is felt *should* attend elite universities. However, these have broadly failed, with little or no change in their social mix over the last fifteen years (Croxford and Raffe, 2015). The latest figures show that the proportion of students in elite universities drawn from the most deprived communities has risen from just 2.4 per cent to 3.3 per cent since 2011 (UCAS, 2015), despite the investment of substantial sums of government and university money; furthermore, most of the improvement is located in a handful of universities, with most seeing a backward slide (Harrison, in press).

One example of this attempted manipulation was the creation of means-tested bursaries, ostensibly to offset the 2006 increase in tuition fees (Department for Education and Skills, 2003). The amounts offered were left to the universities' discretion, but a pseudo-market inevitably formed whereby elite universities offered considerably higher sums than lower-status universities (Callender, 2010; Harrison and Hatt, 2012). These bursaries effectively formed a discount to the cost of higher education, with a distinctly higher discount for students choosing elite universities. Neoclassical economics would predict that a fall in 'price' would increase demand, but Callender, Wilkinson and Hopkin (2009) found that students largely ignored this financial incentive, with evidence that some even felt that larger bursaries were a sign of inferior courses (Davies et al., 2008). Taking a bounded rationality perspective, this 'irrational' behaviour from students that are normally constructed to be the most price-sensitive and risk-averse is more readily understood, with the financial utility of the bursary dimming next to educational priorities and the disutility of spending three years in an institution that feels alien.

Conclusion

This chapter has introduced the theory of bounded rationality and concepts from behavioural economics which emerged from it. It has then applied these ideas to three key decisions made by prospective students, highlighting the potential for new insight, especially with respect to phenomena that other theories have failed to predict.

First, the current obsession with providing endless information to improve students' decision-making is likely to be ineffectual and possibly even counter-productive, simultaneously increasing the complexity of the decision and introducing additional cues of dubious validity. This is not to argue that prospective students should not be given adequate information, but that careful thought needs to be given to its purpose, while not assuming that 'more is better'. Improving access to reliable and high-quality advice and guidance, untainted by normative expectations, is likely to be a more fruitful avenue.

Second, purely financial understandings of student behaviour are inadequate. Evidence is mounting that students do not respond to financial cues in the ways predicted by neoclassical economics. This has been seen both in terms of their response to increasing tuition fees and differential bursaries. Similarly, concepts of risk need to be revised to understand the non-linear nature of expected utility, with higher education often seen by disadvantaged young people as less risky than the alternatives.

Third, that efforts to break down stereotypes about elite universities are not working, with the inherently conservative heuristics around accessibility and representativeness holding sway. Well-intentioned, but misguided, work to 'raise aspirations' has not been successful at the macro-level, which suggests that more radical options to achieve a fairer social mix are needed, especially when the best graduate opportunities are preserved for certain universities. Alternatively, there needs to be a reassessment of the basis on which elite status is conferred, maintained and valorised, towards a more equitable distribution of opportunities.

References

Agosto, D. 2002. Bounded rationality and satisficing in young people's Web-based decision making. *Journal of the Association for Information Science and Technology* 53(1):16–27.

Archer, L., J. DeWitt and B. Wong. 2014. Spheres of influence: What shapes young people's aspirations at age 12/13 and what are the implications for education policy? *Journal of Education Policy* 29(1):58–85.

Barberis, N. 2012. *Thirty Years of Prospect Theory in Economics: A Review and Assessment.* Cambridge, MA: National Bureau of Economic Research.

Becker, G. 1994. *Human Capital: A Theoretical and Empirical Analysis with Special Reference to Education (2nd edition).* Chicago: University of Chicago Press.

Benselin, J. and G. Ragsdell. 2016. Information overload: The differences that age makes. *Journal of Librarianship and Information Science* 48(3):284–297.

Boliver, V. 2013. How fair is access to more prestigious UK universities? *British Journal of Sociology* 64(2):344–364.

Breen, R., H. van de Werfhorst and M. Jaeger. 2014. Deciding under doubt: A theory of risk aversion, time discounting preferences, and educational decision-making. *European Sociological Review* 30(2):258–270.

Brown, P. 2013. Education, opportunity and the prospects for social mobility. *British Journal of Sociology of Education* 34(5/6):678–700.

Callender, C. 2010. Bursaries and institutional aid in higher education in England: Do they safeguard and promote fair access? *Oxford Review of Education* 36(1): 45–62.

Callender, C. and J. Jackson. 2005. Does the fear of debt deter students from higher education? *Journal of Social Policy* 34(4):509–540.

Callender, C., D. Wilkinson and R. Hopkin. 2009. *The Impact of Institutional Financial Support in England: Higher Education Students' Awareness, Knowledge and Take-Up of Bursaries and Scholarships.* Bristol: Office for Fair Access.

Chevalier, A. 2011. Subject choice and earnings of UK graduates. *Economics of Education Review* 30(6):1187–1201.

Coleman, R. and B. Bekhradnia. 2011. *Higher Education Supply and Demand to 2020.* Oxford: Higher Education Policy Institute.

Collet, F. 2009. Does habitus matter? A comparative review of Bourdieu's habitus and Simon's bounded rationality with some implications for economic sociology. *Sociological Theory* 27(4):419–434.

Crawford, C. 2014. *The Link between Secondary School Characteristics and University Participation and Outcomes.* London: DFE.

Croll, P. 2008. Occupational choice, socio-economic status and educational attainment: A study of the occupational choices and destinations of young people in the British Household Panel Survey. *Research Papers in Education* 23(3):243–268.

Croxford, L. and D. Raffe. 2015. The iron law of hierarchy? Institutional differentiation in UK higher education. *Studies in Higher Education* 40(9):1625–1640.

Davies, P. 2012. Can governments improve higher education through 'informing choice'? *British Journal of Educational Studies* 60(3):261–276.

Davies, P., T. Qiu and N. Davies. 2014. Cultural and human capital, information and higher education choices. *Journal of Education Policy* 29(6):804–825.

Davies, P., K. Slack, A. Hughes, J. Mangan and K. Vigurs. 2008. *Knowing Where to Study: Fees, Bursaries and Fair Access.* Stoke-on-Trent: Institute for Educational Policy Research and Institute for Access Studies.

Department for Business, Innovation and Skills. 2016. *Success as a Knowledge Economy: Teaching Excellence, Social Mobility and Student Choice.* London: BIS.

Department for Education and Employment. 2000. *The Excellence Challenge.* London: DFEE.

Department for Education and Skills. 2003. *The Future of Higher Education.* Norwich: HMSO.

Esson, J. and H. Ertl. 2016. No point worrying? Potential undergraduates, study-related debt, and the financial allure of higher education. *Studies in Higher Education* 41(7):1265–1280.

Gigerenzer, G. and D. Goldstein. 1996. Reasoning the fast and frugal way: Models of bounded rationality. *Psychological Review* 103(4):650–669.

Green, F. and Y. Zhu. 2010. Overqualification, job dissatisfaction, and increasing dispersion in the returns to graduate education. *Oxford Economic Papers* 62(4):740–763.

Harrison, N. 2006. The impact of negative experiences, dissatisfaction and attachment on first year undergraduate withdrawal. *Journal of Further and Higher Education* 30(4):377–391.

Harrison, N. In press. Exploring social trends in higher education participation: 2000 to 2015. In R. Waller, N. Ingram and M. Ward (eds.) *Higher Education and Social Inequalities: Getting In, Getting On and Getting Out.* Abingdon: Routledge/BSA.

Harrison, N., F. Chudry, R. Waller and S. Hatt. 2015. Towards a typology of debt attitudes among contemporary young UK undergraduates. *Journal of Further and Higher Education* 39(1):85–107.

Harrison, N. and S. Hatt. 2012. Expensive and failing? The role of student bursaries in widening participation and fair access in England. *Studies in Higher Education* 37(6):695–712.

Holdsworth, C. 2006. 'Don't you think you're missing out, living at home?' Student experiences and residential transitions. *Sociological Review* 54(3):495–519.

Jerrim, J. 2011. Do UK higher education students overestimate their starting salary? *Fiscal Studies* 32(4):483–509.

Kahneman, D. 2003. Maps of bounded rationality: Psychology of behavioural economics. *American Economic Review* 93(5):1449–1475.

Kahneman, D. 2011. *Thinking, Fast and Slow*. London: Penguin.

Kahneman, D., P. Slovic and A. Tversky (eds.). 1982. *Judgment Under Uncertainty: Heuristics and Biases*. Cambridge: Cambridge University Press.

Kahneman, D. and A. Tversky. 1979. Prospect theory: An analysis of decision under risk. *Econometrica* 47(2):263–292.

Kahneman, D. and A. Tversky (eds.). 2000. *Choices, Values, and Frames.* Cambridge: Cambridge University Press.

Kahneman, D., P. Wakker and R. Sarin. 1997. Back to Bentham? Explorations of experienced utility. *Quarterly Journal of Economics* 112(2):375–405.

Koszegi, B. and M. Rabin. 2007. Reference-dependent risk attitudes. *American Economic Review* 97(4):1047–1073.

List, J. 2003. Does market experience eliminate market anomalies? *Quarterly Journal of Economics* 118(1):47–71.

Mangan, J., A. Hughes, P. Davies and K. Slack. 2010. Fair access, achievement and geography: Explaining the association between social class and choice of university. *Studies in Higher Education* 15(3):335–350.

Milburn, A. 2009. *Unleashing Aspiration: The Final Report of the Panel on Fair Access to the Professions*. London: PFAP.

Modood, T. 2012. Capitals, ethnicity and higher education. In S. Tomlinson and T. Basit (eds.) *Social Inclusion and Higher Education*. Bristol: Policy Press. pp. 17–40.

Naylor, R., J. Smith and S. Telhaj. 2016. Graduate returns, degree class premia and higher education expansion in the UK. *Oxford Economic Papers* 68(2):525–545.

Oliver, C. and N. Kettley. 2010. Gatekeepers or facilitators: The influence of teacher habitus on students' applications to elite universities. *British Journal of Sociology of Education* 31(6):737–753.

Purcell, K., P. Elias, G. Atfield, H. Behle, R. Ellison, D. Luchinskaya, J. Snape, L. Conaghan and C. Tzanakou. 2012. *Futuretrack Stage 4: Transitions into Employment, Further Study and Other Outcomes*. Coventry: Warwick Institute for Employment Research.

Purcell, K., P. Elias, R. Ellison, G. Atfield, D. Adam and I. Livanos. 2008. *Applying for Higher Education: The Diversity of Career Choices, Plans and Expectations*. Coventry: Warwick Institute for Employment Research.

Scurry, T. and J. Blenkinsopp. 2011. Under-employment among recent graduates: A review of the literature. *Personnel Review* 40(5):643–659.

Shah, B., C. Dwyer and T. Modood. 2010. Explaining educational achievement and career aspirations among young British Pakistanis: mobilizing 'ethnic capital'? *Sociology* 44(6):1109–1127.

Shiner, M. and P. Noden. 2014. 'Why are you applying there?': 'Race', class and the construction of higher education 'choice' in the United Kingdom. *British Journal of Sociology of Education* 36(8):1170–1191.

Simon, H. 1955. A behavioural model of rational choice. *Quarterly Journal of Economics* 69(1):99–118.

Simon, H. 1979. Rational decision-making in business organisations. *American Economic Review* 69(4):493–513.

Simon, H. 1986. The failure of armchair economics. *Challenge* 29(5):18–25.

Simon, H. 1987. Making management decisions: The role of intuition and emotion. *Academy of Management* 1(1):57–64.

Simon, H. 1997. *An Empirically Based Microeconomics*. Cambridge: Cambridge University Press.

Simon, H. 2000. Bounded rationality in social science: Today and tomorrow. *Mind and Society* 1(1):25–39.

Skeggs, B. 1997. *Formations of Class and Gender: Becoming Respectable*. London: Sage.

Sutton Trust. 2004. *The Missing 3,000: State School Students Under-Represented at Leading Universities*. London: Sutton Trust.

Thomas, L. 2012. *Building Student Engagement and Belonging in Higher Education at a Time of Change: Final Report from the What Works? Student Retention & Success Programme*. London: Paul Hamlyn Foundation.

Todd, P. and G. Gigerenzer. 2003. Bounding rationality to the world. *Journal of Economic Psychology* 24:143–165.

Universities and Colleges Admissions Service. 2015. *End of Cycle Report 2015*. Cheltenham: UCAS.

Walker, I. and Y. Zhu. 2011. Differences by degree: Evidence of the net financial rates of return to undergraduate study for England and Wales. *Economics of Education Review* 30(6):1177–1186.

Whitty, G., A. Hayton and S. Tang. 2015. Who you know, what you know and knowing the ropes: A review of evidence about access to higher education institutions in England. *Review of Education* 3(1):27–67.

Chapter 6

Higher education
Too risky a decision?

Malcolm Brynin

Introduction

Higher education has expanded enormously in the modern era, globally, in response it is generally assumed to an ever-growing demand for higher-level skills. Within this simple framework, often labelled the 'technology bias thesis' (TBT), universities are held to play a specific role, producing the skills required by the economy. This does not mean there need be a balance between this demand for and supply of skills, though many analysts see equilibrium as inherent to the system. Individual entrants into higher education (HE) are characterised as investors in their own education, seeking to raise their own productivity in response to market signals. In deciding whether or not to invest resources (money and time) in HE they are assumed to know the long-term financial value of their investment. More specifically, they are able to cost their prospective expenditure[1] and to balance this against the expected wages from the type of job they have selected (summed over the career), which the qualification makes possible. This 'human capital theory' (HCT), clearly based on the concept of rational action, is still generally favoured by economists despite some internal criticism, such as Manski's: 'Having witnessed the struggles of econometricians to learn the returns to schooling, I find it difficult to accept the proposition that adolescents are endowed with this knowledge' (Manski 1993: 49). Data on graduate recruitment suggest that for the 'majority [of new graduates], moving into employment is a slow transition with many experiencing several years of turbulence and having to compete for jobs with non-graduates' (Pearson 2006: 76).

HCT is a description of how economists believe people might behave if they were economists. A very different approach derived from the sociological literature does away with the need for economic rationality. In this view the demand for high-level qualifications is governed by uncertainty over career intentions and the possible wages associated with these, as well as by a range of non-material motivations to do with the quality of the job. For instance, some people are driven by a desire to help others through their work. There is therefore no necessity or even great likelihood that the rise in demand for university education is strongly or directly related to technological development, even if at the same time the demand for skills is in fact rising. Further, other (more Weberian) facets of rationality are possible. A university education might be deemed necessary regardless of the actual economic returns if this level of education becomes a social norm. Most people want what they would consider to be a good job. As good jobs are increasingly defined as graduate jobs the HE decision in a sense becomes more automatic. It is the natural thing to do to go to university, regardless of the expected returns or perhaps even of job aspirations. The existence of a norm replaces calculation, however uncertain this norm itself might be in relation to an individual's needs and real prospects (Brynin 2013). The uncertainty carries a cost, however. This is the thesis of the argument and analysis presented below.

The problem of risk

Empirically we now have a substantial body of evidence that skill supply exceeds skill demand. While this was asserted long ago (e.g. by Collins 1979), this critique seemingly ignored the fact that there is indeed technological progress and therefore a need for higher-level skills. An additional aspect of this view of educational inflation was that machines would replace human beings as a result of technological change. In turn, though, this ignored the possibility that new skills would be required with the development of new services and products. It is also an empirical fact that the returns to education, in particular the graduate premium (the pay advantage to having a degree), have held up in spite of continued educational expansion. Economists have inferred from this fact support for both the TBT and HCT (e.g. Blundell et al. 2000; Harmon et al. 2001; McIntosh 2005). However, this empirical finding is possibly not as valid as it once was. Some research suggests a decline in the graduate premium (Elias and Purcell 2003; Longhi and Brynin 2009), while in the UK the higher the proportion of graduates in an occupation the lower the average wage (Brynin 2002). Further, in many countries and over a long period of time, a substantial proportion of graduates are overqualified for the work they do (Borghans and de Grip 2000; Hartog 2000; Büchel, de Grip and Mertens 2003), while graduates increasingly do non-graduate work (Dolton and Vignoles 2000; Mason 2000; Purcell et al. 2005; Chevalier and Lindley 2009).

Why then is the demand for places in universities still rising, especially given the huge increase in costs? The question is examined here under three headings: uncertainty, norms, and the risk environment.

The role of uncertainty

While a proportion of students develop stable career plans this masks substantial uncertainty and year-on-year fluctuation, especially for those from families with no prior experience of higher education (Green and Webb 1997; Forsyth and Furlong 2003; Payne 2003; Thomas and Quinn 2007: 48–66; Christie 2009; Croll 2009). Using a large qualitative sample Ball et al. find not only that a substantial proportion eschew planning but that 'the decisions and strategies of those who plan do not appear to be solely or even primarily related to the calculation of economic returns' (2000: 18). Uncertainty derives from unclear career paths, which might often clarify only after time and as a matter of chance and experiment.

Prospective students do not calculate their expected economic returns, because they often do not have clear career aspirations, often do not have the necessary information, but also because money is only one motivation. This does not mean that they act irrationally, only that they need to seek a rational basis for action outside of a narrow calculation of costs and benefits. They do this by seeking and following norms of behaviour very loosely appropriate to their desired social standing.

Graduate jobs as an uncertain norm

The norm for so many jobs is now a degree, or at least appears to be, and this makes the calculation of the return to education for many people irrelevant. Young people simply know that a good job is more likely with a degree. Nevertheless, the norm is itself uncertain because the expansion of higher education itself has blurred the boundary between graduate and non-graduate work, thus altering the capacity of people to assess the risks they are taking. There has in Beck's terms been an increase in the 'risk environment' (Beck 1992, 2009). In this view of the breakdown of modernity, life is more insecure than in the past. Beck uses as one example the world of work, increasingly marked by flexible labour through part-time work, temporary contracts, and reduced job tenure (Beck 2000a). The point is an ironic one. In earlier days there was for many the certainty of poverty. As opportunity rises so does risk – the risk that you might lose what you have or believe you can have. The individual loses control because of the complexity of modern life. Beck did not relate his pessimistic view to higher education, but the extension is compelling. As ever more jobs are undertaken by graduates it becomes less and less clear what constitutes a graduate job. This precisely reflects an increase not merely in risk but in the 'risk environment'. As an example, if clerical work was previously almost totally non-graduate but becomes increasingly selected by graduates then it is less clear to prospective entrants to university whether a degree is needed for this job. The risk increases because it is no longer possible to calculate the risk. A proportion of students will opt for this occupation because they perceive a norm of sorts though without any clear idea of this. As a result more and more graduates enter this occupation and that further reinforces the perceived need for a degree in the occupation, which might eventually become fully graduate even though the nature of the work undertaken within this may not change. The issue here is not whether there is more risk than in the past but that risk is increasingly unavoidable. 'It has become almost impossible *not* to take part in this raffle' (Beck 2000b: 217). The process is neither economic nor technological but entirely social.

This argument is related to the concept of the 'opportunity trap' (Brown 2003; Brown, Lauder and Ashton 2012), which similarly points to the mirage of opportunity prospective students see ahead of them. The reality is that with the globalisation of both education and work many will not find suitable opportunities for their skills. This leads those with the resources to intensify their competitiveness, as predicted by Bourdieu (e.g. Bourdieu and Passeron 1990). There will be many losers as opportunity is highly constrained. In practice, much depends on the relationship between demand and supply of graduates in a particular location at a particular time, and this is an empirical question. However, young people are impelled into higher education not by the quest for higher wages but by the power of social norms. These might be measured financially, but they are social norms nevertheless.

While a norm provides a rational basis for social action, it can be costly. The problem is that a norm is an average and this average masks an underlying distribution. The norm of a 'good' job implies good pay, but wages are hugely skewed, with a small proportion of people earning a very high salary while the vast majority do not. Distributions are far more important than averages. As a hypothetical example: if we estimate that it is worth an individual with a particular occupation in mind to invest in HE because the expected salary after 10 years is £50,000 on average across people doing this kind of work, what the individual actually earns will depend on performance, the quality of the particular job, the part of the country in which the job is located, the industry in which it occurs, the effectiveness of the employer, and sheer luck. Let us say that as a result of these and other factors wages in practice range from £30,000 to £90,000, it is likely that only a small proportion will earn the latter while most will earn far less as incomes are nearly always skewed in this way. It might also be that some good jobs can be obtained without a degree in the same occupation, enabling a proportion of non-graduates to earn over £30,000. For a proportion of people doing this work a degree is in the end not beneficial. However, they will still not wish to run the risk of being in the group of non-graduates who earn less than the average for the occupation. It is this risk that drives them to invest in education almost regardless of the cost and future wage implications.

Defining the risk environment

The existence of the norm of a 'good' job is one reason why governments (especially in Britain) are able to pass an increased proportion of the cost of higher education to students, and why also university administrations do not fear a decline in student numbers. They know that young people are increasingly locked into the system. That change is itself something they have encouraged. Policy-makers contribute to the false certainties offered by the new occupational norms. These mean that educational policy can move towards the individualisation and privatisation of higher education. Risk can be transferred to the individual because policy-makers know that young people have a decreasing choice of options. If they think that a good job needs a degree they will invest in the degree regardless of costs. Policy-makers reinforce the risk environment by making it appear as if the risk is limited or even non-existent:

> The qualifications you earn can help you get a better job with much better money – in fact, over the course of your working life, if you've got an undergraduate degree, you can expect to earn, on average, comfortably over £100,000 more than someone similar with two or more A levels, net of taxes and in today's valuation.
>
> (DBIS 2009)

There is not even a warning that the value of one's education can go down as well as up. The risk environment impels young people into higher education, and so the government's claim becomes a self-fulfilling prophecy: more people enter work as graduates, so more jobs seem to be graduate jobs. This process of defining the risk environment is accentuated through information about the quality of universities through league tables, which some argue are liable to produce contrived and misleading outcomes (Marginson 2007; Oswald 2007). Such information appears to reduce the risk environment while not reducing the actual risk.

Empirical analysis

The aim of the analysis is to identify the occupational norms discussed above, and their effects. To do this we need a measure of these norms, that is, the proportion of graduates typically expected in an occupation and also the wage they would typically receive. The analysis is based primarily on data from the British Labour Force Survey, covering 1993 to 2012. Wage data (in the form of hourly wages) are deflated so that a pound is worth the same whatever the year, taking 2012 as the base value.[2] The analysis covers men and women aged 16 to 60 who work at least 10 hours a week. People with extremely high and low wages are excluded. The analysis is of all occupations in the data but grouped into over 80 categories.

Very few occupations are anywhere near 100% graduate while there is a long tail with very low proportions of graduates. In the period as a whole the mean is around 18% while the median is about 9%. That is, 50% of employees work in occupations with a graduate density of 9% or less. The argument here is that within the range of graduate density there is a set of occupations which are neither clearly graduate nor undergraduate. Any such definition is arbitrary, but here a range of between 10% and 40% is used. The assumption is that where there are fewer than 10% graduates in an occupation prospective students will consider this clearly non-graduate while anything over 40% is clearly graduate. Anything in between is a grey area. Whatever the actual cut-off points the key issue is whether this grey area has grown. As graduate employment has risen generally, has uncertainty as to what constitutes a graduate job risen in tandem with this?

Looking first at all jobs, that is, including manual work, at the beginning of our period of analysis (in fact pooling the first three years) 23.2% of all employees worked in this indeterminate zone of occupations which are 10–40% graduate. By the last three years this had risen to 40.2%. However, this is not the situation that graduates face as very few work in manual jobs. Restricting the analysis to professional, managerial and intermediate occupations produces figures of 40.9% and 59.5%, respectively. In the later period getting on for two thirds of non-manual employees worked in occupations which cannot be defined clearly as either graduate or non-graduate.

This uncertainty about what constitutes a graduate job defines only a part of the risk, which can only be fully quantified in terms of pay. Again using arbitrary cut-off points the analysis is based on three pay bands (using pay data from both graduates and non-graduates, that is, all employees):

Below average: less than 30% below mean pay of all employees
Broad average: between 30% below and 30% above the precise mean
Above average: more than 30% above the mean

To define average pay here the arithmetic mean is used, thus discounting the fact that the wage distribution is highly skewed (with many people receiving low pay while a small number are highly paid). Table 6.1 again pools figures for two groups of three years, the first being 1993–1995, the second 2010–2012. It shows the proportion of employees in the highest NS-SEC classes who are graduates in each pay band as defined above and for each period separately. The bottom row shows a total increase in these graduates in employment across the period from 24.9% to 37.1%. One would expect the bulk of this increase to occur in the above average wage band, but this turns out not to be the case. The first row shows that in the earlier period 6.1% of these employees earning less than average pay were graduates from the top three classes. This rose by over 11 percentage points to 17.6% in the later period while for those on average pay the increase was 13 percentage points. Those in the highest bracket experience the lowest increase, of just under 11 percentage points. Recalling that average pay is

Table 6.1 The percentage of employees who are graduates within wage bands (LFS; employees in upper and lower service as well as intermediate occupations)

Wages	1993–95	2010–12	Increase
Below average	6.1	17.6	11.5
Average	15.3	28.3	13.0
Above average	44.0	54.9	10.9
Average %	24.9	37.1	12.2

Note: Average pay is calculated across all employees but excludes extremely low and high values.

calculated across all occupations, including pay in semi-routine and routine occupations, this suggests that graduate skills are, relatively speaking, of poor value for some workers. Looking at this another way (though this is not shown in the table), in the earlier period 29.3% of these graduates were in the average-wage band. In the later period this had risen to over 36.9%. To earn a merely average pay it is increasingly necessary to be a graduate. The bar is not rising.

This is apparent too in the rise in graduate employment in occupations which are clearly not graduate, as shown in Table 6.2. It is hard to imagine that routine or semi-routine jobs could require a degree. The rise in graduate employment in these is a result of rising supply. Even if some of this is the result of people obtaining a degree and then not wishing to use it, there is no obvious reason why the proportion of graduates in such jobs should on that basis increase.

Even for non-manual jobs there is a cost to this increase. Table 6.3 looks at average hourly pay for the upper service class (USC), that is higher managerial and professional, lower service class (LSC), and intermediate (other non-routine) occupations. Graduates are by far the most common in these types of occupations. Average here is again defined as the mean. For non-graduates average hourly pay rose over the period quite significantly in all three classes, by £1.9 for the USC, £2.1 for the LSC, and £1.6 for employees in the intermediate class. Graduates also enjoyed increases but smaller in each case, namely £1.6, £1.4, and £0.7, respectively. Given that graduate encroachment on intermediate jobs has been the most pronounced, the last fact is worrying.

Table 6.4 shows broadly the same picture through regression analysis. The figure for degrees can be interpreted as showing that having a degree increased hourly wages by roughly 50% compared to those with low or no education (the reference category), which is much higher than the 21% generated by an A-level.

Table 6.2 Percentage of graduates in NSSEC classes over time (LFS)

	USC	LSC	Intermediate	Lower supervisory	Semi-routine	Routine
1993–95	50.7	23.8	6.9	2.0	2.0	1.1
2010–12	57.2	37.7	16.3	5.8	7.5	3.2

Table 6.3 Average pay within the higher and lower service class and intermediate class (LFS; £ per hour)

	Non-graduate employees		Graduate employees	
	1993–95	2010–12	1993–95	2010–12
USC	15.4	17.3	17.8	19.4
LSC	11.9	14.0	15.6	17.0
Intermediate	9.1	10.7	11.2	11.9

Table 6.4 Effects of education on log hourly wages (LFS)

	1993–95	2008–10
Degree	0.50	0.44
A-level	0.21	0.18
(Pseudo) R²	.46	.40
N	62,398	108,653

Note: Controls not shown: age, age squared, gender, ethnicity, job tenure, industry, region, proportion feminine in occupation, year. All results significant to $p < .001$.

However, 15 years later, while it seems that the value of both a degree and an A-level had declined, the drop for the former was twice that of the latter. As Tables 6.1 and 6.3 show, for a significant proportion of graduates their qualification is of limited value. Table 6.4 additionally shows that in the aggregate this value has fallen over time. Factor in the costs of this education and this becomes at the individual level a serious economic issue.

The above analysis using the LFS enables a comparison of the wages of graduates and non-graduates and also the calculation of average wages across all employees. The cost is that we know nothing about the status of the university attended, what course was taken, or school performance (a proxy for ability). Wages will clearly vary on the basis of all three factors. The final analysis uses the Destination of Leavers from Higher Education survey (DLHE), a survey of all graduates leaving education each year. The period analysed here is 2002–03 to 2011–12. Not only is it possible to control for the above factors using these data but they also contain important information on the graduates' perception of the economic value of their qualifications once in employment, both six months and four years after leaving university, though the sample selected for the longer period is only a small subsample of the entire cohort. The analysis shown here is of all graduates, including postgraduates, and both UK and overseas students. It is restricted to those actually in work and in the UK.

Table 6.5 shows that six months after graduation about 46% of graduates are in jobs where they perceive their qualifications as being required or at least expected, 22% say that it gave them an advantage even if it was not required, but as many as 32% believe it was not even an advantage. The salary cost is significant and this is not short-term. While many will be in jobs six months after graduation not intended or expected to be permanent, and indeed such work might often be a stop-gap (though the analysis is only of full-time work), the second column shows that there is a clear wage loss associated with the perception, albeit not large. Those where the degree is perceived to be required or expected earn 4% more than those where it is not even an advantage. Move on 3–4 years, though, and it can be seen that there is long-term scarring from this distinction. Even though the analysis is still of the perceived value of the earlier job, and either the

Table 6.5 Perceived value of education and annual wages (DLHE; 6 months and 4 years after graduation)

Importance of education	%	Salary (6 months) (N = 1,313,814)	Salary (4 years) (N = 63,068)
Required/expected	45.7	22,168	31,532
Advantage	22.4	21,398	29,559
Neither	31.8	21,226	27,531

job or the perception might have changed, after four years the differential is far greater at 14%.

It is of course possible that less able or less motivated people end up in jobs they perceive to be of little value, that they study less remunerative subjects, or that people from less prestigious universities enter such jobs. For this reason the regressions in Table 6.6 control for whether the student went to one of the elite universities known as the Russell Group (an association of universities set up in 1994 to promote the interests of its members, now numbering 24), to a pre-92 university, or to one of the post-92 universities (mostly polytechnics granted university status in 1992, generally obtaining lower research income and attracting less well qualified students than other universities). The analysis also controls for subject studied, as pay varies considerably with this, and the tariff score achieved at school (a score derived from the schools directly of school-leavers' performance – primarily A-level results). As tariff results are not available for many students in the analysis, in particular overseas students, the sample size greatly reduces. The analysis is therefore undertaken both with and without this variable. However, where it is undertaken without, as shown in the second column, the average tariff score for the university is included, which does not reduce sample size and provides a further measure of the value of the university. In both cases, and especially when controlling for individual scores, having a job where a degree is an advantage raises annual wages considerably while where it is required or expected the differential is extremely large (by 11% and 25%,

Table 6.6 Effect of perceived value of education on annual wages (DLHE; 6 months after graduation)

Importance of education	Controlling for individual tariff (N = 189,212)	Controlling for university (N = 840,311)
Required/expected	0.25	0.12
Advantage	0.11	0.05

Notes: Reference category = education neither required nor an advantage. Controls not shown: age, age squared, gender, ethnicity, whether from overseas, whether went to state school, parental education, parental class, whether from low-participation background, whether job is permanent, size of establishment, subject studied, university type.

respectively in the first column). The critical point here is that regardless of ability or selection, for many graduates a university education is perceived to be of no or limited value which often converts into a substantial material loss of value relative to other graduates.

Conclusion

There has been a long-running sociological argument that is opposed to the belief widely held by economists that expanded higher education is beneficial for individuals who participate. It is of course obvious that in general these individuals enhance their labour-market credentials: their learning converts directly into higher wages. Of course this is true at a general level but the argument is based on averages. On average, wages are higher with a university education. However, it has been shown above that many graduates do not benefit in this way. They do not end up in graduate jobs and whether they do or not, many will find that a substantial proportion of non-graduates earn more than they do – and that is putting aside the investment they make into payment of fees and maintenance costs. Why, then, do they invest in higher education? The argument outlined above is that they believe they have little choice. Rising university education creates its own aura, its own magnetism, making more and more jobs seem to be graduate jobs whether or not they are in reality. The risk of entering higher education rises because of the costs and uncertainties involved, but more important, young people are no longer able to make rational judgements as to the true value of their investments. They see an increasing number of jobs becoming graduate so that the risk of not undertaking a university degree seems higher than the risk of taking one. In Beck's terms, there is an increase in the risk environment. This makes it easy for universities and policy-makers to reinforce the idea that the only way forward is through university, and easier for them also to transfer the costs of this additional education to the individual. All that researchers and other commentators can do is to question this easy equation.

Acknowledgements

This work was supported by the Economic and Social Research Council (ESRC) through the Research Centre on Micro-Social Change (MiSoC) (award no. ES/L009153/1).

Notes

1 Reflecting primarily the direct costs such as fees but also the opportunity cost which comes with the postponement of earning a wage.
2 The wages are therefore at 2012 values. Previous and similar analysis by the same author of the period 1993–2008 (Brynin 2013) used 1993 as the baseline, therefore producing lower absolute values than here. Relative values within the period remain the same whatever the baseline.

References

Ball, S., Maguire, M., and Macrae, S. (2000). *Choice, Pathways, and Transitions Post-16: New Youth, New Economies in the Global City*. London: Routledge.

Beck, U. (1992). *Risk Society: Towards a New Modernity*. London: Sage.

Beck, U. (2000a). *The Brave New World of Work*. Cambridge: Polity.

Beck, U. (2000b). Risk Society Revisited: Theory, Politics and Research Programmes. In: Adam, B., Beck, U., and van Loon, J. (eds). *The Risk Society and Beyond: Critical Issues for Social Theory*. London: Sage, 211–229.

Beck, U. (2009). *World at Risk*. Cambridge: Polity.

Blundell, R., DeArden, L., Goodman, A., and Reed, H. (2000). The Returns to Higher Education in Britain: Evidence from a British Cohort. *Economic Journal* 110(461): F82–F99.

Borghans, L., and de Grip, A. (2000). The Debate in Economics About Skill Utilization. In: Borghans, L., and de Grip, A. (eds). *The Overeducated Worker? The Economics of Skill Utilization*. Cheltenham: Edward Elgar, 3–23.

Bourdieu, P., and Passeron, J-C. (1990). *Reproduction in Education, Society and Culture*. London: Sage.

Brown, P. (2003). The Opportunity Trap: Education and Employment in a Global Economy. *European Education Research Journal* 2(1): 141–179.

Brown, P., Lauder, H., and Ashton, D. (2012). *The Broken Promises of Education, Jobs, and Incomes*. Oxford: Oxford University Press.

Brynin, M. (2002). Graduate Density, Gender, and Employment. *British Journal of Sociology* 53(3): 363–368.

Brynin, M. (2013). Individual Choice and Risk: The Case of Higher Education. *Sociology* 47(2): 284–300.

Büchel, F., de Grip, A., and Mertens, A. (eds). (2003). *Overeducation in Europe: Current Issues in Theory and Policy*. Northampton, MA: Edward Elgar.

Chevalier, A., and Lindley, J. (2009). Overeducation and the Skills of UK Graduates. *Journal of the Royal Statistical Society Series A – Statistics in Society* 172: 307–337.

Christie, H. (2009). Emotional Journeys: Young People and Transitions to University. *British Journal of Sociology of Education* 30(2): 123–136.

Collins, R. (1979). *The Credentialist Society*. New York: Academic.

Croll, P. (2009). Educational Participation Post-16: A Longitudinal Analysis of Intentions and Outcomes. *British Journal of Educational Studies* 57(4): 400–416.

DBIS (Department for Business, Innovation and Skills). (2009). *Don't Stop: Aim Higher*. London: Author.

Dolton, P., and Vignoles, A. (2000). The Incidence and Effects of Overeducation in the UK Graduate Labour Market. *Economics of Education Review* 19(2): 179–198.

Elias, P., and Purcell, K. (2003). *Measuring Change in the Graduate Labour Market, Researching Graduate Careers Seven Years On*. Warwick University: Institute for Employment Research (Research Paper No 1).

Forsyth, A., and Furlong, A. (2003). *Losing Out?: Socioeconomic Disadvantage and Experience in Further and Higher Education*. Bristol: The Policy Press.

Green, P., and Webb, S. (1997). Student Voices: Alternative Routes, Alternative Identities. In: Williams, J. (ed). *Negotiating Access to Higher Education: The Discourse of Selectivity and Equity*. Maidenhead, UK: Open University Press, 130–152.

Harmon, C., Walker, I., and Westergaard-Nielsen, N. (eds). (2001). *Education and Earnings in Europe: A Cross Country Analysis of the Returns to Education.* Cheltenham, UK: Edward Elgar.

Hartog, J. (2000). Over-Education and Earnings: Where Are We, Where Should We Go? *Economics of Education Review* 19(2): 131–147.

Longhi, S., and Brynin, M. (2009). Overqualification: Major or Minor Mismatch? *Economics of Education Review* 28: 114–121.

Manski, C. (1993). Adolescent Econometricians: How Do Youth Infer the Returns to Schooling? In: Clotfelter, C., and Rothschild, M. (eds). *Studies of Supply and Demand in Higher Education.* Chicago: University of Chicago Press, 43–60.

Marginson, S. (2007). *Global University Rankings: Where to from Here? Asia-Pacific Association for International Education.* Singapore: National University of Singapore.

Mason, G. (2000). *The Mix of Graduate and Intermediate-Level Skills in Britain: What Should the Balance Be?* London: National Institute of Economic and Social Research, Discussion Paper 161.

McIntosh, S. (2005). Evidence on the Balance of Supply and Demand for Qualified Workers. In: Machin, S., and Vignoles, A. (eds). *What's the Good of Education? The Economics of Education in the UK.* Princeton: Princeton University Press, 169–189.

Oswald, A. (2007). An Examination of the Reliability of Prestigious Scholarly Journals: Evidence and Implications for Decision-Makers. *Economica* 74: 21–31.

Payne, J. (2003). *Choice at the End of Compulsory Schooling: A Research Review.* London: Department for Education and Skills, Research Report RR414.

Pearson, R. (2006). The Demise of the Graduate Labour Market. In: McNay, I. (ed). *Beyond Mass Higher Education: Building on Experience.* Maidenhead, UK: Open University Press, 68–78.

Purcell, K., Elias, P., Davies, R., and Wilton, N. (2005). *The Class of '99.* London: DfES Research Report No. 691.

Thomas, L., and Quinn, J. (2007). *First Generation Entry into Higher Education.* Maidenhead, UK: Open University Press.

Chapter 7

Widening access with success

Using the capabilities approach to confront injustices

Merridy Wilson-Strydom

Introduction

> Justice cannot be indifferent to the lives that people can actually live.
>
> (Sen, 2009, p. 18)

Much research has been published documenting the persistent inequalities in access to higher education based on structural constraints such as race, class, gender, and educational background (for example Archer, 2003; Dudley Jenkins and Moses, 2014; Furlong and Cartmel, 2009; Johnston, 2010; Mountford-Zimdars, Sabbagh, and Post, 2014). Beyond accessing higher education, these inequalities are further mirrored in student success and graduation trends. Selected chapters in this book present evidence of these inequalities. Particularly concerning are the global nature and the persistence of inequalities with respect to participation and performance in higher education, even in contexts where participation rates are relatively high. Clearly, widening participation or improving university access with success is an issue of social justice (Marginson, 2011).

There are several different theoretical frameworks we might use for thinking about social justice in the context of university access. Theories are important in "framing the way issues are seen, shaping perceptions of salience, and thus slanting debate towards certain policies rather than others" (Nussbaum, 2011, p. xi). In this chapter an argument is advanced for the value of the capabilities approach (CA) – originally developed by Amartya Sen and Martha Nussbaum – as a normative framework that enables us to think differently about access and success from a social justice standpoint. With roots in the disciplines of economics, philosophy, and development studies, the CA sets out an alternative to the economic construct of utility and resource-based understandings of social justice within philosophy. As will be argued in this chapter, this alternative conceptualisation is also helpful for rethinking university access. In her useful and accessible book on the CA and development ethics, Deneulin (2014, p. 6) notes that the CA "is an alternative normative language with which to frame decisions and actions, and . . . offers a distinctive analysis of situations." In this chapter I use this alternative normative language for understanding access issues. The chapter will demonstrate how a capabilities-based analysis of university access and success helps us to frame actions in the direction of more just higher education environments.

Being cognisant of the fact that using the CA to study university access specifically is a relatively new and emerging field, the first part of the chapter centres on introducing the key concepts of the CA for readers new to it. In particular, the concepts of freedom, well-being, agency, capabilities, functionings, and conversion factors will be covered, drawing on illustrative examples from access contexts to contextualise the theory. The value added to access research by the CA foundational assumption of human diversity, together with how diverse agents and social structures interact, is emphasised. Drawing on the small, but growing, body of work on access issues using the CA (for some examples, see Hart, 2012; Walker, 2006; Watts, 2009; Wilson-Strydom, 2015a), the remainder of the chapter will make a case for why the CA helps us to think, and so act, differently with respect to the myriad of access challenges globally.

Key concepts of the capabilities approach

The CA has a wide disciplinary audience and application, or to quote Sen, there are a "plurality of purposes for which the capability approach can have relevance" – one of these being access (Sen, 1993, p. 49). While it is common for theories of social justice to focus on theorising what an ideal society ought to look like, such as we see in the work of John Rawls (1999), Sen argues instead that since pragmatically the achievement of a perfectly just society (or university environment) might be unlikely under current conditions, we should thus redirect our energies towards understanding how we might at least reduce the myriad of injustices we see all around us, even if a state of ideal justice seems out of reach. He describes the aim of his work as seeking "to clarify how we can proceed to address questions of enhancing justice and removing injustice, rather than to offer resolutions of questions about the nature of perfect justice" (Sen, 2009, p. ix). While there is debate about the extent to which the CA provides a theory of justice *per se*, it does provide us with a normative framework for assessing and comparing individual well-being and social arrangements in a manner that supports striving for just outcomes for all (Alkire and Deneulin, 2009a).

In essence then, the CA is a normative or moral framework for thinking about people's well-being and agency, and what this means for their freedoms to live the kind of life that they have reason to value (Sen, 1985, p. 169). As noted above, one of Sen's aims was to provide an alternative to the dominant utilitarian and neoliberal approaches to development and well-being. A practical outcome of Sen's work, pioneered by Mahbub ul Haq, is the Human Development Index (HDI) now widely used in development studies and in comparing relative human development[1] levels of countries. Alexander (2008, p. 1) usefully describes the fundamental intent of a capability theorist as being "to defend the idea that social justice consists in creating the greatest possible condition for the realisation of basic capabilities for all." In an access context our focus is thus on creating the greatest possible conditions for the realisation of the capability to participate in higher education.

Six key concepts which form the foundation on which the CA is based are introduced in this section. While each concept is introduced individually, there are important overlaps as these concepts cohere into a capabilities-based normative framework.

Freedoms

The CA makes a cross-cutting distinction between actual achievement (ends) and freedom to achieve (means) (Crocker and Robeyns, 2009). In his book titled *Inequality Reexamined* Sen states that

> A person's position in a social arrangement can be judged in two different perspectives, viz. (1) the actual achievement, and (2) the freedom to achieve. Achievement is concerned with what we **manage** to accomplish, and freedom with the **real opportunity** that we have to accomplish what we value. The two need not be congruent.
>
> (Sen, 1992, p. 31, emphasis in original)

This distinction between actual achievement and freedom to achieve is central and will be built on below as we consider the concepts of well-being, agency, functionings and capabilities. The notion of freedom, as used in the CA, is a positive freedom and takes account of both the opportunity and the process aspects of freedom. Opportunity freedom refers to the ability of a person to achieve what they have reason to value (the real opportunities available to a person) and process freedoms refers to the extent to which the person is able to exercise their agency and freedom of choice, the extent to which a person has autonomy to act in the manner that they value. Thus, this view of freedom "involves both the processes that allow freedom of actions and decisions, and the actual opportunities that people have, given their personal and social circumstances" (Sen, 1999, p. 17). Freedom has both instrumental and intrinsic value.

Well-being

With roots in Aristotelian notions of human flourishing, the CA takes as a starting assumption that when we assess how well someone is doing, we need to focus on the person's state of being – their well-being (Nussbaum, 2011; Sen, 1980, 2009). According to Sen, we need to ask: "What kind of a life is she leading? What does she succeed in doing and in being?" (Sen, 1985, p. 195). Nussbaum (2011, p. x) notes that "this question, though simple, is also complex, since the quality of a human life involves multiple elements whose relationship to one another needs close study." This is the crux of the CA, understanding lives in practice, as opposed to economic growth as the main indicator of development or participation rates of improved university access. As the quotation presented at the outset of this chapter indicates "[J]ustice cannot be indifferent to the lives that people can actually live" – in other words, their well-being (Sen, 2009, p. 18).

Importantly, well-being should not be confused with being well-off (opulence) (Deneulin, 2014). While the later usually refers to a person's wealth or how much a person has, well-being is about a rich conception of the quality of one's life, seen in terms of how a person can 'function', or the extent to which a person can be and do what they value for their life (Sen, 1985). As we will see in the example of two students' lives discussed below, the CA adopts a multidimensional conception of well-being that takes into account "the links between material, mental, and social well-being, or the economic, social, political and cultural dimensions of human life" (Crocker and Robeyns, 2009, p. 65). As such, individual well-being cannot be understood outside of the context in which a person functions (see "Conversion factors" below).

Agency

Agency[2] is the third key concept that requires our attention, distinguishable from well-being, but closely related. Sen defines an agent as someone "who acts and brings about change" (Sen, 1999, p. 19). Thus, agency is the ability of a person to realise the goals that they value. Related are concepts such as self-determination, having a voice, autonomy, and empowerment. The opposite of being able to exercise agency is someone who is passive, forced, or coerced. Sen argues powerfully for the value of agency and freedom as a cornerstone for achieving the types of institutional arrangements needed for development and positive social change (Sen, 1999). Agency is an expression of process freedom discussed above.

Well-being and agency are closely related, but should be seen as analytically distinct. In addition, agency and well-being can sometimes work against each other. For example a student who has paid their fees and is eligible to study may join an illegal protest action in solidarity with other students who are being excluded from university because they cannot pay their student fees, even when there is a risk of suspension for participation in the protest action. This would be an expression of agency on the part of the student, even though his/her personal well-being might be diminished through possible suspension from university.

Functionings and capabilities

Functionings represent achievements or outcomes. They are the things that a person is able to be or to do within their given life context. Thus, an individual or group's achieved functionings provide a metric of well-being. At a broad level, functionings encompass being adequately nourished, being employed, being literate, doing a job that is meaningful and fulfilling, and so on. If we consider university access, functionings would include, for example being able to read academic texts, being able to take part in university life, taking responsibility for oneself, or being able to pass an examination. The second important element of the concept of functionings is that it refers to outcomes or achievements that a person values or has reason to value. In this way individual autonomy and choice (agency) is explicitly recognised. An achievement or outcome may not be regarded as a functioning if it is not something that is valued by the person concerned (Alkire and Deneulin, 2009b, p. 32). For example a university student who completes a business degree because that was the only study direction his parents would pay for, despite wanting to become a pre-school teacher, may not regard his business degree as a functioning he has reason to value. The business degree, whilst creating certain opportunities for employment, does not contribute to the graduate's well-being because he wishes to be a teacher.

The concept of capabilities combines the concept of functionings with opportunity freedom. While a functioning is an outcome or an achievement, a capability is the potential to achieve. As such, capabilities can be seen as the freedom, or choices and options, a person has to achieve functionings that are of value to them. This distinction between functionings and capabilities is fundamental for both Sen and Nussbaum, and provides an additional means through which agency can be exercised as was shown above with the example of the student protesting in solidary (Nussbaum, 2011; Sen, 1999). In sum, when thinking about inequality we need to be concerned not only with what people have been able to achieve, but also with the opportunities that have (or not) been available to them.

Conversion factors

Recognition of human diversity is a central assumption within the CA, which is particularly generative for thinking differently about social justice concerns, and for how diversity is accounted for in university access policy and practice. The concept of conversion factors provides a useful conceptual tool for taking explicit account of diversity. People differ in many ways and these differences affect the extent to which they can convert opportunities (capabilities) into achievements (functionings). While differences do not inherently imply inequality, differences become inequalities when they impact on capabilities and functionings. Sen reminds us that "there is evidence that the conversion of goods to capabilities varies from person to person substantially, and the equality of the former may still be far from the equality of the latter" (Sen, 1980, p. 219). For example a student who is deaf is different from a hearing student. This difference is not inherently an inequality. However, if specific support, such as sign language interpreting, is not available then the capability to learn at university will be limited for the deaf student compared to the hearing student. The deaf student thus requires different resources for learning compared to the hearing student. Working towards equality of resources would not result in equality of capabilities or educational functionings.

Adapting Sen's conceptualisation, Robeyns (2005, p. 99) outlines three groups of conversion factors: personal conversion factors (e.g. physical condition, reading ability, intelligence, health, etc.), social conversion factors (e.g. power relations, policies, social norms, gender roles, family relations, practices of discrimination, etc.), and environmental conversion factors such as geographical locations, rural versus urban, climate, and so on. These personal, social, and environmental conversion factors impact on the extent to which a person is able to make use of the resources available to them to create capabilities or opportunities. Paying attention to conversion factors provides a mechanism for understanding what is needed in practice to realise potential outcomes (functionings) (Walker and Unterhalter, 2007, p. 10). Thus, when assessing equality or social justice within a given situation (such as within universities) we need to ask whether "some people [students] get more opportunities to convert their resources into capabilities [for accessing education] than others?" (Walker, 2005, p. 109). As Sen points out, "[I]nterpersonal variability of the relation between goods and functionings turns out to be quite central to many important policy issues" (Sen, 1985, p. 199). University access and success is one such policy issue.

Access for human capital or capabilities formation

> It is people who matter ultimately, profits are only instrumental to human lives.
>
> (Nussbaum, 2011, p. 185)

Many authors have argued that the dominant ideology informing higher education policy with its foundations deeply rooted in neoliberal ideology and politics is the human capital understanding of education (Assie-Lumumba, 2005; Boni and Walker, 2013; Giroux, 2008; Nussbaum, 2010; Robeyns, 2006; Tikly and Barrett, 2011; Walker, 2006). However, human capital theories are limited in that they focus exclusively on the instrumental economic benefits of education; "human qualities that can be employed as 'capital' in production in the way that physical capital is" (Sen, 1997, p. 1959). Thus the purpose of higher education as a public good has been replaced by neoliberal market models that prioritise producing graduates who can contribute to economic advancement and so help to make countries more competitive in capitalist knowledge-based economies. In this context the purpose of widening participation or increasing access to university is to contribute skilled graduates to the global knowledge economy. As will be shown below, the CA contends that this instrumental understanding of the role higher education plays in society is limited, and also limits our thinking when we consider issues of access. Since the creation of human capital has, arguably, become the pervasive purpose of higher education, and also because there are both overlaps and fundamental differences between the human capital and the CA, it is necessary to briefly highlight the similarities and differences.

The notion of human capital, first introduced by Becker (1964), made a significant contribution to economic theory, particularly in drawing attention to the human element of development. With a focus on building human capital through investment in education and skills development, this approach was critical in drawing attention to the importance of education for development (Lanzi, 2007; Robeyns, 2006; Sen, 1997, 1999). Despite redirecting attention towards investment in higher education – and by implication underpinning calls for increased access – human capital theories are limited because they emphasise only the instrumental economic benefits of education (Sen, 1997). It is also commonly assumed that labour markets work rationally and hence that once a person has completed higher education that the labour market will allocate them to appropriate employment (Unterhalter, 2009). In this way, human capital frameworks take scant account of the multiple injustices at play within higher education, labour markets, and broader society. This injustice limits certain groups' access to educational opportunity, and labour markets often do not function as a just allocator of employment. As we saw above, using the concept of conversion factors, the CA explicitly seeks to understand the personal, social, and environmental conditions or factors that influence well-being, the well-being of each and every person as an end in their own right. Human capital concepts of the individual, in contrast, position the person as a means of development through expansion of human capital and so, economic development.

The CA extends human capital conceptions to take account of *both* instrumental and intrinsic values of higher education. Further, it draws attention to the role that education plays in the expansion of individual freedoms and agency, so also facilitating development (Nussbaum, 2006; Sen, 1997). Like freedom which has both instrumental and intrinsic value, being educated can be both a functioning in its own right and an enabler of other capabilities and functionings. From a capabilities perspective, the *actual lives* of people, what they are able to be and do, is foregrounded. This means that the approach is directly concerned with *practical, everyday forms of inequality and injustice*. Within a CA account, each and every individual is viewed as an end in themselves, and not the means to some other (larger) end such as building the knowledge economy, contributing to economic growth, or achieving access equity targets. As such, individuals, and how individuals' lives are going, is positioned as the ultimate moral concern within the normative lens of the CA. Importantly, this is evidence of the CA's assumption of *ethical* individualism which is "the view that what ultimately matters is what happens to every single individual in society [university]" (Alkire and Deneulin, 2009b, p. 35). Ethical individualism is not the same as *ontological* or *methodological* individualism. The former assumes that society consists only of the individuals that make it up, and hence no emphasis is placed on social structures or institutions. Methodological individualism, which is rooted in an assumption of ontological individualism, assumes "that all social phenomena can be explained in terms of individuals and their properties" (Alkire and Deneulin, 2009b, p. 35). Individual well-being is positioned as the normative goal towards which we should strive, but individuals are explicitly located in social contexts which enable and constrain action in multidimensional ways.

A capabilities-based understanding of access and success

> [W]hilst public education does benefit everyone, it necessarily also benefits some more than others, with those gaining most likely to be those who start out better placed, whether that is by nature or circumstance.
>
> (Jonathan, 2001, p. 49)

In his 1979 Tanner Lecture on Human Values, Sen posed his central question as 'equality of what?' (Sen, 1980). The CA provides a powerful answer to this question. Other social justice theories also seek to answer this question, but, Sen and Nussbaum argue that all have limitations that can be overcome with a capabilities-based formulation. In particular, both Sen and Nussbaum present strong critiques of utilitarianism and the Rawlsian notion of primary goods (Alexander, 2008; Nussbaum, 2011; Sen, 1980, 1999) – two approaches to social justice that have been particularly influential.[3] In making a case for the value of the CA for work on access, it is useful to begin by posing Sen's central question, 'equality of what?' in relation to university access. Typically, in access research and policy discussions, the focus is on the participation rates of young people – often comparatively across various groupings – entering and successfully completing their studies. Where participation rates and completion rates are similar, we assume equality of access. To explore this further, we will use the stories of two students currently participating in a longitudinal qualitative study[4] at a South African university. Bellah and Miguel (pseudonyms chosen by the students) are both enrolled at the given university for a Bachelor of Science degree. They both started their studies in 2014 and completed their first-year – in comparison to the approximately 30% of first-year students in South Africa who drop out of their studies (CHE, 2012). When counted using typical access and success measures, Bellah and Miguel would be regarded as equal – having achieved equality of access and retention in the first year. However, the CA asks us to broaden our metrics of assessment to take account of how people's lives are going, their well-being or quality of life. Further, as noted earlier, individual differences, or human diversity, is central, rather than incidental, and as Sen reminds us, "[T]he recognition of the fundamental diversity of human beings does, in fact, have very deep consequences" (Sen, 1980, p. 202).

Returning to the two students – more in-depth consideration of their lives as students points to important differences, which have 'deep consequences' for how we think about social justice with respect to university access. Bellah grew up prominently with her mother as her father is a politician and was mostly away from home. Both her parents have university degrees and her mother now works at the state Education Department where she is responsible for school-related planning activities. The importance of education was always emphasised in her home. Bellah attended a relatively well functioning school in the township[5] in which she lived. Although not always well stocked, the school did have facilities such as science laboratories, a computer lab, and a library which is not common at township schools. On the whole, most of Bellah's teachers were committed to their teaching and encouraged the learners to work hard and perform well. Bellah applied to three different universities, and made her final selection because of a family member living in the university town who was able to provide support while she is away from home. She was fortunate to obtain a place to live in a university residence. She speaks highly of the additional support provided by virtue of living on campus and having access to senior students as mentors, easy access to computers and the Internet as well as the university library. Bellah has a bursary from a private company that covers her tuition and accommodation costs and her family is able to assist with money for daily living expenses and book purchases. She enjoyed her first-year of university and describes the university environment as conducive for studying, she is involved in various activities on campus, and at the end of her first year she successfully ran for a leadership position in her residence.

Miguel was orphaned at the age of 16, from which time he became responsible for himself and his two younger siblings. His parents migrated from Mozambique to South Africa before his birth and Miguel does not know or have any contact with his extended family for additional support. Miguel was able to complete high school due to the kindness of members of his church and one of his teachers who provided food for him and his siblings to complement the meagre child support grants that his siblings qualified for. He attended a local township school which was extremely poorly resourced. He was not able to afford electricity or candles and so studied for his final high school examinations under the street light outside his shack. Despite these conditions, he obtained good school leaving marks and qualified to enter university. Miguel had to put his dream of higher education on hold for five years while he worked as an underground miner to earn enough to put his siblings through school. Thus, Miguel was older than most of his fellow first-year students when he started university and found it difficult to identify with his peers and make friends. He qualified for a government loan, but needed to send much of the money home as his siblings were unemployed. As a result, Miguel lived in very poor quality illegal housing to save money, and was unexpectedly evicted late in the year and in effect became homeless. He was often not able to afford to buy food and would survive on water, one apple per day, and any food his fellow students shared with him. Nonetheless, he was committed to his studies and worked extremely hard, spending much of his time in the university library and the 24/hour study area. Miguel managed to complete most of his first-year courses.

With this additional contextual information about Bellah and Miguel's lives and their well-being, should we still assume equality of access and success? Can we conclude that since both Bellah and Miguel were able to enter university and complete their first-year that the situation is a just one? How do we answer Sen's central normative questions – "What kind of life is she leading? What does she succeed in being and doing?" (Sen, 1985, p. 195). Like assuming that equality of income implies equality of well-being, assuming equality of access and success based on participation, retention, and completion rates is insufficient. Instead, our answer to the question of 'equality of what?' ought to be: equality of the capabilities to meaningfully participate in higher education and so achieve well-being as a student. For example drawing on her research on widening participation in the United Kingdom, Hart argues that the CA

> highlights the way current policy tends to be evaluated in terms of outcome, based on achievements such as numbers applying to, and being accepted at, higher education institutions, as well as the level and number of qualifications achieved [none of which take] account of the well-being an individual has achieved, or indeed the range of opportunities the individual has been able to choose from.
>
> (Hart, 2007, pp. 37–38)

The growing body of research that applies the CA to access and widening participation is opening up our understanding of what the capability to participate in higher education might look like in different contexts (Hart, 2012; Unterhalter and Brighouse, 2007; Unterhalter and Carpentier, 2010; Walker, 2006; Wilson-Strydom, 2015a, 2015b). Hart's research has usefully highlighted the central role that aspirations play in widening participation, as well as the manner in which aspirations may be encouraged or silenced by various conversion factors at play across different social contexts (Hart, 2012). Okkolin (2013) applied the CA to understand how highly educated Tanzanian women were able to access higher education even when structural conditions limited women's educational opportunities. Watts and Bridges (2006) used CA to critique widening participation policy in the UK from the perspective of working-class young people who chose not to attend higher education. They argue that "the twin agendas of social inclusion and economic development lead to the reformation rather than the resolution of injustice" (Watts and Bridges, 2006, p. 143). In the US context, Deprez and Wood (2013) apply the CA to pedagogic practice as they argue for teaching that promotes well-being. Drawing on a large scale multi-year study in South Africa, a list[6] of capabilities for socially just university access and success has been developed (Wilson-Strydom, 2014, 2015a). The study took place between 2009 and 2012 and involved 2,816 high school learners in their final three years of schooling and 270 first-year university students. While the contextual specificity of the empirical data underpinning the list is that of South African higher education, the theoretical and literature-based underpinnings of this conceptualisation of capabilities are global, and the capabilities are formulated at a general level. As such, the capabilities listed are likely to resonate in contexts other than South Africa, although the specificities and particular areas of emphasis will need to be contextually determined.

Table 7.1 Capabilities for university access and success

Dimension	Capabilities
Practical reason	Being able to make well-reasoned, informed, critical, independent, and reflective choices about post-school study.
Knowledge and imagination	Having the academic grounding for chosen university subjects, being able to develop and apply methods of critical thinking and imagination to identify and comprehend multiple perspectives and complex problems.
Learning disposition	Having curiosity and a desire for learning, having the learning skills required for university study and being an active inquirer (questioning disposition).
Social relations and social networks	Being able to participate in groups for learning, working with diverse others to solve problems or complete tasks. Being able to form networks of friendships for learning support and leisure.
Respect, dignity, and recognition	Having respect for oneself and for others, and receiving respect from others, being treated with dignity. Not being devalued, or devaluing others because of one's gender, social class, religion, or race. Valuing diversity and being able to show empathy (understand and respect others' points of view). Having a voice to participate in learning.
Emotional health	Not being subject to anxiety or fear that diminishes learning. Having confidence in one's ability to learn.
Language competence and confidence	Being able to understand, read, write, and speak confidently in the language of instruction.

Returning to the stories of Bellah and Miguel – using the capabilities listed in Table 7.1 as the metric for assessing equality with respect to access and success, rather than enrolment and retention statistics only, would provide a much richer informational basis (Sen, 1999) for identifying the inequalities and injustices at play in students' lives, and so points towards interventions that universities might consider in an effort to achieve greater equality of student experiences and well-being rather than equality of participation rates across groups. In particular, we see how different Bellah and Miguel's experiences were with respect to their freedoms, agency, and well-being, and particularly with respect to the capabilities for social relations and social networks, emotional health, knowledge and imagination, and respect, dignity, and recognition. Revisiting Sen's question of 'equality of what?' – if we see expansion of university access as an issue of social justice, then we cannot be indifferent to the lives that our students can actually live once they enter university (Sen, 2009, p. 18, see quotation at the start of the chapter). Interventions[7] that seek to improve access should then take account of these capabilities – and the personal, social, and environmental conversion factors that impact on their realisation. From this basis, institutions are better placed to create university environments that enable the multidimensional capabilities for participation.

Conclusion

This chapter set out to introduce the CA as a theoretical framework that helps us to think about university access in new ways, and explicitly in a manner that foregrounds social justice concerns. After a short conceptual tour of the key concepts within CA, the approach was applied to university access, using the stories of two students to illustrate the arguments. In this way, the chapter has sought to follow the call made in the opening quotation, namely, that justice cannot be indifferent to the lives that people actually live. Since the CA foregrounds an understanding of what people can actually be and do, the boundaries between conceptual critique and practical action for change are potentially blurred, so opening up spaces for action (Walker, 2006, p. 142). In this way, the CA provides both a conceptual lens for theoretically exploring access and widening participation from a social justice point of view, as well as the basis for proposing interventions, drawing on the actual experiences of students.

Notes

1 The concept of human development seeks to move discussions about what development means beyond the dominant approaches focusing only on income as measured by Gross National Product (GNP). Human development is defined as follows: "Human development aims to enlarge people's freedoms to do and be what they value and have reason to value. In practice, human development also empowers people to engage actively in development of our shared planet. It is people-centred. At all levels of development, human development focuses on essential freedoms: enabling people to lead long and healthy lives, to acquire knowledge, to be able to enjoy a decent standard of living and to shape their own lives. Many people value these freedoms in and of themselves; they are also powerful means to other opportunities" (Alkire, 2010, p. 43).
2 For a more fully developed account of agency in the capability approach than is possible in this chapter, please see Crocker and Robeyns (2009).
3 Space does not permit a deeper engagement with these debates in this chapter, see Wilson-Strydom (2015a, 2015b) for detailed argument about theories of social justice in relation to university access.
4 This longitudinal study (2014–2016) is focused on understanding students' lives with a view to exploring how students, as agents, interact with university structures. Forty students who entered the university as first-year students in 2014 were selected to participate in the study. All students attended relatively poorly resourced township schools. They are enrolled in courses across five major fields of study and both male and female students are participating. Methodologies include annual in-depth interviews and a series of four participatory workshops per year using a variety of qualitative methodologies such as group discussions, photo voice, student drawings, written reflections on experiences, and others. The study is funded with a grant from the South African National Research Foundation (NRF), grant number: 87922.

5 The term 'township' refers to large, poor, and often underdeveloped urban areas that house many of South Africa's unemployed. Townships have their roots in apartheid policies of race-based segregation. Despite major legislative and policy changes since 1994, townships remain poorly serviced, with high levels of poverty and violence.
6 There is a robust debate in the CA literature about whether or not to propose specific lists of capabilities. Space does not permit this issue to be considered here. For more information about these debates see (Alexander, 2008; Nussbaum, 2003; Robeyns, 2003, 2005; Sen, 2004; Walker, 2006).
7 Since the role of context is critical, this chapter does not propose specific interventions as the interventions needed to foster capabilities for participation that are appropriate in one university context would not necessarily apply in another. Nonetheless, the list of capabilities for university access provides a general entry point from which contextual specificities can be identified and addressed.

References

Alexander, J. (2008). *Capabilities and Social Justice. The Political Philosophy of Amartya Sen and Martha Nussbaum*. Surrey, England: Ashgate.

Alkire, S. (2010). *Human Development: Definitions, Critiques, and Related Concepts. Human Development Research Paper 2010/01* (No. 2010/01). New York: UNDP.

Alkire, S., and Deneulin, S. (2009a). A Normative Framework for Development. In S. Deneulin and L. Shahani (Eds.), *An Introduction to the Human Development and Capability Approach. Freedom and Agency* (pp. 3–21). London: Earthscan.

Alkire, S., and Deneulin, S. (2009b). The Human Development and Capability Approach. In S. Deneulin and L. Shahani (Eds.), *An Introduction to the Human Development and Capability Approach. Freedom and Agency* (pp. 22–48). London: Earthscan.

Archer, L. (2003). Social Class and Higher Education. In L. Archer, M. Hutchings, and A. Ross (Eds.), *Higher Education and Social Class. Issues of Exclusion and Inclusion* (pp. 5–20). London: RoutledgeFalmer.

Assie-Lumumba, N. (2005). Critical Perspectives on the Crises, Planned Change, and the Prospects for Transformation in African Higher Education. *Journal of Higher Education in Africa*, *3*(3), 1–29.

Becker, G. (1964). *Human Capital: A Theoretical and Empirical Analysis with Special Reference to Education* (Third Edition). Chicago: Chicago University Press.

Boni, A., and Walker, M. (Eds.). (2013). *Human Development and Capabilities: Re-Imagining the University of the Twenty-First Century*. London: Routledge.

CHE. (2012). *Vital Stats: Public Higher Education 2010*. Pretoria: Council on Higher Education (CHE). Retrieved from http://www.che.ac.za/documents/d000249/vital_stats_public_higher_education_2010.pdf

Crocker, D., and Robeyns, I. (2009). Capability and Agency. In C. J. Morris (Ed.), *Amartya Sen: Contemporary Philosophy in Focus* (pp. 60–90). Oxford: Oxford University Press.

Deneulin, S. (2014). *Wellbeing, Justice and Development Ethics*. Abingdon: Routledge.

Deprez, L. S., and Wood, D. R. (2013). Teaching for Well-Being: Pedagogical Strategies for Meaning, Value, Relevance and Justice. In A. Boni and M. Walker (Eds.), *Human Development and Capabilities: Re-Imagining the University of the Twenty-First Century* (pp. 145–161). London: Routledge.

Dudley Jenkins, L., and Moses, M. S. (Eds.). (2014). *Affirmative Action Matters: Creating Opportunities for Students around the World*. London: Routledge.

Furlong, A., and Cartmel, F. (2009). *Higher Education and Social Justice*. Berkshire, England: Society for Research into Higher Education and Open University Press.

Giroux, H. A. (2008). *Against the Terror of Neoliberalism: Politics beyond the Age of Greed*. Boulder, CO: Paradigm Publishers.

Hart, C. S. (2007). The Capability Approach as an Evaluative Framework for Education Policy: the Example of Widening Participation in Higher Education in England. *Prospero, 13*(3), 34–50.

Hart, C. S. (2012). *Aspirations, Education and Social Justice: Applying Sen and Bourdieu*. London: Bloomsbury.

Johnston, B. (2010). *The First Year at University. Teaching Students in Transition*. New York: Society for Research into Higher Education & Open University Press.

Jonathan, R. (2001). Higher Education Transformation and the Public Good. In *Re-Asserting the 'Public Good' in Higher Education, Kagisano Discussion Series (Report 1)* (pp. 28–63). Pretoria: Council on Higher Education.

Lanzi, D. (2007). Capabilities, Human Capital and Education. *The Journal of Socio-Economics, 36*, 424–435.

Marginson, S. (2011). Equity, Status and Freedom: A Note on Higher Education. *Cambridge Journal of Education, 41*(1), 23–36.

Mountford-Zimdars, A., Sabbagh, D., and Post, D. (Eds.). (2014). *Fair Access to Higher Education: Global Perspectives*. Chicago: University of Chicago Press.

Nussbaum, M.C., 2000. *Women and Human Development. The Capabilities Approach*. Cambridge: Cambridge University Press.

Nussbaum, M. C. (2003). Capabilities as Fundamental Entitlements: Sen and Social Justice. *Feminist Economics, 9*(2–3), 33–59.

Nussbaum, M. C. (2006). Education and Democratic Citizenship: Capabilities and Quality Education. *Journal of Human Development, 7*(3), 385–395.

Nussbaum, M. C. (2010). *Not for Profit: Why Democracy Needs the Humanities*. Princeton, NJ: Princeton University Press.

Nussbaum, M. C. (2011). *Creating Capabilities: The Human Development Approach*. Cambridge, MA: Harvard University Press.

Okkolin, M.-A. (2013). *Highly Educated Women in Tanzania. Constructing Educational Well-being and Agency* (PhD Thesis). University of Jyväskylä, Jyväskylä, Finland.

Rawls, J. (1999). *A Theory of Justice* (Revised Edition). Cambridge, MA: Harvard University Press.

Robeyns, I. (2003). Sen's Capability Approach and Gender Inequality: Selecting Relevant Capabilities. *Feminist Economics, 9*(2–3), 61–92.

Robeyns, I. (2005). The Capability Approach: A Theoretical Survey. *Journal of Human Development, 6*(1), 93–114.

Robeyns, I. (2006). Three Models of Education: Rights, Capabilities and Human Capital. *Theory and Research in Education, 4*(1), 69–84.

Sen, A. (1980). *Equality of What? The Tanner Lecture on Human Values*. California: Stanford University.

Sen, A. (1985). Well-Being, Agency and Freedom: The Dewey Lectures 1984. *The Journal of Philosophy, 82*(4), 169–221.

Sen, A. (1992). *Inequality Reexamined*. New York: Russell Sage Foundation.

Sen, A. (1993). Capability and Well-Being. In M. Nussbaum and A. Sen (Eds.), *The Quality of Life* (pp. 30–53). New Delhi: Oxford University Press, India.

Sen, A. (1997). Editorial: Human Capital and Human Capability. *World Development, 25*(12), 1959–1961.

Sen, A. (1999). *Development as Freedom.* Oxford: Oxford University Press.

Sen, A. (2004). Capabilities, Lists, and Public Reason: Continuing the Conversation. *Feminist Economics, 10*(3), 77–80.

Sen, A. (2009). *The Idea of Justice.* Cambridge, MA: Harvard University Press.

Tikly, L., and Barrett, A. M. (2011). Social Justice, Capabilities and the Quality of Education in Low Income Countries. *International Journal of Educational Development, 31*, 3–14.

Unterhalter, E. (2009). Education. In S. Deneulin and L. Shahani (Eds.), *An Introduction to the Human Development and Capability Approach. Freedom and Agency* (pp. 207–227). London: Earthscan.

Unterhalter, E., and Brighouse, H. (2007). Distribution of What for Social Justice in Education? The Case of Education for All by 2015. In M. Walker and E. Unterhalter (Eds.), *Amartya Sen's Capability Approach and Social Justice in Education* (pp. 67–86). New York: Palgrave Macmillan Ltd.

Unterhalter, E., and Carpentier, V. (2010). *Global Inequalities and Higher Education: Whose Interests Are We Serving?* Hampshire, England: Palgrave Macmillan Ltd.

Walker, M. (2005). Amartya Sen's Capability Approach and Education. *Educational Action Research, 13*(1), 103–110.

Walker, M. (2006). *Higher Education Pedagogies.* Berkshire, England: Society for Research into Higher Education and Open University Press.

Walker, M., and Unterhalter, E. (2007). The Capability Approach: Its Potential for Work in Education. In M. Walker and E. Unterhalter (Eds.), *Amartya Sen's Capability Approach and Social Justice in Education* (pp. 1–18). New York: Palgrave Macmillan Ltd.

Watts, M. (2009). Sen and the Art of Motorcycle Maintenance: Adaptive Preferences and Higher Education. *Studies in the Philosophy of Education, 28*, 425–436.

Watts, M., and Bridges, D. (2006). Enhancing Students' Capabilities? UK Higher Education and the Widening Participation Agenda. In S. Deneulin and N. Sagovsky (Eds.), *Transforming Unjust Structures: The Capability Approach* (pp. 143–160). Dordrecht, Netherlands: Springer.

Wilson-Strydom, M. (2015a). *University Access and Success: Capabilities, Diversity and Social Justice.* Abingdon: Routledge.

Wilson-Strydom, M. (2015b). University Access and Theories of Social Justice: Contributions of the Capabilities Approach. *Higher Education, 69*(1), 143–155.

Chapter 8

Reflexivity and agency

Critical realist and Archerian analyses of access and participation

Peter Kahn

Introduction

It is often claimed that higher education represents an emancipatory project. Barnett (1990) argued that the overall project of higher education entails students learning to engage in critical self-reflection and to question what is taken for granted. Significant intellectual and personal growth can accompany participation in higher education. There have been suggestions also that society as a whole benefits. Gutmann (1987), for instance, claimed that higher education has an important part to play in establishing and maintaining democratic societies consisting of free citizens. It is evidently thus a cause for concern when rates of participation in higher education vary according to socio-economic status or ethnicity, for instance, given the inequalities that are likely to occur on a range of levels.

Such variation in participation is, indeed, widespread. There are significant differences in participation rates in the UK that result from socio-economic background (Chowdry, Crawford, Dearden, Goodman, & Vignoles, 2013). The participation in higher education of Black male students in the United States remains a particular challenge (Harper, 2012). Vally and Spreen (2014) have highlighted how inequality is pervasive across higher education in South Africa. Chien, Montjouridès and van der Pol (Chapter 1, this volume) pointed out that rates of participation in higher education vary from one region of the world to the next, and that rates of female participation are particularly low in countries with limited resources.

At the same time, though, various researchers have argued that the overall purpose of higher education has shifted towards the pursuit of economic ends. Bok (2009) has suggested that higher education now primarily serves to prepare students for employment. Lynch (2006) has argued that students are increasingly seen by institutions as consumers of education. Such shifts have also been seen in relation to policy designed to widen the participation of under-represented groups. Archer (2007) suggested that there has been an emphasis on the economic benefits of participation in higher education in widening participation policy within the UK. She argued that a focus on 'aspirations' within one national programme could be linked to justifications for widening participation that have been framed in terms of economic flourishing. Sheeran et al. (2007) similarly identified an agenda that sought to widen participation for the sake of a more economically able workforce. Emancipation, though, involves far more than an economic flourishing. Bhaskar (1993) argued that emancipation pertains to desired rather than undesired sources of determination. Emancipation occurs when needs are identified by individuals or groups on their own behalf, rather than when they are determined for them by others. It can hardly be assumed that an economic focus is always best suited to the diversity of students' aspirations, responsibilities and needs.

It is also clear that significant weaknesses remain in what might be termed the dominant approach to explaining and addressing levels of participation in higher education. Gorard, Smith, May, Thomas, Adnett and Slack (2006) demonstrated that the research literature in this field emphasises the notions of situational, institutional and attitudinal barriers to participation in higher education. They have identified a tendency for policy and practice in the field within the UK to focus on 'removing' barriers. Critics, however, have drawn attention to weaknesses in this conceptual framework. Gorard and Smith (2007) contended that while introducing strategies and policy to overcome identified barriers may be significant for some individuals, addressing barriers has only had a marginal effect on participation rates. They argued that the research on barriers pays minimal attention to reasons why non-participants do not engage. Where non-participants are investigated a different picture can emerge, as in research by Fuller, Paton, Foskett and Maringe (2008). This study illuminated ways in which participation is rooted in complex social, historical and biographical factors. One can assume that a barrier is transferred directly to the actions of individuals, rather than look to explore more sophisticated models of causation. It remains the case, though, that a focus on barriers can be straightforwardly framed and addressed through an economic lens.

A critical realist and Archerian contribution

It is thus important to explore perspectives that both offer a comprehensive account of the decision-making processes involved and remain open to the complexities of social justice. Critical realism (Bhaskar, 1986) constitutes a paradigm that is predicated on explanatory critique in relation to social structure, with criticality stemming from the underlying focus on emancipation that non-reductionist analyses allow. As a field, critical realism offers a non-reductive explanatory critique that draws attention to the underlying basis for the actual events that we experience. Critical realist studies seek to identify the mechanisms that give rise to events and to our subjective experience of those events. A mechanism is said to be real in the sense that it constitutes a causal tendency, while still allowing for the possibility that a mechanism will not necessarily be triggered in any given setting. Sayer (1992) contrasted this notion of causality with one in which discrete events are linked together in a direct relationship of cause and effect. The notion of explanatory critique is important, as Bhaskar (1986, 169–179) argued that 'accounts of social reality are not only value-impregnated but value-impregnating' and that this provides social science with an impulse towards emancipation. The field is 'critical' in the sense that it is attuned to isolating grounds of error, focusing first of all on explanatory critique in relation to social structure rather than, say, on exposing the will to power. In identifying structures and mechanisms in play, it will then be possible to consider the varying ways in which identified sources of determination might be desired. It is clear that this determination can occur on a communal as well as an individual basis. The use of the terms 'wanted' and 'desired' by Bhaskar (1986) in relation to sources of determination implies a reflexive awareness on the part of the subjects concerned in relation to what they do want or desire.

Critical realism primarily represents a meta-theory rooted in philosophy, with a need to develop directly applicable theoretical frameworks. In particular, the sociologist Margaret Archer has developed a set of mediating frameworks under the banner of realist social theory (Archer, 1995, 2000, 2012). This chapter explores Archer's account of the interplay between social structure and human agency. Her account seeks to explain the ways in which agents use their personal powers to act 'so rather than otherwise' in given social situations. Her approach takes seriously the uncertainties that are present in all decision making, highlighting the reflexive basis on which actions are progressed. This chapter further presents an approach to adapting and developing this framework proposed by Kahn (2009, 2014), in order to help explain interplay between personal and socio-cultural factors that relate to student access, participation and engagement in higher education. What is it that determines whether a student seeks to engage with higher education, initially in taking the application process forward or in engaging with their studies as a university student? The argument here illustrates the power of a critical realist approach to the field of widening participation, in considering issues that relate to research and practice on access and participation.

The pursuit of varied courses of action

Archer (2003) suggested that there is a range of socio-cultural constraints and enablements that exist in relation to one's actions as an agent. For instance, one's prior educational experience and the knowledge that one possesses about higher education are significant factors in determining whether one enters higher education. However, she argued that these factors do not 'produce a uniformity of response from those similarly situated in relation to them' (Archer, 2007, 19). Rather, we arrive at answers to the questions 'What do I want?' and 'How will I secure this?' through a dynamic interplay between our own concerns and our context. Interplay between contexts and concerns is mediated by internal conversation or reflexive deliberation. Archer defined 'reflexivity' as the ordinary exercise of the mental ability by which someone considers himself or herself in relation to (social) contexts. It involves such patterns of internal conversation as rehearsing, imagining, reliving, projecting ahead and prioritising. As such, reflexive deliberation provides a basis on which an individual determines intentions in relation to possible future courses of action. It is clear that any account must deal with the range of variation that does indeed exist. For instance, Johnston, MacDonald, Mason, Ridley and Webster (2000) identified how young people from a disadvantaged neighbourhood in North East England exhibited diverse and unpredictable careers and transitions, despite their similar socio-economic backgrounds and common location of residence.

Archer (2003) identified three phases to one's reflexive deliberations. The first phase comprises the discernment through which we identify possible concerns. These concerns relate to our well-being in three orders of natural reality, namely nature, practice and the social. Nature pertains to our physical well-being, employment provides a key focus for practice and our relationships with others are at the heart of social reality. This initial phase is followed by the deliberation through which we rank these concerns, and then by the dedication through which we decide whether we are able to embark upon a particular way of life, or *modus vivendi*. Alongside this, we progressively specify concrete courses of action, so that concerns lead to projects, and projects lead to stable practices. It is in pursuing specific projects that an individual engages most directly with the constraints and enablements that stem from social and cultural structures. We adjust our projects as we perceive their feasibility in the given context. Thus an individual who has begun to experience failure at educational examinations may conclude that they are unable to enter university.

On this basis, Archer (2007) traced how experiences of socio-cultural contextual continuity or discontinuity contribute to the development of characteristic modes of reflexivity and the prioritisation of different configuration of concerns. Archer (2007) traced how different modes of reflexivity could be linked to different outcomes for social mobility. As a result of pursuing a particular mode of reflexivity, she argued that individuals remake their own social worlds in different ways. In particular, she identified the following modes of reflexivity within the subjects that she researched:

- *Communicative reflexives* share their deliberations with others before deciding on a course of action. Someone for whom communicative reflexivity dominates their internal deliberations might be more likely to take much greater account of the views of close friends and relatives before making a decision on whether or not to apply for university entry. The exercise of communicative reflexivity has links with the networks of intimacy identified by Heath, Fuller and Paton (2008) as relevant to non-participation in higher education. Archer found that communicative reflexivity was more predominant where individuals remained in the same locality on a long-term basis, were able to maintain stable relationships, and had scope to pursue a range of occupations locally (2007, 145).

- *Autonomous reflexives* typically prioritise performance in relation to practice, relying on their own internal deliberations to navigate their way in the world. Archer identified ways in which autonomous reflexivity develops as an individual prioritises employment-related concerns. She further argued that the pursuit of such concerns typically leads to contextual discontinuity, as one moves locations in order to realise one's ambitions. We can illustrate this with reference to a decision to embark on a university degree: an autonomous reflexive might be more inclined to consider comparative data on several different possible degree programmes or institutions, optimising their decision on the basis of their aspirations for a successful career in relation to the data.

- *Meta-reflexives* are characterised as those whose reflexive deliberations pay critical attention to social ideals. Experiences of contextual discontinuity also play an important role in the development of this mode of reflexivity, as one sees that it is possible to pursue different social ideals. A meta-reflexive might give serious consideration to the consequences for others of a decision to study, or to how studying for a particular degree might affect his or her capacity to make a difference in the world.

- *Fractured reflexives*, meanwhile, engage in deliberation that intensifies personal distress rather than results in purposeful courses of action. The transition that is entailed in entering higher education effectively demands at least some exercise of agency, posing challenges for those for whom this triggers anxiety and distress. Archer (2012) suggested that students pursuing this mode of reflexivity are still admitted to university, but that process by which this occurs is relatively closely dependent on circumstances or on the initiative that others take.

It was through such modes of reflexivity that Archer sought to explain the varied ways in which individuals engage with structural constraints as they pursue those concerns that matter to them.

Gaining entry into higher education involves a whole sequence of decisions and activities, and may be regarded as a project that extends beyond the acquisition of a set of admitting qualifications. This chapter now looks to draw out the implications of this overall account as to how individuals exercise agency when making decisions around entry into higher education. The chapter concludes by considering the agency of those already participating in higher education.

Decision making around access to higher education

Structural and cultural factors constrain the ease with which it is possible to gain entry into higher education, and affect the presence or absence of alternative courses of action. The discourse within the field around barriers to participation does acknowledge these constraints quite directly. There are constraints that are linked to institutions, as with the nature of the programmes that are offered, the timetabling of classes, admissions procedures, institutional location and so on. There are factors that apply to the desired lifestyle of a prospective learner, such as the costs of the programme that McGivney (1992) highlights, and the reduced time available for a social life or to care for dependents. Whether or not one possesses the requisite qualifications to enter higher education is also important, as Gibbons and Chevalier (2007) have emphasised.

According to Archer's model such structural and cultural factors operate as barriers in significant part because they influence both the subjective concerns held by the individual and the projects that are then pursued or not pursued. The subjective concerns connect to dispositional factors identified within the literature. Gorard and Smith (2007), for instance, highlighted subjective opportunity structures. They suggested that structural and cultural factors can engender a negative attitude towards learning, in which it is perceived as alien and imposed. Prior educational experiences (Gorard & Rees, 2002) and one's family (San-Segundo & Valiente, 2003) constitute a particular influence on these concerns. Participation is strongly related to parents' education, with familiarity with higher education and levels of satisfaction with readily available alternatives all influenced by family background.

However, the way in which an individual takes forward subjective concerns remains central to the exercise of agency. An individual seeking to establish a way forward in his or her life within a given socio-cultural context must still decide upon which concerns to prioritise, and how best to pursue these concerns through specific courses of action, whether or not these involve seeking entry into higher education. According to Archer (2003), reflexive deliberation plays an important role in this progressive specification of courses of action, such that employing a given mode of reflexivity will lead one to prioritise different concerns and thus pursue different actions. Archer (2007) argued that communicative reflexives seek to prioritise their relations with others in making decisions. There is a tendency for those engaged in communicative reflexivity to give close attention to the needs and aspirations of the partners in their dialogues. Autonomous reflexivity, meanwhile, is associated with the prioritisation of concerns that are centred on performative achievement. Concerns that are related to the pursuit of higher education thus fall naturally within the purview of such deliberation. Archer (2007) specifically identified autonomous reflexivity as a mechanism for upward social mobility. In this case, rates of participation in higher education from amongst autonomous reflexives might be expected to depend on the extent to which performance in employment is dependent on capacities developed through higher education. As well as taking a concern for the nature of their own reflexive deliberations, meta-reflexives are characteristically concerned about the pursuit of a set of values. Archer (2007) linked meta-reflexivity to lateral social mobility, and to a prioritisation of social values above performance in employment. One might expect that the extent to which higher education allows one to pursue a range of social ideals would affect participation rates for meta-reflexives, with scope for participation rates to vary given the extent to which higher education serves the needs and aspirations of given groupings of students. If the focus of higher education narrows further towards economic priorities, though, then further tensions can be expected.

Communicative reflexivity and fractured reflexivity, furthermore, both take on particular importance for access to higher education, partly as Archer identified a correlation between lower, or no, qualifications and these two modes of reflexivity (2007). She argued that communicative reflexives play an active role in choosing their own social immobility, avoiding enablements such as higher education in order to prioritise inter-personal concerns. Rather than pursue social mobility, they choose to maintain a web of social relationships. One has to work to pursue a way of life that is predicated on taking up employment locally, but in so doing one may side-line inducements to enter higher education. Furthermore, various studies point to the communicative basis for decisions to participate in higher education, with parents and other significant interlocutors closely involved. Both Fuller et al. (2008) and Heath et al. (2008) explored how decisions to participate or not in higher education are linked to networks consisting of family members and friends. Johnston et al. (2000) investigated how within Willowdene a plurality of informal social networks was in evidence, which assisted individuals to manage their lives, secure employment and generally to experience social inclusion.

Many elements of the process to gain entry into higher education, however, are potentially alien to communities or groups with little experience of higher education. Weil (1989) argued that university entry involves a dislocation which is intensified according to the number of ways in which the learner may be identified as 'non-traditional', with class, gender and ethnic difference playing key roles in this. Entry into an elite institution poses further scope for unfamiliarity, as Jary (2008, 112) has noted. We have seen poor performance of elite institutions in recruiting from lower socio-economic groups on an on-going basis since then in the UK (Chowdry et al., 2013). The argument here is not that communicative reflexivity is more prevalent in social categories with low rates of participation in higher education. Archer saw no correlation between one's dominant mode of reflexivity and socio-occupational class background (2007, 96). Rather, we would suggest that what is important is the lack of familiarity with higher education amongst those with whom communicative reflexives share their deliberations. Someone who engages in communicative reflexivity from within a social setting that is unfamiliar with higher education may well experience an encouragement of other concerns or even outright disdain. This is particularly important given that Archer has suggested that communicative reflexivity is more prevalent in younger age groups, as contextual discontinuity is often only experienced as one becomes an adult.

The large differences in HE participation rates that Chowdry et al. (2013) identified at high-status universities by socio-economic background may be related to the particular difficulties that students from lower socio-economic backgrounds may face in pursuing communicative reflexivity in settings that stretch beyond their familiar context. If we draw on the notions from Bernstein (2005) of restricted and elaborated codes, then capacity to engage in communicative reflexivity will be affected according to the capacity of prospective students to communicate with others on the basis of an elaborated code that does not assume understanding on the part of one's interlocutors at the outset. Such communications across difference is an integral feature of engaging with bureaucratic institutions such as universities.

Fractured reflexives also form an important category in considering the variation that emerges from individual agency. Archer (2007) argued that it is the reflexivity of communicative reflexives that is most likely to become fractured. The study by Johnston et al. (2000) identified a series of crucial points in young people's lives such as bereavement, family break-up or the imprisonment of one's father that give rise to particular challenges to advisory services looking to support young people. Such experiences strike at the heart of communicative reflexivity by removing trusted interlocutors. Pursuing an extended personal project is assisted by the capacity to engage in a functioning form of reflexive deliberation. Someone who waits for events to unfold rather than seeks to shape those events, as is characteristically the case for fractured reflexives, may be less likely to explore the possibility of entering higher education on their own initiative, unless personal support is available.

Understanding student engagement in higher education

This model of the interplay between social structure and human agency can also be used to frame the engagement of students in their studies, as Kahn (2014) has argued. According to this perspective, student engagement is framed as that process by which learners establish concerns within given educational settings, and translate these concerns into projects and practices as learners. Kahn (2014) suggested that educational settings specifically include requirements for students to engage with specific sets of tasks and social relations, so that the agency entailed needs to be considered on a corporate as well as an individual basis. As such, the way that students exercise agency is relatively tightly constrained. Macfarlane (2015), indeed, has highlighted how students are expected to comply with rules on class attendance, actively interact with each other in order to succeed and display desired forms of emotional development.

Archer (2003) suggested that the prioritisation of different sets of concerns alongside experiences of social continuity or discontinuity can lead one to adopt a distinctive mode of reflexivity, with different outcomes for social mobility emerging as a result. An empirical study by Kahn, Everington, Kelm, Reid and Watkins (2016), though, saw that a specific group of learners needed to manifest a range of modes of reflexivity in response to structural constraints rather than rely on a single dominant mode of reflexivity as Archer (2007) had seen in her more open setting. For instance, if an academic task requires students to demonstrate competence in group work, then there will be advantages in place if a given student is able to engage in communicative reflexivity with their peers. If one does not share a common social background with the main body of one's peers, such reflexivity may well be harder to establish. Archer (2003) indicated that communicative reflexivity is integrally linked to the presence of common understanding, relations, values and so on between the interlocutors; as manifested also in relation to one's capacity to employ an elaborated code in communication with others.

Kahn (2014) further highlighted the collective dimension to student learning more widely, with university study often involving the exercise of corporate agency as an integral feature of what is required to address required tasks or to navigate one's way within educational environments. Archer used this term of 'corporate agency' (2003, 133) to refer to the way that a group of individuals articulate a set of aims and develop organisation to realise those aims. Particular constraints are thus again present in relation to corporate agency if one's own interests are disdained by a large majority of the other students, with scope to affect whether or not one remains in higher education.

This study by Kahn (2014) also explored the scope for students to manifest modes of extended reflexivity, contrasting this with both the restricted reflexivity that involves formulaic stances and the fractured reflexivity that does not directly progress intentional courses of learning. Kahn (2014) argued that there is a clear element of uncertainty in the way that students respond to such tasks and social relations, and that this allows for a range of responses. Archer (2003) specifically highlighted the role that uncertainty plays in generating the need for reflexivity. There may be different ways, though, in which educational actions are directed away from the intrinsic uncertainty that is associated with learning, as when taking what might be regarded as a short cut in relation to a required task. Mechanisms may exist, though, that trigger the exercise of fractured reflexivity, for instance, from students who are from minority groups within higher education. Burke (2015) argued that pedagogical relations that involve misrecognition have potential to shame students. We would highlight the implications of such misrecognition for reflexivity on the part of students, and for their capacity to act as agents in educational settings. Flann (2010) has identified ways in which relations of domination constitute an important factor in silencing reflexivity more widely. More widely, though, choices may remain as to whether one remains as a student and how much time is devoted to one's studies; and these are also underpinned by one's willingness to engage in reflexivity. This touches on student aspirations in relation to learning, so that weaker retention might be expected from students who find themselves unable to act as agents, or who choose other priorities above learning.

Access and participation in a wider perspective

This chapter has argued that one particular explanatory framework offers significant insight into issues of access and participation in higher education. There is scope for those considering entry into higher education, and for students, to act so rather than otherwise in their given structural settings. It is clear, though, that the reflexivity exhibited in these settings is itself influenced by structural constraints. Such influences on reflexivity represent an additional element that extends beyond the immediate restrictions afforded by a structural constraint. The analysis here offers a way forward in understanding causal mechanisms that relate to access and participation in higher education. The complexities of establishing and sustaining a *modus vivendi* that is predicated on participation in higher education extend far beyond the notion of overcoming a set of 'barriers', with a value in considering wider frames of reference than one simply predicated on economic concerns.

The analysis has implications for practice, policy and research into access and participation. The account has highlighted the importance of reflexivity in the interactions between structure and agency as far as access and participation are concerned. Kahn (2009) offered a range of ways to support the reflexivity of individuals within the practice of widening access to higher education. In this there will be scope to consider further the role that social relations play in shaping reflexivity, given recent critical realist theorising in this area. Donati (2011) has argued that interpersonal relations frame the reflexivity of the subjects involved. He argued that this is particularly so where a reciprocal dimension is present to the relation, given that this helps to sustain the reflexivity. It is already clear, though, that social relations have an important role to play in the field. Johnston et al. (2000) suggested that, in cases where one is looking to widen access to higher education to individuals who have experienced broken lives, advisers with detailed long-term personal knowledge are required in order to support their reflexivity. Thomas (2006) similarly noted the need for personal tutors for students in the target groups for widening participation. There will be ways to strengthen the extent to which given individuals, such as personal tutors, supervisors and departmental administrators maintain a longstanding and personal knowledge of their students.

Alongside this, it will be important to explore further the corporate basis for access and participation in higher education, something that is relevant also to the way that one's needs and aspirations are framed through a social lens. A greater awareness of the importance of corporate agency has potential to open up avenues to participation, while recognising that may jar with many current stances in policy and practice. Taylor (1993) argued that bureaucratic approaches typically prize economic flourishing above stable trusting communities, thus isolating individuals from each other. Widening participation activities, approaches to student admissions or the way that learning is configured within higher education could be predicated in part on groups rather than individuals, as when a group of people enter an alien context together and are thus able to offer each other mutual support in framing suitable courses of action. Mountford-Zimdars (Chapter 13, this volume) highlights how such an approach has long been a characteristic of admissions practices in private universities in the United States.

Kahn (2009) explored a range of ways in which higher education might be adapted and restructured on the basis of collective considerations that align with our analysis of interactions between structure and agency. It would be possible to develop curricula so that there is greater scope for programmes of higher education to align with concerns held by students, including those based around notions of human flourishing that extend beyond a preparation for employment. There is scope to develop curricula that address the concerns and priorities held by meta-reflexives who prioritise social ideals, as in relation to environmental issues. Taylor (1993) argued that an instrumental mode of life tends to dissolve the intermediate social structures that are a feature of culture, religion and ethnicity. Our analysis suggests that there would be value in establishing structural features within higher education that pertain, for instance to programmes, halls of residence, outreach activity or so on. Such approaches require substantive partnerships between universities and other groups, but potentially serve to make higher education more accessible to communicative reflexives and fractured reflexives from groups with low rates of participation in higher education. However, at the same time, there is scope for approaches that build in social relations across difference, as the hermeneutic tradition has long argued (Gadamer, 1989). The value of including difference within a cohort of students, for instance, has developed as a particular feature of the cultural system that is associated with higher education, as has Harrison (2015) argued. However, it also offers scope to challenge pre-judgements of all those involved.

One analysis points to the limitations of relying solely on structural considerations in seeking to widen access and participation within higher education, as when focusing primarily on barriers to access and participation. The theory of practice developed by Bourdieu (1977), for instance, has been widely employed in studies on widening participation, but it downplays any significant role for reflexivity. Meanwhile, while socio-material perspectives (Fenwick, Edwards, & Sawchuk, 2011) have not been widely applied to studies around widening access, there is scope for further applications from this field. Socio-materialism highlights ways in which education is determined by dynamic networks of actors, resources and surroundings. As a whole, however, the field similarly downplays human intentionality. A critical realist account would acknowledge the constraints under which students operate, but would recognise further that some scope remains for the agent to act so rather than otherwise in any given situation.

It is helpful to frame both issues of access to higher education and participation in learning through a critical realist lens. There is significant scope to make use of further theoretical resources that have been developed from within critical realism. An extensive range of theoretical constructs has been developed by Archer in recent years that extends beyond the role of reflexivity in interactions between structure and agency, to include theories of personal and social identity (Archer, 2000), morphogenesis of social structures (Archer, 1995) and social relations (Donati & Archer, 2015). Beard, Clegg and Smith (2007), for instance, draw on such perspectives to consider the importance of the affective domain in the lifeworld of students, without reducing the discussion to therapeutic consideration alone. Case (2013), meanwhile, draws on these constructs to account for student success in higher education in ways that go beyond a consideration simply of inputs. In opening up the possibilities for non-reductive explanatory critique, critical realism offers significant scope for theorising to assist in advancing the emancipatory agenda around widening participation in higher education.

References

Archer, L. (2007). Diversity, equality and higher education: A critical reflection on the ab/uses of equity discourse within widening participation. *Teaching in Higher Education* 12, 635–653.

Archer, M. S. (1995). *Realist Social Theory: The Morphogenetic Approach*. Cambridge: Cambridge University Press.

Archer, M. S. (2000). *Being Human: The Problem of Agency*. Cambridge: Cambridge University Press.

Archer, M. S. (2003). *Structure, Agency and the Internal Conversation*. Cambridge: Cambridge University Press.

Archer, M. S. (2007). *Making Our Way through the World: Human Reflexivity and Social Mobility*. Cambridge: Cambridge University Press.

Archer, M. S. (2012). *The Reflexive Imperative in Late Modernity*. Cambridge: Cambridge University Press.

Barnett, R. (1990). *The Idea of Higher Education*. Buckingham: Society for Research into Higher Education & Open University Press.

Beard, C., Clegg, S., & Smith, K. (2007). Acknowledging the affective in higher education. *British Educational Research Journal*, *33*(2), 235–252.

Bernstein, B. (2005). *Theoretical Studies Towards a Sociology of Language*. London: Routledge.

Bhaskar, R. (1986). *Scientific Realism and Human Emancipation*. London: Verso.

Bhaskar, R. (1993). *Dialectic: The Pulse of Freedom*. London: Verso.

Bok, D. (2009). *Universities in the Marketplace: The Commercialization of Higher Education*. Princeton, NJ: Princeton University Press.

Bourdieu, P. (1977). *Outline of a Theory of Practice*. Cambridge: Cambridge University Press.

Burke, P. J. (2015). Re/imagining higher education pedagogies: Gender, emotion and difference. *Teaching in Higher Education*, *20*(4), 388–401.

Case, J. M. (2013). *Researching Student Learning in Higher Education: A Social Realist Approach*. London: Routledge.

Chowdry, H., Crawford, C., Dearden, L., Goodman, A., & Vignoles, A. (2013). Widening participation in higher education: Analysis using linked administrative data. *Journal of the Royal Statistical Society: Series A (Statistics in Society)*, *176*(2), 431–457.

Donati, P. (2011). *Relational Sociology: A New Paradigm for the Social Sciences*. London: Routledge.

Donati, P., & Archer, M. S. (2015). *The Relational Subject*. Cambridge: Cambridge University Press.

Fenwick, T., Edwards, R., & Sawchuk, P. (2011). *Emerging Approaches to Educational Research: Tracing the Socio-Material*. Abingdon: Routledge.

Flann, H. (2010). Emotion, and the Silenced and Short-circuited Self. In (Ed). M. S. Archer, *Conversations about Reflexivity*, 187–205. London: Routledge.

Fuller, A., Paton, K., Foskett, R. and Maringe, F. (2008). Barriers to participation in higher education? Depends on who you ask and how. *Widening Participation and Lifelong Learning, 10*, 6–17.

Gadamer, H. G. (1989). *Truth and Method*. New York: Crossroad.

Gibbons, S. and Chevalier, A. (2007). *Assessment, Achievement and Participation*. London: London School of Economics.

Gorard, S. and Rees, G. (2002). *Creating a Learning Society?* Bristol: Policy Press.

Gorard, S. and Smith, E. (2007). Do barriers get in the way? A review of the determinants of post-16 participation. *Research in Post-Compulsory Education, 12*, 141–158.

Gorard, S., Smith, E., May, H., Thomas, L., Adnett, N. and Slack, K. (2006). *Review of Widening Participation Research: Addressing the Barriers to Participation in Higher Education*. Bristol: Higher Education Funding Council.

Gutmann, A. (1987). *Democratic Education*. Hoboken, NJ: Wiley.

Harper, P. D. (2012). *Black Male Student Success in Higher Education: A Report from the National Black Male College Achievement Study*. Retrieved from http://works. bepress.com/sharper/43

Harrison, N. (2015). Practice, problems and power in "internationalisation at home": Critical reflections on recent research evidence. *Teaching in Higher Education, 20*(4), 412–430.

Heath, S., Fuller, A. and Paton, K. (2008). Network-based ambivalence and educational decision-making: a case study of 'non-participation' in higher education. *Research Papers in Education, 23*, 219–229.

Jary, D. (2008). The continued importance of widening participation. *Widening Participation and Lifelong Learning, 10*, 1.

Johnston, L., MacDonald, R., Mason, P., Ridley, L. and Webster, C. (2000). *Snakes & Ladders: Young People, Transitions and Social Exclusion*. Bristol: The Policy Press.

Kahn, P. E. (2009). On establishing a modus vivendi: The exercise of agency in decisions to participate or not participate in higher education. *London Review of Education, 7*(3), 261–270.

Kahn, P. E. (2014). Theorising student engagement in higher education. *British Educational Research Journal, 40*(6), 1005–1018.

Kahn, P. E., Everington, L., Kelm, K., Reid, I. and Watkins, F. (2016). Understanding student engagement in online learning environments: the role of reflexivity. Accepted for publication in *Educational Technology Research and Development*.

Lynch, K. (2006). Neo-liberalism and Marketisation: The implications for higher education. *European Educational Research Journal, 5*(1), 1.

Macfarlane, B. (2015). Student performativity in higher education: Converting learning as a private space into a public performance. *Higher Education Research and Development, 34*(2), 338–350.

McGivney, V. (1992). *Motivating Unemployed Adults to Undertake Education and Training*. Leicester: National Institute of Adult Continuing Education.

San-Segundo, M. and Valiente, A. (2003). Family background and returns to schooling in Spain. *Education Economics, 1*, 39–52.

Sayer, R. A. (1992). *Method in Social Science: A Realist Approach*. London: Routledge.

Sheeran, Y., Brown, B., and Baker, S. (2007). Conflicting philosophies of inclusion: The contestation of knowledge in widening participation. *London Review of Education, 5*, 249–263.

Taylor, C. (1993). *Sources of the Self.* Boston: Harvard University Press.

Thomas, L. (2006). Widening participation and the increased need for personal tutoring. In (Eds). L. Thomas and P. Hixenbaugh, *Personal Tutoring in Higher Education*, 21–31. Stoke-on-Trent: Trentham.

Vally, S., and Spreen, C. A. (2014). Globalization and Education in Post-Apartheid South Africa: The Narrowing of Education's Purpose. In (Eds) N. P. Stromquist and K. Monkman, *Globalization and Education: Integration and Contestation Across Cultures* (2nd Edition), 267–284. New York: Rowman and Littlefield.

Weil, S.W. (1989). Influences of lifelong learning on adults' expectations and experiences of returning to formal learning contexts. PhD dissertation, University of London, Institute of Education.

Section 3

Contemporary challenges

This section builds on the previous two sections to explore seven theorised examples of access challenges from around the world, highlighting the inequalities (and some possible solutions) from a diverse range of countries including the US, Australia, Japan and Russia.

Chapter 9

Framing and making of access policies

The case of Palestinian Arabs in higher education in Israel[1]

Ayala Hendin, Dalia Ben-Rabi and Faisal Azaiza

Introduction

Discourse on access of disadvantaged groups is traditionally framed in the context of representation and is concerned with questions of over-, under- or equal representation of groups. Such framing is rooted in principles of equality and social justice. However, it carries additional unique significance in higher education as a meritocratic system, where access is essential for the potential creation of knowledge. The importance of access is apparent in various policy discourse and framing, linking it to economic development, demographic sustainability, diversity and more.

As a society of many migrant groups, religious groups and a large indigenous minority, Israel has diverse access patterns between sub-populations. Access, or group participation, is defined as a challenge and is far from reaching its potential, especially among the Palestinian Arab indigenous minority, ultra-Orthodox Jewish population, Ethiopian-origin Jewish population, and other socio-economically and geographically peripheral groups. In this chapter, we examine the way this challenge is framed in the context of the Palestinian Arabs in Israel. We focus specifically on Arab, Druze and Circassian citizens of Israel.[2] We claim that on the rhetorical level, access is currently linked to economic development. This framing acts as a catalyst for current access-oriented policy making.

We begin by setting the theoretical framework for access discourse and policy problem framing, and the local context of access patterns and challenges. We then delve into a case of policy framing and making of an access-oriented intervention for Palestinian Arabs in Israel. We show how the policy framing interacts with the policy making through the plan's strategy, components and scope. We conclude with a number of messages from the case, bringing theory and practice together and offering a new perspective on access policy initiatives in light of changing discourses.

Access discourse, policy framing and policy making

We look at access and participation patterns through the lens of access literature and analyze the current access policy through theories of policy problem framing and policy making.

Discourse on access of disadvantaged groups typically employs the terms 'integration', 'participation', 'diversity' or 'inclusion' while discussing student experience in higher education, and vertical or horizontal disparities when comparing between groups of students. Participation, we suggest, best fits the reality of indigenous groups, as it is based on demographic patterns and does not bear a normative dimension. Integration, in contrast to participation, occurs when a group accepts the hegemonic culture while preserving the culture of origin, as commonly occurs with immigrants (Berry, 1997). Inclusion terminology has been widely used since the democratization and growth in accessibility of higher education (Gidley, Hampson, Wheeler, & Bereded-Samuel, 2010; Gurin, Dey, Hurtado, & Gurin, 2002). It hints to opportunities among those previously excluded, and has various degrees of policy making: access-oriented policies, active participation or engagement initiatives or the highest degree of empowerment interventions aimed at achieving success (Gidley et al., 2010). The term 'inclusion' is hardly used with regard to Arabs. On the contrary, while Israeli society has many cultures and is empirically pluralistic, this is not the normative case, as individual choices to separate or to assimilate are not perceived as equally legitimate (Smooha, 2001). Moreover, much research leans on the conflict approach, emphasizing exclusion practices and policies within higher education and claiming that the educational system – both schools and academic institutions – is in effect, a state-control system over indigenous minorities (Abu-Saad, 2006; Al-Haj, 2012; Arar, 2012).

Comparative discourse on group access and participation uses the term 'vertical inequality' when referencing the highest degree attained on average by each group, or 'horizontal inequality' when referring to disparities in quality of education of each group, as reflected in prestige and/or selectiveness of common fields and institutes of study (Shavit, Yaish, & Bar-Haim, 2007). While there is a general decrease in 'vertical' disparities measured by enrollment and degree attainment, 'horizontal' disparities are increasing with disadvantaged groups participating at higher rates in less selective and less prestigious institutions and fields of study (Ayalon & Yogev, 2005; Ayalon, Grodsky, Gamoran, & Yogev, 2008; Dar & Getz, 2007; Feniger, Mcdossi, & Ayalon, 2014; Gerber & Cheung, 2008).

As we examine the local discourse and its interaction with access-oriented policy, we employ problem definition theory and frame analysis. Rochefort and Cobb suggest problem definition is "what we choose to identify as public issues and how we think and talk about these concerns" (Rochefort & Cobb, 1994, p. vii). Dery shows how problem definition serves to legitimize an issue and creates an opportunity for action (Dery, 2000). Kingdon and Thurber (1984) add that the transformation from problem definition to policy intervention accrues at the meeting point between three streams: problems, politics and policy ideas. As problems become urgent, a window of opportunity opens for policy change. As the window opens, convergence between problems, politics and policies raises the potential for significant change (Kingdon & Thurber, 1984).

Frame analysis is concerned with policy making and focuses on how social or economic phenomena interact with policy decisions. It allows for a more integrative approach for understanding complex, multi-dimensional policies (Rein,

1983; Schön & Rein, 1995). Pick (2006) differentiates between 'rhetorical frames' and 'policy frames', stating that whereas rhetorical frames are relevant for policy process and refer to broad discourse interpretation, policy frames are relevant to a particular policy or intervention (Pick, 2006). Van Hulst and Yanow (2014) suggest the use of 'framing' rather than 'frame' as a more dynamic and interactive process sensitive to political aspects and better enables the tracing of policy developments over time.

Palestinian Arabs in higher education in Israel: participation patterns and hurdles along the way

Access and participation patterns

Arabs, Druze and Circassians are indigenous groups to the land of Israel. These three groups enjoy some educational and cultural autonomy, yet suffer from many socio-economic disparities, some of which are state-created. In higher education, individuals from each of these populations are enrolling and attaining degrees at all levels in higher rates than ever before (Shaviv et al., 2013). However, both vertical and horizontal inequalities continue to exist.

Higher rates of native Hebrew-speaking high school graduates continue to higher education within eight years of completing high school than native Arabic-speaking graduates (49% versus 30%). In 2013, while 26% of young adults (ages 18–25) in Israel were Arab, only 9.7% of undergraduate degree recipients were Arab, 8.7% of master's recipients, and 3.2% of Ph.D. recipients (CBS, 2015). Among undergraduates, Arab students, like many disadvantaged groups, are over-represented in professionally oriented fields of study such as pharmaceutical studies, nursing, dental studies, optometry and teaching, and are under-represented in high-earning professions such as industrial engineering, marketing, business and management (CBS, 2015). Moreover, Arab students take longer to attain degrees, with only 40% enrolled between 1998–2000 attaining a degree in the standard time, compared to 50% of their Jewish counterparts, and 31% of Arab students who do not complete their degree within five years of the standard time, compared to 22% of Jewish students (CBS, 2012).

Vertical and horizontal disparities among the Arab population are tied to socio-economic disparities, including lower education, employment and income rates. A number of local-related characteristics, which we describe in the coming sections, help contextualize unique challenges of Arabs in higher education in Israel.

Separate educational tracks within one education system

For most young adults, higher education is the first formal encounter within the education system between the different religious groups. Public schools throughout compulsory education are divided into a number of 'Hebrew language tracks' and 'Arabic language tracks', and are therefore divided by ethnicity.

Independent, private and semi-private schools are also mostly divided by ethnic and religious group, as well as by language. All public schools follow a national core curriculum, taught in the language of the population of the school. On average, graduates of the Arabic tracks complete high school with lower rates of academic level matriculations than their Hebrew-speaking counterparts (43% vs. 57%)[3] (Ministry of Education, 2014), and thus have more difficulty meeting higher education admissions requirements. For those enrolling in a selective research university, admissions is also based on a psychometric exam where, in recent years, a 95-point gap (on a 200–800 scale) has existed between Hebrew- and Arabic-speaking exam takers, creating a disadvantage for Arabic speakers upon enrollment in selective institutions and prestigious fields of study (National Institute for Testing & Evaluation, 2013).

Variables such as socio-economic status, parental education, school resources, infrastructure and quality commonly impact the relationship between abilities and achievements and influence admission and preparation for higher education (Jabareen & Agbaria, 2011; Seginer & Vermulst, 2002). Aside from the challenge of Arab students enrolling without prior formal Hebrew learning experiences (Amara & Mar'i, 2002; Olshtain & Nissim-Amitai, 2004; Roer-Strier & Haj-Yahia, 1998), research suggests that disparities between the Hebrew and Arabic tracks lead to disparities in successful higher education participation. Arab students are equipped with fewer higher education role models, fewer advising and counseling opportunities (Khattab, 2005; Roer-Strier & Haj-Yahia, 1998; Weiner-Levy, 2006), as well as fewer study methods fully correlated with analytical skills that are essential in higher education (Roer-Strier & Haj-Yahia, 1998).

Different starting point: age and life experience

Enrollment age and life experience also shape differences in quality and success of participation in higher education. For instance, in the 2014/15 academic year, the median undergraduate enrollment age of Arabs was 3.4 years younger than their Jewish counterparts (CBS, 2015). While most Arab students commence their studies shortly after high school graduation, most Jewish students enroll as 'mature students' after compulsory military service and, commonly, additional time for travel or work. This reality contributes to gaps in personal, social and professional skills and experience. The system, institutions and academic departments, although catering to all students, are oriented to the experience of the typical Jewish-Israeli student.

An example on the system level is the admissions process for selective institutions that requires a high school diploma based on national matriculations, although the timeframe for applications does not correlate with the timeframe of national matriculation exams. On the institutional level, institutions are generally very academically focused and are less involved in student services related to personal, social, economic and professional needs. Such needs are met on an individual or group basis and on a partial, low and local scale, once again oriented to the typical 'mature' Jewish-Israeli student. Lastly, the academic curriculum in various departments is also less adapted to those right out of high school. For example, in some fields, a professional practicum is scheduled in the second year of undergraduate studies, assuming, inaccurately, prior professional experience (Hendin, 2009).

Chilly climate for non-Jewish students

As in the case of age and life experience, other aspects of the system make it 'chilly' as described in minority student experience literature, for non-Jewish students. Aside from Arabic teachers colleges, courses at Israeli institutions are all taught in Hebrew and are Jewish-oriented, with those preferring an Arabic education generally studying in the Palestinian Authority or in Jordan (Abu-Rabia-Queder & Arar, 2011; Arar & Haj-yehia, 2010).

Chilliness or lack of cultural competency is apparent in many institutional policies and practices. Examples include: (1) Academic calendars not taking into account non-Jewish holidays and some institutions lacking clear and accessible policies regarding absences on non-Jewish holidays and other celebrations (Hendin & Ben-Rabi, 2015); (2) Minimal presence of Arabic language on campuses – in signs, official documents and website and conference translation options, despite Arabic being an official national language (Abu-Ras & Maayan, 2014); (3) Non-Jewish holidays and cultural events barely mentioned or celebrated (Hendin & Ben-Rabi, 2015); (4) Low to no Arab representation in official student organizations (Hendin & Ben-Rabi, 2015) or in faculty and institutional organizations and committees (Ali, 2013); (5) Curriculum requirements not always fitting a diverse student body, such as a social science requirement to participate in research experiments not taking into account that a basic prerequisite for many experiments is Hebrew language as the mother tongue. Another example is that social work fieldwork placements are mostly in Jewish organizations that cater to exclusively Jewish populations and are seldom relevant to the experience needed in Palestinian Arab communities (Hendin, 2009); (6) Scholarships and other available support frequently require military service as a prerequisite (Dagan-Buzaglo, 2007); (7) Having no publicly funded university or college located in a strictly Arab region (Abo El-Hija, 2005) and a poor public transportation infrastructure in many Arab residential areas, challenging physical access to the available institutions (Hendin & Ben-Rabi, 2015).

Framing and making of access policies

In an attempt to reduce barriers and increase vertical and horizontal equality in access, in 2010/11, the Planning and Budgeting Committee (PBC) of the Council for Higher Education (CHE) launched a widening-participation multi-year plan for Arabs, Druze and Circassians. Many institutions already realized the need for intervention, and applied local institutional programs that sought to impact access patterns. However, the multi-year plan grounded such initiatives for the first time in a comprehensive framework with sufficient on-going public budgeting, making it one of the largest national efforts to actively promote inclusive participation of a specific population group. Public discourse and contextualizing of the access 'problem' are key to understanding the policy that was put into place, as well as its motivations and potential for access pattern changing.

Policy framing: access as an economic development opportunity

We propose three main incarnations of local access discourse, representing different contextualization of the 'problem', the policy options and the political interest in change making. In the early years of the state of Israel, the policy problem was defined in terms of state and nation building, and the higher education policy options focused on enhancing the capacity of the three existing elite universities, in line with principles of meritocracy (Guri-Rozenblit, 1993; Troen, 1992). The mid-years focused on access barriers as the problem, whereas the policy motivation was an aspiration for social justice with specific focus on geographically peripheral populations. Interventions concentrated on widening the capacity of the system through establishing four new universities, and in the 1990s, accrediting and publicly budgeting 21 colleges across the country (Volansky, 2005). Those years were also characterized by questioning 'just' tuition in various public committees (Katzav, 1983; Kubersky, 1991; Maltz, 1996; Navon, 1977; Winograd, 2001), improving college readiness through pre-academic programs (Volansky, 2005) and experimenting with admissions policies, especially in the selective research universities (Volansky, 2005). In recent years, we suggest a third incarnation with a rhetorical frame shift defining the problem as not meeting international economic development standards. The leading policy ideas focus on the Arab and ultra-Orthodox Jewish communities as potentially enhancing economic development, allowing for a group-oriented, wide, all-inclusive intervention (Shaviv et al., 2013; Shochat, 2007).

From the individual perspective, access of disadvantaged groups to higher education has always been framed in terms of personal mobility opportunity (Al-Haj, 2012; Mar'i, 1978). However, framing access as a national opportunity is a more recent renovation. Discourse has shifted from individual benefits of access to group and society benefits. As the Arab population gains more attention in the public sphere as potential propellers of national economic development, attention spills over to higher education placing Arabs in the access discourse spotlight.

Former chairperson of the PBC, Professor Manuel Trajtenberg, joined the PBC after serving as the first chair of the Israeli National Economic Council. Thus, his national economic development rhetoric comes as no surprise as he continually states that "Increased participation of Arab citizens in higher education will enhance their socio-economic status in Israeli society, and will contribute greatly to the State of Israel as a whole" (Shaviv et al., 2013, p. 3).

Earlier rhetoric linking group access to economic development are in CHE/ PBC recommendations from January 2002 and in the 2006 Shochat Public Committee. In 2002, CHE/PBC called to actively encourage Arab participation in higher education. In 2006, the Shochat Public Committee recognized the need to continue making higher education more accessible to Arab high school graduates. The committee report stated that access of Arabs to higher education is "vital to the society and market in Israel as they aspire to modernization, economic growth and equality" (Shochat, 2007, p. 30).

The economic development framing is intertwined with similar national and international notions. As of 2006, economic development efforts are institutionalized through the establishment of the National Economic Council, and in 2007 the Authority for the Economic Development of the Arab, Druze and Circassian population (Israel Prime Minister's Office, 2007). Additionally, a number of government resolutions and plans for the Arab, Druze and Circassian population were put in place. Examples include the five-year plan for economic development (Israel Prime Minister's Office, 2010a); a policy for increased participation of minorities in the workforce (Israel Prime Minister's Office, 2010b); a four-year program for promoting the Druze and Circassian populations' economic development and growth (Israel Prime Minister's Office, 2011a); a five-year program for economic development and growth of the Bedouin population in the Negev (Israel Prime Minister's Office, 2011b); and more (Shaviv et al., 2013).

Internationally, all national economic development plans, as well as the access to higher education plan, are connected to Israel joining the Organisation for Economic Cooperation and Development (OECD) in 2010. In its review of the labor market and social policies in Israel, the OECD stated that poverty rates and social inequality are higher in Israel than in any other OECD country (OECD, 2010). The report gave special attention to Arabs and ultra-Orthodox Jews as two communities challenging Israel's development and ability to reduce socioeconomic disparities. The convergence between this problem definition, the political interest in meeting OECD standards and the policy ideas already in the discourse created a window of opportunity for policies focusing on these populations. Four out of 16 recommendations in the report addressed the Arab community specifically (OECD, 2010) and many national efforts, including the access to higher education plan, have passed through the window and are now implemented as policies (State of Israel & Ministry of Industry, Trade & Labour, 2012).

Policy making: strategy, components and scope of access-oriented intervention efforts

The policy framing process helped put in place the strategy of the expanding access multi-year plan. The plan mounted six leading principles as a framework for systematic change: First is the integration of minorities into the existing system and into the regular programs with adaptations to their needs. Integrative frameworks, in the PBC's eyes, will eventually provide the best preparation for integration in employment or further academic study.

Second is comprehensiveness. The program addresses various student life situations, before and after academic studies, as essential to successful participation in higher education.

Third is the program's holistic nature. The PBC aims to create a holistic response to the multiple challenges of Arabs in higher education resulting from obstacles created in the formal education system, the labor market and Israeli society.

Fourth, and linked to the third, is the intention to deal with challenges external to the higher education system. Such efforts include Hebrew language training, transportation to institutions and employment guidance. The PBC is not replacing the ministries in charge of those issues, but participating in collaborative efforts to encourage initiatives in these areas, which will support the efforts to increase access to higher education for Arabs.

Fifth is the program design, focusing on improving the quality of integration, support and outcomes of students once they are already enrolled in higher education. The PBC states that emphasis on quality within the system is the best way to ensure long-term successful participation.

Last is implementation flexibility with accountability. The program sets a framework and basic principles that are essential for success. Institutions are required to show clear accountability and commitment using long-term action plans, clear goals and objectives for absorbing minority students, diversification of courses of study, enrollment of graduate students and improvements in the quality of their studies. However, institutions have the flexibility to adapt implementation to fit their specific characteristics and populations.

In line with these principles, the multi-year plan budgets programming in all 28 public institutions that have Arab students and that are not teachers colleges. Each institution is required to set up an implementation platform supported by the highest levels of institutional management. This platform includes a unit director, who is a senior faculty member – ideally an Arab – responsible for coordinating the programming, as well as an institutional steering committee for the program with key Arab representatives from the institution. The institutional platform is an opportunity for Arab faculty members and administration to take an active role in tailoring the national plan to specific institutional needs and desires. It is also an opportunity to support the plan with local policies and initiatives, some of which feed back to the national policy and reshape it. Examples include defining quality standards for Arabic language accessibility on campus and implementing these standards; initiatives to promote academic conferences in Arabic on campus; and adjusting the academic year to include vacation days on Muslim and Christian holidays.

Each institution included in the plan can request funding for programs that are under the umbrella of the plan. These include a pre-academic preparatory program, a shorter academic preparatory program for those already accepted to institutions and academic, social, professional and personal supports throughout undergraduate studies. As the plan is comprehensive and holistic, it also includes a national fund for scholarships granted on the bases of socio-economic measures and fields of study, higher education guidance for high school students, career centers available to those completing degrees and scholarships for graduate students and faculty.

Policy framing as a catalyst for policy making

Access problem framing in economic development terms interacts with inclusive participation policy efforts, as is seen in the strategy, components and scope of the multi-year plan. The principles of the general strategy link increased access with an increase in general degree attainment, attainment in standard time and decreased dropout rates. Access alone, without attainment, may affect personal mobility but will likely have minimal impact on national economic development. Therefore, the plan's strategy, which stresses attainment, reflects the rhetorical discourse of economic development. Second, the plan focuses on improving quality, support and outcomes throughout higher education, as opposed to just focusing on the period before higher education. This, too, supports the access framing in terms of attainment, in line with determents of economic development. Third, the plan's comprehensive and holistic structure places, yet again, a large weight on degree attainment and successful transition from higher education to the local workforce.

Some specific components of the plan interact with the economic development framing as well. First is the higher education guidance component, implemented in selected high schools. Individual-focused guidance usually utilizes personal orientation assessment tools. However, as the plan focuses on systematic change, guidance is mostly informative and employs tools aimed at assistance in reaching enrollment requirements and understanding professional implications of decisions on institutes and field of study.

Second is the scholarship fund, addressing both the vertical and horizontal aspects of access inequality. Eligibility for a scholarship is determined by field of study and by socio-economic criteria, and gives advantage to fields with labor market demand. Once again, framing access in economic development terms sets the infrastructure for the policy. Third, the career centers component ties between participation in higher education, career planning and transition to work. Once again, long-term economic outcomes are used as indicators of successfully widening access, rather than purely educational outcomes.

Lastly, the exceptionally large scope of the current plan reflects how it is contextualized as part of a greater national effort, external to higher education. The budget for higher education support to the Arab population grew from 7 million NIS in the 2009/10 academic year to 90 million NIS in the 2015/16 academic year, and is now designed as an ongoing five-year budget. The program layout is also wide in scope with cross-institution, cross-country and cross-sub-population characteristics, all oriented at significant national change in educational and economic trends. Similarly, the implementation platform, which grounds the program in institutions and encourages inter-institutional learning, is ensuring the plan's sustainability, once again, in correlation with the discourse of importance attributed to the policy in and out of higher education.

Conclusions

Concurrent with public discourse, there is a growing academic interest in enrollment, participation and inclusion trends of Arabs in Israeli higher education institutions, especially in regard to how these trends correlate with economic development and workforce participation. In this chapter, we showed how framing the Palestinian Arabs access 'problem' in economic development terms opened a window of opportunity for access-oriented policy making. As of the 2014/15 academic year, implementation of the access policy is close to complete, and changing participation trends are being monitored.

We draw a number of lessons from policy framing and making in the context of Arabs in higher education in Israel.

First, we suggest that the term 'inclusion', not commonly used in the context of Arabs in Israel, may in fact best describe the current efforts of the Council of Higher Education. We do not attempt to claim that Israeli higher education institutions are normatively pluralistic, nor that the system and institutional environment is past its 'chilly' characteristics. However, attention to patterns of inclusion alongside those of exclusion may create a reality enabling inclusive practices. Attention must be paid to the different degrees of inclusion as they relate to various population groups, and as they reflect different levels of capacity and commitment among institutions.

Second, and leaning on theories of policy problem definition, we suggest that as policy makers deal with one problem, special attention should be given to the potential creation of other problems. As access patterns and barriers are monitored, there is a need to consider potential spillover of increased access to slowed degree completion or increased dropout rates. There is also a need to examine how encouragement or incentives for participation in specific areas of study may affect participation in other areas of study.

Last, as the current policy framing is reflected in policy-making efforts, it will be interesting to trace additional developments of discourse and framing, and their potential triggering of policy making. Seeds of new discourse relate to increased participation of Arabs in higher education as a demographic need of institutions trying to fill their enrollment quotas for budgeting purposes, or as an opportunity to promote a shared experience of positive relations between Arabs and Jews, thus contributing to social cohesion (Shaviv et al., 2013).

Notes

1 We thank Aran Zinner and Ronli Rotem for comments on earlier drafts of this chapter. We also thank the Myers-JDC-Brookdale Institute's Marshall Weinberg Fund for Professional Collaboration and Development, which helped support this research project.

2 In this chapter we refer to all three of these communities as 'Arab'.
3 Data on 12th-grade achievements of all Arabs (including Druze and Bedouin), and all Jews (including ultra-Orthodox Jews). Excluding ultra-Orthodox Jews increases the gap with 64% eligibility for academic-level matriculation among non-ultra-Orthodox Jews.

References

Abo El-Hija, Y. (2005). Why was an Arab university not established in Israel? In I. Gur-Ze'ev (Ed.), *The End of Israeli Academia?* (pp. 303–311). [In Hebrew].

Abu-Rabia-Queder, S., & Arar, K. (2011). Gender and higher education in different national spaces: Female Palestinian students attending Israeli and Jordanian universities. *Compare, 41*(3), 353.

Abu-Ras, T., & Maayan, Y. (2014). *Arabic and Arab Culture on Israeli Campuses: An Updated Look.* Israel: Dirasat, The Van Leer Jerusalem Institute, Sikkuy. [In Hebrew].

Abu-Saad, I. (2006). State-controlled education and identity formation among the Palestinian Arab minority in Israel. *American Behavioral Scientist, 49*(8), 1085–1100.

Al-Haj, M. (2012). *Education, Empowerment, and Control: The Case of the Arabs in Israel.* New York: SUNY Press.

Ali, N. (2013). *Representation of Arab Citizens in the Institutions of Higher Education in Israel.* Israel: Sikkuy. [In Hebrew].

Amara, M., & Mar'i, A. R. (2002). *Language Education Policy: The Arab Minority in Israel.* Dordrecht: Springer.

Arar, K. (2012). Israeli education policy since 1948 and the state of Arab education in Israel. *Italian Journal of Sociology of Education, 1*, 113–145.

Arar, K., & Haj-yehia, K. (2010). Emigration for higher education: The case of Palestinians living in Israel studying in Jordan. *Higher Education Policy, 23*(3), 358–380.

Ayalon, H., Grodsky, E., Gamoran, A., & Yogev, A. (2008). Diversification and inequality in higher education: A comparison of Israel and the United States. *Sociology of Education, 81*(3), 211–241.

Ayalon, H., & Yogev, A. (2005). Field of study and students' stratification in an expanded system of higher education: The case of Israel. *European Sociological Review, 21*(3), 227–241.

Berry, J. W. (1997). Immigration, acculturation, and adaptation. *Applied Psychology, 46*(1), 5–34.

CBS. (2012). *Statistical Abstract of Israel 2012.* Israel: The Central Bureau of Statistics.

CBS. (2014). *Statistical Abstract of Israel 2014.* Israel: The Central Bureau of Statistics.

Dagan-Buzaglo, N. (2007). *The Right to Higher Education in Israel: A Legal and Fiscal Perspective.* Israel: Adva Center. [In Hebrew].

Dar, Y., & Getz, S. (2007). Learning ability, socioeconomic status, and student placement for undergraduate studies in Israel. *Higher Education, 54*(1), 41–60.

Dery, D. (2000). Agenda setting and problem definition. *Policy Studies, 21*(1), 37–47.

Feniger, Y., Mcdossi, O., & Ayalon, H. (2014). Ethno-religious differences in Israeli higher education: Vertical and horizontal dimensions. *European Sociological Review, 31*(4), 383–396.

Gerber, T. P., & Cheung, S. Y. (2008). Horizontal stratification in postsecondary education: Forms, explanations, and implications. *Annual Review of Sociology, 34*, 299–318.

Gidley, J. M., Hampson, G. P., Wheeler, L., & Bereded-Samuel, E. (2010). From access to success: An integrated approach to quality higher education informed by social inclusion theory and practice. *Higher Education Policy, 23*(1), 123–147.

Gurin, P., Dey, E., Hurtado, S., & Gurin, G. (2002). Diversity and higher education: Theory and impact on educational outcomes. *Harvard Educational Review, 72*(3), 330–367.

Guri-Rozenblit, S. (1993). Trends of diversification and expansion in Israeli higher education. *Higher Education, 25*(4), 457–472.

Hendin, A. (2009). *Integration of Arab Students in Israel's Higher Education System.* Master's thesis, Hebrew University of Jerusalem, Israel [In Hebrew].

Hendin, A., & Ben-Rabi, D. (2015). *The Access Plan for Higher Education of Arabs, Druze and Circassians: Preliminary Findings from an Evaluation Study on the Implementation of the Student Support Services.* Jerusalem, Israel: Myers-JDC-Brookdale Institute. [In Hebrew].

Israel Prime Minister's Office (2007). Government resolution 1204: Establishment of the national economic council. Jerusalem [In Hebrew].

Israel Prime Minister's Office (2010a). Government resolution 1539: Five-year plan for economic development. Jerusalem [In Hebrew].

Israel Prime Minister's Office (2010b). Government resolution 1994: Increased participation of minorities in the workforce. Jerusalem [In Hebrew].

Israel Prime Minister's Office (2011a). Government resolution 2861: Four-year program for promoting the Druze and Circassian populations' economic development and growth. Jerusalem [In Hebrew].

Israel Prime Minister's Office (2011b). Government resolution 3708: Five-year program for economic development and growth of the Bedouin population in the Negev. Jerusalem [In Hebrew].

Jabareen, Y. T., & Agbaria, A. (2011). *Education on Hold: Israeli Government Policy and Civil Society Initiatives to Improve Arab Education in Israel.* Nazareth, Israel: Dirasat, Arab Center for Law and Policy.

Katzav, M. (1983). The Committee Setting Tuition for Higher Education. Report of the Committee Examining and Determining the System, the Level of Tuition, and the Student Assistance Resources for Higher Education in Israel from 1983 Onwards. Jerusalem: The Committee.

Khattab, N. (2005). The effects of high school context and interpersonal factors on students' educational expectations: A multi-level model. *Social Psychology of Education, 8*(1), 19–40.

Kingdon, J. W., & Thurber, J. A. (1984). *Agendas, Alternatives, and Public Policies.* Boston: Little, Brown.

Kubersky, H. (1991). Report of the Public Committee Setting the Level of Tuition and the Student Assistance Resources in Higher Education for 1995/96–1991/92. Jerusalem: The Committee.

Maltz, J. (1991). The Public Committee Setting the Level of Tuition and the Student Assistance Resources in Higher Education for 1996/97–2000/01. Jerusalem: The Committee.

Mar'i, S. K. (1978). *Arab Education in Israel.* Syracuse, NY: Syracuse University Press.

Ministry of Education. (2014). *Matriculation Files.* Israel: Ministry of Education. [In Hebrew].

Navon, M.K.Y. (1977). The Committee Setting Tuition for Higher Education. Report of the Committee Examining and Determining a System and Level for Tuition in Higher Education in Israel from 1977 Onwards. Jerusalem: The Committee.

National Institute for Testing & Evaluation. (2013). *Psychometric Entrance Test: Annual Report 2013.* Israel: National Institute for Testing & Evaluation. [In Hebrew].

OECD. (2010). *Review of Labor Market and Social Policies: Israel.* Paris: OECD.

Olshtain, E., & Nissim-Amitai, F. (2004). Curriculum decision-making in a multilingual context. *International Journal of Multilingualism, 1*(1), 53–64.

Pick, D. (2006). The re-framing of Australian higher education. *Higher Education Quarterly, 60*(3), 229–241.

Rein, M. (1983). Value-critical policy analysis. In S. Callaghan and B. Jennings (Eds.), *Ethics, the Social Sciences, and Policy Analysis* (pp. 83–111). New York: Springer.

Rochefort, D. A., & Cobb, R. W. (1994). *The Politics of Problem Definition: Shaping the Policy Agenda.* Lawrence: University Press of Kansas.

Roer-Strier, D., & Haj-Yahia, M. (1998). Arab students of social work in Israel: Adjustment difficulties and coping strategies. *Social Work Education, 17*(4), 449–467.

Schön, D. A., & Rein, M. (1995). *Frame Reflection: Toward the Resolution of Intractable Policy Controversies.* New York: Basic Books.

Seginer, R., & Vermulst, A. (2002). Family environment, educational aspirations, and academic achievement in two cultural settings. *Journal of Cross-Cultural Psychology, 33*(6), 540–558.

Shavit, Y., Yaish, M., & Bar-Haim, E. (2007). The persistence of persistent inequality 1. In S. Scherer, R. Pollak, G. Otte & M. Gangl (Eds.), *From Origin to Destination: Trends and Mechanisms in Social Stratification Research* (pp. 37–57). Chicago: University of Chicago Press.

Shaviv, M., Binstein, N., Stone, A., & Fudem, O. (2013). *Pluralism and Equal Opportunity in Higher Education Expanding Access for Arabs, Druze and Circassians in Israel.* Jerusalem: Council for Higher Education.

Shochat, A. (2007) *Report of the Committee for the Examination of the System of Higher Education in Israel* [in Hebrew]. Jerusalem: Government of Israel.

Smooha, S. (2001). Arab-Jewish relations in Israel as a Jewish and democratic state. In Ephraim Yaar and Zeev Shavit (Eds.), *Trends in Israeli Society* (pp. 231–363). Tel Aviv: The Open University.

State of Israel, & Ministry of Industry, Trade & Labour. (2012). *Progress Report on the Implementation of the OECD Recommendations: Labour Market and Social Policies – ISRAEL.* Israel: Myers-JDC-Brookdale Institute.

Troen, S. I. (1992). Higher education in Israel: An historical perspective. *Higher Education, 23*(1), 45–63.

Van Hulst, M., & Yanow, D. (2014). From policy "Frames" to "Framing" theorizing a more dynamic, political approach. *The American Review of Public Administration, 46*(1), 92–112.

Volansky, A. (2005). *Academy in Changing Environment: Higher Education Policy in Israel 1952–2004.* Israel: Hakibbutz Hameuchad Publishing House. [In Hebrew].

Weiner-Levy, N. (2006). The flagbearers: Israeli Druze women challenge traditional gender roles. *Anthropology & Education Quarterly, 37*(3), 217–235.

Winograd, E. (2001, April). The Public Committee for the Gradual Reduction of Tuition in Higher Education and the Examination of Possible Additional Student Accommodations. Jerusalem: The Committee.

Chapter 10

Widening access in a vast country

Opportunities and challenges in Australia

Ann Jardine

Introduction

With the identification of underrepresented groups in higher education and the setting out of a methodology for monitoring sector performance in the 1990s, Australia could justifiably claim to be at the forefront of the establishment of a national equity framework. However, over the next 15 years, few inroads were made in widening access to university for the majority of the cohorts of society targeted within the framework. It could be argued that this is in part due to the Australian context.

Australia is by its very nature a vast and sparsely populated country. Of the 23 million inhabitants 35% live in the two cities of Sydney and Melbourne. Approximately 70% live in one of the major cities that hug the coastline (Australian Bureau of Statistics, 2013). For the remaining 30% of the population, distance from one another and from resources is a major challenge that adds another layer of complexity to the barriers to going to university. This is the case for universities when implementing widening access strategies and for students when choosing to go.

This chapter explores the policy settings from 1990 until 2015, the opportunities that have emerged from changes to the setting, and through the use of a case study from the University of New South Wales Australia (UNSW), a member of the research-intensive Group of Eight (GO8) universities, discusses the particular challenges that are faced in putting in widening access initiatives in a vast country.

The Australian policy framework: establishing the groundwork

The agenda for widening the access of underrepresented cohorts within Australia can trace its origins back to the Government policy document *A Fair Chance for All: National and Institutional Planning for Equity in Higher Education* (Department of Employment, Education and Training, 1990). The document is regarded as a landmark moment in the development of a national equity policy framework and in future efforts to widen access. Not only did it state the clear intent of government policy to make university education accessible to all Australians, it also made it clear that it was to be the university sector itself that was to provide the strategies to achieve the overall objective.

As a result of the document, two important cornerstones were established for future strategies, both of which have largely remained in place. First, six target groups within Australian society were identified within the framework. Members of the population could fall into multiple target groups. The focus of this chapter is primarily on students from two of the target groups, those from low socio-economic status (SES) backgrounds and those from rural and isolated areas (now separated out into regional and remote). Low SES is currently defined by the geocoded Sa1 statistical area where using Socio-economic Indexes for Areas (SEIFA) the bottom 25% are regarded as low SES. Regional and remote are defined using codes derived from the Australian Standard Geographical classification (Department of Education and Training, 2015b).

Second, in 1994 measures of the performance of the sector were established which remain in place today. Individual institutions and the sector overall were to be measured on the access, participation, retention and success rates of each of the six identified groups (Department of Employment, Education and Training, 1994). Performance against these four indicators is still published annually by the relevant Federal department.

The policy framework remained largely untouched until 2003 with the publication of *Our Universities: Backing Australia's Future* (Department of Education Science and Training). Changes were made to the overall framework. Significantly, the policy framework for widening access for people from Indigenous backgrounds was uncoupled to be given more emphasis through specifically focused initiatives.

A major shake-up in the Australian equity policy framework came in 2008 with *The Review of Australian Higher Education* (Bradley, Noonan, Nugent & Scales, 2008) known colloquially as the Bradley Review. This report represented one of the most comprehensive and significant reviews of the sector ever undertaken. Its impact on efforts to widen access in Australia cannot be underestimated.

The report highlighted in particular the lack of progress for people from rural and isolated areas, low SES backgrounds and from Indigenous backgrounds. A number of wide-ranging recommendations were made covering the establishment of national targets for particular groups, targeted funding for universities and income/financial support for students. In refining the national priorities two major sector targets were established. The first target set the percentage of 25- to 34-year-olds holding an undergraduate degree at 40% by 2020. The second target, that by 2020 20% of undergraduates would be from low SES backgrounds, identified a clear national priority for widening access.

Financial incentives for university widening access programs

Opportunities for universities to systematically address widening access remained limited until 2008. Up until that time, annual funding based on the individual performance of the institutions against the four measures of access, participation, retention and success was modest. Funding was viewed as seed funding, and as a result initiatives tended to be small scale, in their depth, breadth and in their timescale. Separate funding was also made available for supporting Indigenous students through the Indigenous Support Funding Program (Coates & Krause, 2005).

From 2008 funding was significantly increased, particularly under the Higher Education Partnerships and Participation Program (HEPPP). While HEPPP did not preclude strategies focused on any equity group, the focus was heavily on students from low SES backgrounds. Specific funding streams to support students with a disability within institutions and work with people from Indigenous backgrounds remained separate (Department of Education and Training, 2015a).

The aim of HEPPP was two-fold: first, to support outreach and in doing so encourage universities to work collaboratively, and second, to provide support to students from equity groups once they entered university. To support outreach, $108M AUD was set aside for a four-year period. Performance-based funding was provided annually to every publicly funded university. In addition, competitive funding (approx. $117M AUD) was made available through two rounds of bidding (Department of Education and Training, 2015c). An important difference in this competitive funding was that it ran over a three-year period rather than one year. This enabled the establishment of longitudinal projects.

Alongside the increase in equity funding was another major policy decision that was also in part designed to support the widening access agenda. In 2011 the cap on domestic undergraduate places was removed, enabling universities to set their own numbers under a demand-driven system. This represented a radical shift in both funding universities and in how individual universities chose to respond to the supply and demand of students (Norton, 2013).

Challenges for widening access within Australia

The policy framework post-2008 has facilitated a growth in university initiatives aimed at widening the access of underrepresented groups. Many of the reasons underpinning low progression rates in Australia are not unique to the country. The challenges of putting in place programs that achieve positive outcomes are however exacerbated by the context of a vast geography, with a small population concentrated heavily in a few geographical pockets hugging the coastline and widely dispersed across the interior.

Focusing on educational attainment, cost of going to university and raising the social capital of students, the challenges in widening access can be explored further.

Arguably one of the major challenges in widening access in all developed countries is the educational attainment gap between students from low SES backgrounds and their peers. As in other countries this gap in Australia begins before students reach school age and continues across their schooling. A recent 2013 report *PISA 2012: How Australia Measures Up* (Thomson, De Bortoli & Buckley) examining the PISA data for 15-year-olds found that in mathematical, scientific and reading literacies students from low SES backgrounds were an average 2.5 years behind their high SES peers.

While the issue of distance and isolation is not only experienced in Australia there is evidence that the gap for students outside metropolitan areas is more significant than the average in other OECD countries. In mathematical and reading literacies, students in remote areas were almost two years behind their metropolitan peers and almost 15 months behind their peers in more populated regional areas. The gap between Indigenous and non-Indigenous students was also approximately 2.5 years across the three literacies (Thomson et al, 2013).

For students from very remote parts of Australia the educational attainment gap starts before school with children in Kindergarten likely to be more developmentally vulnerable than their metropolitan peers (NSW Department of Education, 2013). In New South Wales (NSW) metropolitan students in Year 5 achieve higher National Assessment Program: Literacy and Numeracy (NAPLAN) scores than Year 7 students in remote NSW.

The educational attainment gap is also evident when the Year 12 Australian Tertiary Admissions Rank (ATAR) is examined. ATAR is a ranking of students who have taken academic subjects within their Higher School Certificate in the final two years of schooling. Ranking is from 99.95 down. The ATAR forms the basis for entry into university through the setting of a cut-off rank for each degree program. Cut-offs are set at the discretion of the individual institutions. The ATAR is used by the sector as both a supply-and-demand mechanism to control numbers into specific degree programs and a measure of academic achievement, and in many cases a proxy for academic potential. In 2014 the percentage of students from low SES backgrounds with an ATAR above 90 was 14.6% compared with 39.8% from high SES backgrounds (Department of Education and Training, 2015d). Internal unpublished UNSW analysis of high school median ATAR (HSMA) in NSW indicates that there is a strong negative correlation ($r = -0.798$) between HSMA and the level of disadvantage of the school as measured by the Family Occupation and Education Index (FOEI) used by the NSW State Government. The more disadvantaged the school, the lower the overall school academic achievement. This could be regarded as reflecting the educational advantages available to certain sections of Australian society across the 12 years of primary and secondary education.

To put the challenge of distance into context it is worth briefly examining some of the issues in providing an equitable school education system. NSW is the most populated state in Australia. Though one of the smaller states overall, it is over three times the size of the United Kingdom. Within NSW there are over 440 state high schools with over 180 being provincial and remote as defined by the

Schools Geographic Location Classification. This specific classification for schools (rather than regional and remote used at the student level) is based on population size and distance from nearest town or service centre (Jones, 2004). Due to size and location, there can be challenges for many of these schools in terms of staffing and in subject offerings in senior high school. The 2013 NSW Department of Education report *Rural and Remote Education: A Blueprint for Action* highlights the difficulty of provincial and remote schools employing teachers in key subject areas, particularly math and science, as well as other specialist teachers. The workforce is also more likely to be inexperienced or unstable, with recently trained graduates moving in and out of less populated areas.

The attainment gap is reflected in the access rates across the university sector. Mirroring international trends, access rates of low SES students are lowest to the research-intensive GO8 universities which sit highest in world rankings, have the highest entry requirements and whose admissions policies centre on use of the ATAR. As the focus on the wider access has increased, so has discussion about the use of ATAR as the mechanism for accepting students into university increased. Opportunities to address the attainment gap have been identified in university admissions policies. In recent years, universities have introduced a plethora of different schemes to accompany ATAR as the admissions mechanism. These include articulation pathways from other parts of the education sector, sub-degree programs as alternative pathways, ATAR bonus point schemes, and conditional offer or early entry schemes. Recently, using the example of UK universities such as Bristol, UNSW is exploring the use of contextualised data in order to make differential offers. However it is also recognised that broadening admissions policies alone is not sufficient to address widening access and that outreach has a very important place in an overall approach (Moore, Mountford-Zimdars & Wiggans, 2013).

The financial cost of going to university is a second major challenge in widening access. Within the Australian context this is compounded by the distance factor and the deficiencies in Governmental student income support and institutional financial support through scholarships and bursaries. Unlike other OECD countries Australia has had a strong tradition of university students being commuter students: 85% study within their own state, over 35% live at home and less than 10% live in halls of residence (Australian Bureau of Statistics, 2013). For regional and remote students, living at home is not an option unless studying by distance education. Moving away from home results in significant costs associated with travel, accommodation and living expenses.

Taking NSW as the example, 5 of the state's 10 public universities are situated in Sydney. Three additional universities are also situated on the Eastern seaboard with two within two hours of the Sydney CBD. The other two universities are inland with campuses in the west, south and north of the state. The greatest degree choice lies in Sydney, yet the living costs in Sydney are recognised as very high in the global context. While university-provided housing has increased over recent years, there is still a shortage of affordable student accommodation in the city. A recent survey conducted by Universities Australia (2013) found 50% of undergraduates relied on some financial support from family and two thirds of them reported living below the poverty line. Financial distress for students from low SES and Indigenous backgrounds was even worse (Universities Australia, 2013). To put living expenses in a broad context, international students studying in Australia are required to have funds of approximately $18,600 AUD per annum (Brett, Sheridan, Harvey & Cardak, 2015). To put them in an institutional context, to live in self-catering accommodations on campus at UNSW in 2015 cost from approximately $13,500 AUD per annum (www.unsw.edu.au).

All Australian students are provided with income-contingent loans for students to cover all tuition fees. Australia was the first country to put such loans in place with the establishment of the Higher Education Contributions Scheme (HECS). HECS has since provided the basis of a model for several other countries including England. Through the HECS-HELP scheme, students are able to defer payment of the student contribution until they are earning a threshold amount ($54,126 as of 2015) (Department of Education and Training, 2015a).

Currently, three contribution bands are applied at subject level, with subjects in disciplines such as the Arts, Humanities, Education and Nursing in the lowest band and subjects in disciplines such as Law and Medicine in the highest band. The bands were based on perceived future earnings capacity, rather than the cost of teaching (Department of Education and Training, 2015a). To give a global context to student contributions, as of 2015 these stand at the following per annum maximums: $6,152 AUD for band 1, $8,768 AUD for band 2 and $10,266 AUD for band 3 subjects.

What has never been provided within the Australian context is any substantial loan scheme to cover living expenses. This may be as a result of the trend in Australia for metropolitan students to be commuter students. However within a widening access framework that includes targeting students from regional and remote Australia who are forced to move from home, it could be argued that this is a failure to address a very real barrier for certain national priority equity cohorts.

Attempts have been made to negate the impact through government income support schemes. As with other parts of the overall policy framework there have been several iterations of the types of support available to students on low incomes. However with just over $6,000 AUD per annum available in Commonwealth scholarships and a huge variance in the number and value of institution scholarships, it cannot be claimed that these meet the actual costs incurred in undertaking university study, especially if living away from home is necessary. As earlier figures indicate, the provision of meaningful scholarships to regional and remote students requires substantial investment from government, institutions and through philanthropy.

It could be argued that it is university outreach initiatives that play a key role in raising social capital. It is done through a focus on awareness and aspirations where students are provided with multiple opportunities to experience the university context. There are however differing views on whether students from disadvantaged backgrounds lack educational aspirations. James and his colleagues (2008) suggested it may be the case. However findings in *Expectations and Destinations of NSW Senior Secondary Students* (Polesal, Leahy, Gillis, Dulhunty & Calvitto, 2013) indicated that while students and families in disadvantaged communities can and do have high aspirations these may not match outcomes in terms of their access to university. Interestingly, the research also found that teachers in regional areas have lower expectations than their students and families, and that their expectations were lower than the outcomes for their students in going to university. The research supports the notion of enabling aspirations rather than raising them. It also indicates that students in regional areas do wish to progress their education past school.

Widening access through outreach: a case study from one Australian university

Post-2011, supported by the substantial Federal Government funding, much work has taken place within the outreach space. The following section explores the UNSW ASPIRE outreach program working primarily with students from low SES backgrounds (www.aspire.unsw.edu.au). Initiated in 2007, from a small pot of seed funding, the growth of the program from two metropolitan Sydney high schools to 57 primary and high schools across Sydney and regional NSW has been assisted through securing nearly $5M (AUD) in competitive funding (in 2008 and 2011) which has predominantly funded the program up to the end of 2015. Government funding has been supplemented by a small amount of corporate funding and in kind support from UNSW.

An evidence-based approach was taken in establishing the program. In 2007 Australia lacked a robust history of longitudinal outreach programs, so it was decided to examine the work of practitioners internationally. Given the strong similarities in educational systems, the focus was on work in the UK. UNSW provided the Director of ASPIRE with a travelling scholarship to undertake a two-month study of the English Aimhigher partnership approach (now disbanded). Research focused on the regional partnerships in the north of England encompassing both urban partnerships (e.g. Greater Manchester) and smaller rural partnerships (e.g. North Yorkshire).

Extant literature (e.g. Moore & Dunworth, 2011) has also formed part of the evidence underpinning ASPIRE. It informs practitioners that successful actions begin at an early age, are longitudinal and sustained providing multiple opportunities for engagement with students and families. Engagements include providing role models, linking school and university study with career opportunities and enabling school students to experience the university environment. Increasing social capital by raising awareness of university study, raising knowledge of how the sector works, enabling aspirations and supporting schools to raise educational attainment lie at the core of the work.

Taking what was learnt, the ASPIRE program contains many of the elements of Aimhigher strategies. At its core is a longitudinal approach built on a learning framework which addresses aspirations, awareness and supporting attainment through a stepped process. The framework builds on the work undertaken the previous year and includes, as fundamental elements, workshops that take place in schools and events at key stages (Years 5/6, 8, 9,10 and 11) that take place on the University campus. Fundamental to the program is the establishment of strong partnerships with schools where the individual context of the school is taken into consideration and as a result, the program contains many bespoke elements. Where the program has significantly differed from Aimhigher is through working with students from Kindergarten through to Year 12 (final school year) and working in school with whole-year groups particularly below Year 11 rather than targeted cohorts.

From 2007 until 2010 the focus of the program was firmly on potential partner schools in metropolitan Sydney. It is acknowledged that this was largely because of the comfort zone of those of us driving the program. Examining this in more detail, undertaking outreach in Sydney was working within known environments. The team had a good understanding of the geography, the potential partner schools and the demographics of the communities in which the schools resided.

The establishment of Regional ASPIRE in provincial and remote NSW schools came about for two reasons. First came a chance conversation with a teacher from a provincial high school situated 470 kilometres from UNSW and a request from the school to join the program. This was followed by the successful securement of government funding which enabled consideration of such a venture. Since the first small cluster of five schools in 2010, ASPIRE has built a strong commitment to working outside Sydney and at the time of writing is working with 30 provincial and remote partner schools.

Given that regional and remote students remain underrepresented in universities (Department of Education and Training, 2015b) there is a need for universities to work in this space. However, implementing a program with the crucial core elements has had particular challenges. To put some scale to the regional program, schools range from between 350 kilometres to over 700 kilometres from UNSW. Travel requires an hour flight and up to a four-hour drive to engage with the communities. In 2014 over 30,000 kilometres were travelled by road and over 70 flights taken to just deliver the in-school program.

Strategies to address the challenges of distance and cost coupled with a recognition of the differences in communities have led to an acceptance that the model developed for metropolitan schools did not lend itself to being lifted and placed within our regional partners. This has enabled and in some cases necessitated different ways of engagement. The reach of the program has expanded not only geographically but also in terms of student engagement. Working with small communities and often in schools that encompass Kindergarten to Year 12 enabled the program to focus on the early years in a way that logistically has not been possible in metropolitan schools.

The delivery and content of the program has been adapted from the original metropolitan model. Activities have been rewritten to include material relevant to the communities in which partner schools sit. In Sydney the program works within multicultural communities where English is not the language spoken at home. Regionally, the program works in communities that can be predominantly monoculture (English-speaking backgrounds) or include a significant Indigenous population. In recognition of this, the team includes an Indigenous project officer and works collaboratively with the Indigenous Unit of the University.

As an ongoing exercise, case studies of those in the communities with degrees are sought and shared. This in turn assists in highlighting that there are wider degree choices than education and the health disciplines and that there are opportunities to return to work in communities post-degree. Anecdotally students are surprised at the range of degrees held by members of their communities. In some instances ASPIRE has been able to utilise UNSW alumni to emphasise this point. The size of schools (ranging from less than 10 to approximately 350 students) has meant in some year groups there are very small numbers. To gain efficiencies and also enable students to learn from others, some in-school sessions are run in one school using a centralised model with other schools travelling to that location. Likewise, a major event for Year 9 students has been moved to a central regional location.

Giving regional and remote students opportunities to engage with different parts of the University and gain an important understanding of universities has required particular strategies. Centralising some events provided an opportunity for a large number of school students to engage with UNSW staff and students while overcoming the practical and logistical problems of taking UNSW representation off campus for large blocks of time. Learning from Aimhigher (Rodger & Burgess, 2010) the importance of school students being able to interact with university students has been a core component of the metropolitan model through on-campus and in-school activities. The latter has been difficult to replicate in the regional model. Online engagement has to date not been successful due mainly to technical difficulties. The program continues to examine ways to address this.

However, taking note of the success of Aimhigher summer schools (HEFCE, 2009), engagement with university students and assisting students to learn about university life has occurred through intensive residential experiences in Sydney in Years 8, 10 and 11 which include on-campus focused activities and off-campus activities (e.g. negotiating public transport) that sit outside their normal experiences. These residentials are also in recognition that it is primarily regional and remote students who have the residential university student experience. In 2015, the Year 11 academic skills building experience was piloted as an online experience. This has not been successful, with low take-up rates and high drop-out rates. As mentioned, virtual engagement with regional schools has its own challenges, with a range of technological issues ranging from Internet access to software compatibility. However, internal qualitative feedback from teachers in partner schools indicates that it is the visibility of UNSW within their communities and the personal contact with school students that is highly valued.

Addressing the logistics of managing a program across large distances has been an iterative process and has included developing the most successful communication channels with schools, revisiting how regional trips (usually of five days duration) are scheduled and refining how resources are moved. To manage the time in moving the team and materials from UNSW to multiple school locations, one central point for flights was established with that town used as a repository for program resources.

The program continues to examine ways to address the challenges it faces in delivering high-quality outreach. It continues to be an iterative process informed by an ongoing cycle of feedback, evaluation and reflection to put refinements in place.

The impact of outreach

The ongoing evaluation of the program has been an important component since inception. Comprehensive qualitative evaluations of the program undertaken in 2011 and 2014 indicated that school staff valued the ASPIRE program highly and reported a positive impact on students. The value placed on the program is further evidenced by the ongoing requests from schools in the regional areas to join. However, corroborating evidence on impact is harder to produce. Attitudinal shifts in students have been tracked and shown to have become more positive in terms of going to university. Analysis of data provided by the NSW University Admissions Centre indicates that offer rates to university from partner schools have increased during the life of the program and more so than at a control group of schools outside the program (a range of data can be found at www.aspire.unsw.edu.au). The problem for ASPIRE is making any clear causal link between the program and the results. In Sydney where the results are strongest, schools are often working with multiple university partners and external agencies. Therefore it is difficult for one program to lay claim to increased progression rates. Regionally, ASPIRE is the only program working systematically and longitudinally with its partner schools. While increased offer rates are evident in individual schools, the results show little overall increase. This in part is due to the fluctuating numbers of students in senior schools across years. This adds to the complexity of evaluating the impact. More longitudinal evidence is needed.

Sector-wide, there is some cause for optimism on the collective impact from the outreach activities of universities. The years 2009 onwards represent the time of the most significant changes to the equity policy framework in Australia and the entering of a demand-driven system. The growth sector-wide is indicated by an overall increase in applications in 2014 of 10.3%, in offers of 19% and in acceptances of 15.7% (Department of Education and Training, 2015d). It is not necessarily surprising that some gains have been made in bridging the gap for underrepresented groups. The largest increase in access rates for students from low SES backgrounds has been experienced in the period between 2009 and 2013 (latest available figures). While the rise has not been as high across the elite Group of Eight (GO8) universities, the upward trend is still evident. Encouragingly the highest increase in the number of applications and offers to university has been from students from low SES backgrounds. While numbers have risen, what is not so encouraging is that students from medium and high SES backgrounds are still more likely to get an offer than their low SES peers (Department of Education and Training, 2015d). The picture is not as encouraging for students in regional areas. During the same period access rates for students in regional areas have risen only marginally with rates for those in remote areas falling.

The next steps

At the time of writing, the next steps for widening access in Australia are unclear as universities grapple with potential shifts in the national higher education policy framework and current concerns around funding levels within the sector. Although government funding still exists for widening access initiatives, the substantial funding for multifaceted programs such as ASPIRE has ceased. However, it is unclear whether such large-scale widening access programs will be a priority across institutions in the future. Up until now (2015) the sector narrative has been that the major aim of programs was to widening access into the sector. If recognised through institutional funding, the tension between social good and return for institutional dollar comes into focus. Widening access may become less about access to university per se and more about bringing students into the funding institution. This need not necessarily be viewed as a negative. There are sound arguments that could be made for suggesting that widening access into elite universities such as UNSW should be of importance for those institutions. What would be a negative is if the primary measure of success was the rate of return for the institution through enrolments from partner schools. If that is the case then high cost programs with poorer rates of return such as regional programs may be at risk.

The equity policy framework of recent years suggests that the programs that have been implemented can make a difference to sector-wide access rates. However the job is not finished and underrepresentation still exists. Funding is critical for progress to continue to be made. The answer to maintaining existing and growing new programs may lie in closer partnership between universities, industry and philanthropic donors. Certainly continuing to address widening access has both a moral and economic imperative. It is a matter of social justice for individuals, and the economic prosperity for all of society.

References

Australian Bureau of Statistics. (2013). *Australian Social Trends*. Retrieved from http://www.abs.gov.au/AUSSTATS/abs@.nsf/Lookup/4102.0Main+Features30 April+2013 and http://www.abs.gov.au/AUSSTATS/abs@.nsf/Lookup/4102.0 Main+Features20July+2013#p3

Bradley, D., Noonan, P., Nugent, H., & Scales, B. (2008). *Review of Australian Higher Education*. Retrieved from http://www.deewr.gov.au/HigherEducation/Review/Documents/PDF/Higher%20Education%20Review_one%20document_02.pdf

Brett, M., Sheridan, A., Harvey, A., & Cardak, B. (2015). *Four Barriers to Higher Education Regional Students – and How to Overcome Them*. Retrieved from www.ncsehe.edu.au

Coates, H., & Krause, K. (2005). Investigating ten years of Equity Policy in Australian Higher Education. *Journal of Higher Education Policy and Management*, 27(1), 35–46.

Department of Education and Training (2015a). *Higher Education Support Act 2003*. Retrieved from https://www.education.gov.au/higher-education-support-act-2003-and-guidelines

Department of Education and Training (2015b). *Higher Education Statistics, Student Data*. Retrieved from https://education.gov.au/higher-education-statistics

Department of Education and Training (2015c). *Higher Education Participation and Partnerships Program*. Retrieved from https://education.gov.au/higher-education-participation-and-partnerships-programme-heppp

Department of Education and Training (2015d). *Undergraduate Applications, Offers and Acceptances*. Retrieved from https://education.gov.au/undergraduate-applications-offers-and-acceptances-publications

Department of Employment, Education and Training (1990). *A Fair Chance for All*. AGPS, Canberra.

Department of Employment, Education and Training (1994). *Equity and General Performance Indicators in Higher Education: Equity Indicators*, Vol. 1 (L M Martin). AGPS, Canberra.

Higher Education Funding Council of England (2009). *Aimhigher Summer Schools: Analysis of Provision and Participation 2004 to 2008*. HEFCE, London, UK.

James, Richard, Bexley, E., Anderson, A., Devlin, M., Garnett, R., Marginson, S. & Maxwell, L. (2008). *Participation and Equity: A Review of the Participation in Higher Education of People from Low Socioeconomic Backgrounds and Indigenous People*. Centre for the Study of Higher Education, Melbourne.

Jones, R. (2004). *Geolocation Questions and Coding Index*. Report to Ministerial Council on Education Employment Training and Youth Affairs, Canberra.

Moore, J., & Dunworth, F. (2011). *Review of Evidence from Aimhigher Area Partnerships of the Impact of Aimhigher*. Aimhigher, UK.

Moore, J., Mountford-Zimdars, A., & Wiggans, J. (2013). *Contextualised Admissions: Examining the Evidence*. Report to the Supporting Professionalism in Admissions Programme, Cheltenham, UK.

New South Wales Department of Education. (2013). *Rural and Remote Education: A Blueprint for Action*. Retrieved from www.det.nsw.edu.au/media/downloads/about-us/our-reforms/rural-and-remote-education/randr-blueprint.pdf

Norton, A. (2013). *Keep the Caps Off! Student Access and Choice in Higher Education*. Grattan Institute, Melbourne.

Polesal, J., Leahy, M., Gillis, S., Dulhunty, M., & Calvitto, L. (2013). *Expectations and Destinations of NSW Senior Secondary Students*. Melbourne Graduate School of Education, Melbourne.

Rodger, J., & Burgess, M. (2010). *Qualitative Evaluation of Aimhigher Associates Program: Pathfinder.* Report to Higher Education Funding Council of England, London, UK.

Thomson, S., De Bortoli, L., & Buckley, S. (2013). *PISA 2012: How Australia Measures Up.* ACER, Camberwell, Vic.

Universities Australia. (2013). *University Student Finances in 2012.* Retrieved from https://www.universitiesaustralia.edu.au/news/commissioned-studies/Australian-University-Student-Finances-in-2012#.VZyBYWNwyxg

Chapter 11

Accessing postgraduate study in the United States for African Americans

Relating the roles of family, fictive kin, faculty, and student affairs practitioners

Carmen M. McCallum, Julie R. Posselt and Estefanía López

Introduction

Graduate education is an increasingly important part of the opportunity structure in the United States (US) and United Kingdom (UK).[1] With many sectors of the labor market saturated with baccalaureate degrees, many employers have come to expect graduate degrees for hiring and/or promotion (Collins, 2002; Wakeling, 2007), in such middle-class fields as education, business, social work, nursing, and other health sciences and health services. The choice to pursue graduate education is thus closely related to career choice for many, but it is most fully explained empirically by a combination of internal (e.g. personal, psychological) and external (e.g. environmental, contextual) factors. Perna (2004) found that academic and financial resources, as well as social and cultural capital, contributed to graduate school enrollment outcomes. Other studies of postgraduate enrollment in the U.S. have examined characteristics of a student's undergraduate institution (e.g. Millett, 2003; Mullen, Goyette, & Soares, 2003), debt accumulated as an undergraduate (Chen & Bahr, 2012; Malcom & Dowd, 2012), socioeconomic status (Stolzenberg, 1994; Zhang, 2005), and the availability of funding (Millett, 2003; Nevill & Chen, 2007) in relation to pursuit of graduate or professional education.

A major theme in research about postgraduate education in the U.S. is the persistence of racial/ethnic, gender, and socioeconomic inequalities (Posselt & Grodsky, forthcoming). Among these inequalities, African Americans are underrepresented in most fields at the doctoral level and in some fields at the master's level. To work towards reducing these gaps, a clear understanding of factors affecting their access to graduate education and choice to pursue is needed. To that end, in this chapter we examine trend data and current research on graduate school pursuit among African Americans. Following a discussion of national enrollment and attainment trends, we review the available research and conclude that strategies for increasing their participation must account for the types and ways in which interpersonal relationships shape African Americans' graduate school choice.

A few key assumptions underlie our analysis. First, we assume that the diversity of students and the various pathways in which they enter graduate school require that diverse forms of support may also be required for students to be successful (Barefoot, 2008). We do not believe there is a single model of teaching and advising that meets all students' needs. Second, existing research suggests that a culturally specific model of teaching and advising takes an individualized approach to reaching students and fostering their success (e.g. Ladson-Billings, 2006). Finally, while recognizing that customizing teaching and advising to individual needs can be taxing on those providing the support and will require additional time and resources, we assume that if educators are committed to providing all types of students with a quality education, that they will willingly make the investment.

Some readers may appreciate a broader view of graduate school pursuit in the United States. To that end, we present patterns across racial/ethnic groups in graduate degree enrollment and attainment at the bachelor's, master's, and doctoral levels. Then, we outline gender and academic discipline trends for African American students specifically. We draw from several federal datasets. The Current Population Survey (CPS) is a survey initiative sponsored jointly by the U.S. Census Bureau and the U.S. Bureau of Labor Statistics. The Survey of Earned Doctorates is an initiative of the National Science Foundation that serves as an annual census of new doctorates. Finally, the Survey of Doctorate Recipients, the National Survey of College Graduates, and the National Survey of Recent College Graduates are made available through the National Center for Education Statistics' Integrated Survey Data system.

Degree attainment across race/ethnicity

Continuation to postgraduate education is conditional on baccalaureate attainment, and in the U.S., only about half of students who start college obtain any degree within six years. Six-year degree completion rates for Latinos/Hispanics (41%) and African Americans (37%) are significantly lower than the national average (Radford et al., 2010). Still, the shares of the young adult populations possessing both baccalaureate and postgraduate degrees have risen considerably. In 1960, 11% of persons between 25 to 29 years old held a B.A. degree or higher. Twenty years later, in 1980, the proportion had doubled to 22%, and by 2010 it was up to 32% (U.S Census Bureau, 2013). Figure 11.1 depicts the percent of adults with a B.A. or higher degree from 1990–2013.

Figure 11.2 captures the rising percentage of 25- to 29-year-olds with an M.A. or higher degree by race and gender. On average, educational attainment rates in the U.S. have been higher for females than males at every level of education since 2000 (U.S. Department of Education, 2014). A larger share of women than men are attaining advanced degrees in every racial/ethnic group except for Asians.

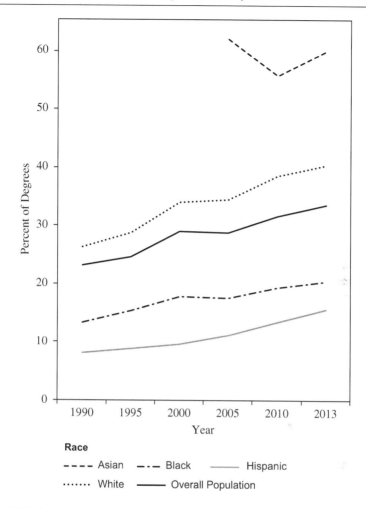

Figure 11.1 Percentage of persons 25 to 29 years of age with B.A. or higher degree (1990–2013)

However, inequities persist in doctoral education and in some disciplines at all levels. For example, clear disparities can be observed between males and females and between Asians, Whites, and underrepresented minorities[2] with respect to doctoral degree attainment in science and engineering. Figure 11.3 uses SESTAT Integrated Survey Data to display the total number of science and engineering doctoral degrees that have been awarded over time between 1995 and 2010, and makes plain the stark racial and gender imbalances in who is earning degrees in these fields.[3] While underrepresented minorities have nearly doubled their share of doctoral degrees awarded (a total of 10% in 2010), it remains less than half of their share of the U.S. population. Similarly, although there are upward doctoral

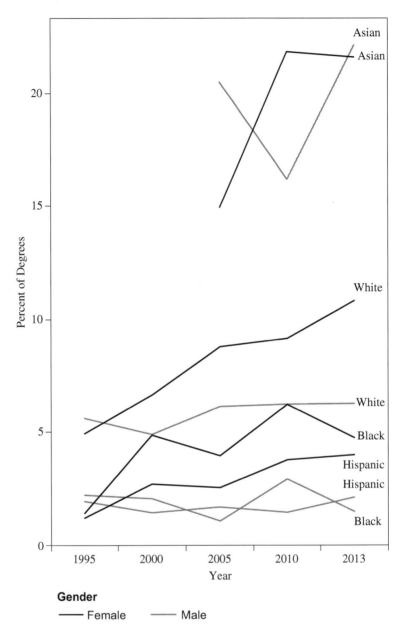

Figure 11.2 Percentage of persons 25 to 29 years of age with an M.A. or higher degree, by race and gender (1995–2013)

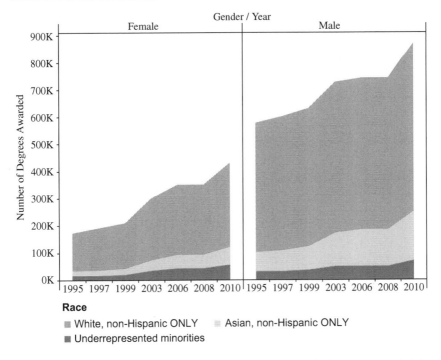

Figure 11.3 Number of science and engineering doctoral degrees awarded by race and gender (1995–2010)

attainment trends for both females and males, women by 2010 had yet to earn as many doctorates in science and engineering as men had obtained by 1995.

Degree attainment among African Americans

African Americans constitute 12.5% of the total population of graduate students, which closely reflects their share of the U.S. population (U.S. Census Bureau, 2013). Figure 11.4 displays the rising percent of degrees awarded to African Americans between 1981 and 2009, relative to the total U.S. population. In 2009 African Americans obtained 9% of the bachelor's, 10% of the master's, and 6% of the doctorate degrees granted in the U.S.

Across each racial/ethnic group, African Americans have the largest gender gap for educational attainment, with females surpassing males at the associate and bachelor's degree levels (Buchmann, DiPrete, & McDaniel, 2008). Between 2007 and 2013, the bachelor's or more degree attainment gap between African American female and males appears to have widened. However, as Buchmann et al. (2008) explain, this pattern does not signify a reversal in the African

American gender gap, as is the case for other racial/ethnic groups in the U.S. Rather, the pattern is indicative of a long historical trend for American women in higher education since the Census Bureau began tracking bachelor's degrees by race and gender in 1974 (Buchmann et al., 2008). Finally, as Figure 11.5 indicates, in all disciplines except Engineering and Physical Sciences, African American women earn a greater share of doctoral degrees than men.

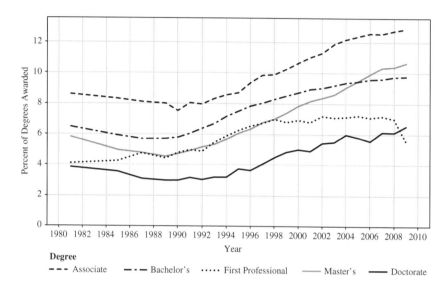

Figure 11.4 Percent of degrees awarded to African Americans by degree type (1981–2009)

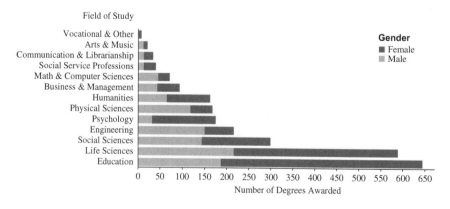

Figure 11.5 Number of doctoral degrees awarded to African Americans by field of study and gender (2012)

The role of relationships in African Americans' graduate school choice

African American college students have a higher probability than White students of intending to enroll in STEM doctoral programs (Eagan, Hurtado, Chang, Garcia, Herrera, & Garibay, 2013). Yet as the data above show, they remain underrepresented in doctoral studies and in STEM disciplines. For academic departments to help turn African American students' high educational aspirations and intentions into increased enrollment and attainment, professors and administrators require a more sophisticated understanding of what influences African Americans to pursue and enroll in graduate degree programs.

Although there have been important studies in recent years on the factors that influence African Americans' decision to enroll in graduate and professional degree programs, most research has been based on small sample sizes (e.g. Louque, 1999; McCallum, 2012). This work has generated deep understanding, but its generalizability is limited. The few quantitative studies have focused on a single institution's data and/or aggregates African Americans with other underrepresented racial/ethnic groups (e.g. Bersola, Stolzenberg, Love, & Fosnacht, 2014). In the largest study of the choice to enroll in graduate programs, Perna (2004) found that proxies for social capital (i.e., parental financial contributions to college and characteristics of one's bachelor's degree–granting institution) and cultural capital (i.e., parental educational attainment and whether English was the primary language spoken in the home) were significantly associated with graduate school enrollment in the 1992 bachelor's degree cohort. Including these variables and academic and financial resources in her model significantly increased African American students' odds of enrolling in graduate school relative to Whites. Given the important roles of social capital and interpersonal relationships in prior research, we closely examine the available literature on this theme and how the findings intersect with established norms in the African American community.

Cultural norms among African Americans

Some scholars have found that motivation to earn a graduate degree is related to African Americans' understanding of what it means to be a productive member of the African American community (Louque, 1999; Williams, Brewley, Reed, White, & Davis-Haley, 2005). That vision unfortunately often conflicts with entrenched assumptions about what is needed to be a productive member of American society, generally. The U.S. and other Western societies are generally founded upon Western European Protestant values and an individualistic worldview that encourages individual choice, personal freedom, and self-actualization (Nobles, 2006; Oyserman, Coon, & Kemmelmeier, 2002; Triandis et al., 1988). They also applaud those who base their identity on personal accomplishments (Oyserman et al., 2002). Contrastingly, African Americans and Eastern societies tend to have a worldview that embraces "common fates, common goals and common values" with others whom they share familial, ethnic, and religious ties (Oyserman et al., 2002, p. 5). This orientation, referred to as collectivism, compels African Americans to make decisions based on the needs of their community over their own needs (Nobles, 2006; Oyserman et al., 2002; Triandis et al., 1988). They believe earning the degree will provide them with skills and knowledge required to become role models and social justice advocates for the African American community (Loque, 1999; Schwartz et al., 2003; Williams et al., 2005).

The ideology of collectivism amongst African Americans can be traced back to their African roots. African people believed that all things were connected: animals, plants, people, and the environment (Oyserman et al., 2002). The success or failure of any one of those entities meant the success or failure of all of them (Oyserman et al., 2002). This ideology remained with Africans as they were brought to the United States as slaves. Although some argue that the institution of slavery diminished a collectivist worldview (Fine, Schwebel, & James-Myers, 1987), others posit that slavery, Jim Crow laws, and other discriminatory practices in the U.S. strengthened it (Carson, 2009; Nobles, 2010). In order to survive in a country that continually creates policies geared towards their failure, African Americans understand that they must depend on each other.

Fictive kinship as cultural norm

Their interconnectedness and interdependency reinforces the norm of depending on extended family members for support. It also encourages African Americans to create familial-like relationships with African Americans with whom one has no blood ties to in order to maximize resources and obtain moral support often lacking from societal institutions (Littlejohn-Blake & Darling, 1993). These relationships, referred to as *fictive kinship*, can be as important as blood relationships to African Americans (Barnett, 2004; Herndon & Hirt, 2004; Triandis, 1995). Prior to Stack's (1974) examination of poor urban African American families, fictive kinships were thought to have little or no value. However, his study revealed that these social-cultural networks provide African Americans with adaptive strategies, resources, and resiliency to cope with racism. Although other populations may also have relationships that resemble fictive kinships, comparative research has found they are most common among African Americans (Taylor, Chatters, Woodward, & Brown, 2013).

Given evidence of African Americans' collectivist orientation, commitment to interpersonal relationships and the well-established role of social capital in educational transitions, we examined research about African American college students' interpersonal relationships and how they may encourage pursuit and enrollment in graduate and professional degree programs. A review of relevant literature revealed several key relationships. Family members and fictive kin play critical roles, as expected, but professors and student affairs personnel may also come to play a role that resembles fictive kin. Importantly, we find that only when there is clear alignment between a student's expectations for these relationships and the support that students find them to offer are they likely to influence the development of graduate school aspirations and prospective students' decisions to apply and enroll.

Family relationships in the pursuit of graduate education

In the U.S., the role of parents in college enrollment is well established (Bettinger, Long, Oreopoulus, & Sanbonmatsu, 2012; Wartman & Savage, 2008); however, few scholars have explored how parents and other family members shape students' graduate and professional degree aspirations or enrollment decisions (Hearn, 1987; McCallum, 2015a; Stolzenberg, 1994). Those who have explored the role of family have primarily focused on parents' socioeconomic status (SES), and have concluded that parent SES is not directly related to aspirations or enrollment in law school, master's programs in the disciplines, or Master's of Business Administration (MBA) programs (Hearn, 1987; Stolzenberg, 1994). Empirically, students' college experiences and/or human capital development during those years decreases or eliminates the effect of parents' SES on graduate or professional degree plans (Hearn, 1987, Stolzenberg, 1994). Stolzenberg (1994) suggested college provides a "socioeconomic liberation of college students from their status origins" (p. 1068). Mullen et al. (2003), however, found that parents' SES was positively associated with enrollment in professional, doctoral and master's degree programs. They noted that this relationship was indirect, operating through the prestige of the undergraduate institution that students attend (Mullen et al., 2003).

Research specifically focusing on African Americans indicates that family members are extremely influential to students' pursuit of graduate and professional degree programs (Loque, 1999; McCallum, 2015a; Williams et al., 2005). Some studies conclude that African American students considered family members to be the *most* influential individuals to their graduate school decisions (Loque, 1999; McCallum, 2015a; Schwartz et al., 2003; Williams et al., 2005). Family members included immediate and extended relatives, such as husbands, children, mother, father, siblings as well as fictive kin (Loque, 1999; McCallum, 2015a). For example, in a historical analysis of five African American women who obtained their Ph.D., Loque (1999) found that family helped with day-to-day tasks (i.e., cooking, cleaning, etc.) in the period before application, permitting greater time for prospective graduate students to study and prepare, and that once enrolled, family members provided tangible supports (e.g. by delivering drafts of their dissertation to committee members' homes). Schwartz et al. (2003) and McCallum (2015a) found that African Americans received encouragement and support through conversations with family members, and that these conversations were even more influential than those they had with professors, support professionals on campus, and friends.

An important theme in this small literature is that family members' support and encouragement includes the advice that enrollment in a graduate degree program should be more than an individualistic decision to better one's life. Family frequently connect pursuit of an advanced degree to the larger historical and social context, in which African Americans have been denied the opportunity to earn such degrees (Loque, 1999; Schwartz et al., 2003; Williams et al., 2005). Thus, African Americans with the opportunity should take advantage of educational opportunities to better oneself *and* the broader African American community. Among African Americans who do enroll, this ideology appears to be an important motivating factor (Loque, 1999; McCallum, 2015a; Williams et al., 2005). For example, Williams et al. (2005) found that a desire to give back to the community and "pass it forward" – meaning pass along knowledge and opportunities obtained in school to other African Americans – motivated African American students to pursue advanced degrees. Likewise, McCallum's (2015a) study, which focused on pursuit and enrollment in Ph.D. programs, found that students were motivated to pursue advanced degrees by stories of family members and other African Americans who desired to pursue a graduate degree, but who did not have the opportunity to do so. With the understanding that family relationships play a critical role, it is natural to ask how relationships with professors and staff on campus may also affect African American student enrollment. We turn to this literature next.

Relationships with professors

For over six decades, scholars have examined the impact of student–professor relationships on educational outcomes (e.g. Astin, 1977, 1993; Kuh & Hu, 2001; Pascarella & Terenzini, 2005). These interactions affect students' satisfaction with college (Astin, 1993; Pascarella & Terenzini, 2005), academic achievement, cognitive and social development (Pascarella & Terenzini, 2005), and postgraduate aspirations (Carter, 2001; Hearn, 1987; Weidman, 1989). Students who interact frequently with professors inside and outside of the classroom also report graduate and professional degree aspirations more than students who do not (Carter, 2001; Hearn, 1987; Weidman, 1989).[4] Identifying college experiences that support or increase aspirations is important because, nationally, the proportion of African American students who report graduate/professional education aspirations or expectations tends to attenuate during the college years (Carter, 1999). And, indeed, the frequency of student–professor interactions is positively associated with the decision to pursue graduate education (Hathaway et al., 2002; Lammers, 2001).

One common context for student–professor contact outside the classroom, for both African Americans and students from other underserved backgrounds, is graduate school preparatory programs and undergraduate research programs (e.g. Barlow & Villarejo, 2004; Hathaway et al., 2002). Quantitative research has been useful for establishing *that* student–professor interactions matter, while qualitative studies have illuminated how they matter. A review of 54 articles focused on undergraduate research programs by Seymour, Hunter, Laursen, & Deantoni (2004) concluded that undergraduate research programs encourage graduate school enrollment, strengthen graduate school aspirations, and/or influence choice of graduate school. Similarly, Eagan et al. (2013) found that mentoring from professors was positively associated with STEM graduate degree intentions; through methods that permit causal inference, they also found that undergraduate research maintained or strengthened those intentions.

Other studies evaluating student research programs have concluded that the interactions with professors that they facilitate come with multiple benefits for students – one being a desire to pursue a graduate degree (Bauer & Bennett, 2003; Hathaway et al., 2002; Posselt & Black, 2012; Seymour et al., 2004). Using data compiled from oral interviews of 33 undergraduates, however, Ishiyama (2007) came to the conclusion that first-generation, low-income White students had different expectations of their research mentors than did African American students. African American students expected to form a personal connection with their mentor and expected that their mentor would express concern and extend support for their professional and personal wellbeing.

These findings are aligned with those of other studies that explore the mentoring expectations of African American students (Fries-Britt & Griffin, 2007; Griffin, 2013; Guiffrida, 2005; Patton, 2009). Fries-Britt and Turner (2002), who examined student–professor relationships at a historically Black college, determined that African American students expect professors to go "beyond the call of duty" to help them succeed (p. 321). Building upon Fries-Britt and Turner's (2002) work, Guiffrida (2005) determined that going beyond the call of duty meant that professors were willing to provide "intrusive academic, career and personal advising" (p. 714). Most recently, Griffin (2013) noted that African American students sought "socio-emotional support, active advocacy, . . . and high academic expectations" (p. 180) from professors.

The type of student–professor relationship that African Americans expect has been described as *othermothering*, defined as behaviors that can be likened to the behavior of relatives – similar to fictive kin – and which support students during their academic journey (Foster, 1993; Griffin, 2013; Guiffrida, 2005). Strong socio-emotional support and a family-like ethic of care are essential to African Americans' vision of a student-centered professor, and are rooted historically in how African Americans show that they care for one another. Historically, the type of caring present in othermothering relationships, within institutions of higher education and beyond, has been viewed as a form of social justice that empowers African Americans through an education system filled with racist and discriminatory policies that prevent their success (Mawhinney, 2011; Roseboro & Ross, 2009; Walker & Tompkins, 2004).

The closeness and intensity of othermothering make these types of relationships different than typical student–professor mentoring relationships – both the normative type of relationship in the U.S. (which is strictly professional in most cases) and the typical mentoring experienced by African American college students (which research repeatedly finds to be characterized by negative experiences, especially on predominantly White campuses) (e.g. Fleming, 1984; Nettles, 1991). When professors fall short of student expectations, African American students become disappointed in the student–faculty relationship and often their college experience (Griffin, 2013; Guiffrida, 2005). In these situations, mentoring from professors is unlikely to support African Americans' pursuit of graduate education.

Relationships with student affairs professionals

The experiences that U.S. college students have outside the classroom can be as influential to their development and learning as those that they have inside the classroom (Boyer, 1987; Chickering & Risser, 1993; Love, 1995; Pascarella & Terenzini, 1991, 2005). It is therefore important to increase understanding of the relationships that students form with student affairs professionals in general, and more specifically the way those relationships may affect graduate degree aspirations and enrollment. In the U.S., student affairs is roughly comparable to student services in the United Kingdom. It includes professionals in residence halls/dorms, student activities, centers that serve specific student populations, and in some cases, academic advising offices. Student affairs professionals work with students to enhance their growth, learning, and development outside the classroom environment (e.g. Hirt, Amelink & Schneiter, 2004).

Although there are only a few papers that directly address the topic, there is a large body of literature that implies student affairs professionals may influence students' graduate and professional degree aspirations and enrollment plans (Astin, 1977, 1993; Boyer, 1987; Chickering & Risser, 1993; Pascarella & Terenzini, 1991, 2005). For example, scholarship that focuses on undergraduate research programs often mentions "staff," but does not elaborate on their role in helping students reach their academic and career goals (Hathaway et al., 2002; Lammers, 2001). We know, however, that whereas professors' attention may be divided, student affairs professionals' role is focused exclusively on serving students. They may therefore be more willing to cultivate the types of deep othermothering relationships that African American students seek (e.g. Hirt et al., 2004). For example, in a study of the nature of student affairs work at liberal arts colleges, student affair administrators described their job as service-oriented and student-centered rather than business-oriented and administrative-centered. They prided themselves on being better attuned to the needs of students than faculty and other professionals, because they are present with students every day. In a similar study, student affairs professionals at historically Black colleges and universities described feeling obligated to go above and beyond their job description to help students succeed (Hirt, Strayhorn, Amelink, & Bennett, 2006). They reinforced the idea with students that all African Americans have an obligation to "pay forward" their knowledge and opportunities to other African Americans in the pipeline (Hirt et al., 2006).

A recent study by the lead author of this chapter considered the direct contribution of student affairs professionals across a variety of institutions to African Americans' decision to pursue the Ph.D. (McCallum, 2015b). They challenged students to pursue their goal of obtaining a graduate school degree while supporting them emotionally, financially (through work study), and physically (providing resources) (McCallum, 2015b). The relationships that students formed with student affairs professionals were often described as "safe"; therefore, students utilized those relationships to discuss topics they were unwilling to discuss with professors. The patterns of care exemplified in these relationships are aligned with fictive kinship patterns embedded in the concept of *othermothering*. Although the majority of research to date has focused on professors and family members (relatives and fictive kin) in influencing graduate school choice for African Americans, McCallum's study suggests that a culturally relevant framework for understanding graduate and professional school choice among African American students should also include student affairs professionals.

Conclusion

Why, one might ask, is it important that we seek more equitable representation of African Americans in graduate education? There are several answers and angles on this question. One concerns doctoral education as a pathway to the professoriate. Recent evidence indicates that greater diversity among diverse faculty and staff enhances the learning environment for all students. Relatedly, we need to increase the representation of African Americans in graduate programs leading to other professions if we wish to reduce racial stratification in the upper strata of the labor market. Third, the quality of collaborative efforts in academia and other professions is on the line: research by Scott Page (2008) indicates that diverse groups of amateurs out-perform homogenous groups of experts on tasks involving problem solving and creativity. Last, but not least important, the U.S. carries an educational debt to African Americans for centuries of discriminatory economic, political, and social policy (Ladson-Billings, 2006).[5] The debt began to accrue during the period of enslavement and continues today (Harper, Patton, & Wooden, 2009). Because resources have been deliberately withheld, deliberate measures must be taken to erode their negative, intergenerational effects. We contend that such measures require an understanding of culturally specific dynamics that continue to shape African Americans' educational experiences and opportunities.

The research is clear about the importance of interpersonal relationships in African Americans' college choice process. Embedded within any relationship is the potential to motivate another person to achieve more than they might have imagined or to dampen that individual's goals and aspirations. In the context of interpersonal relationships with African American college students, the literature is clear that family, fictive kin, faculty, and student affairs practitioners each can serve as sources of emotional and tangible support, access to networks, advice, and other resources that make the transition to graduate school a more feasible pathway. Too often, however, relationships with faculty members – who ostensibly can exert the most direct influence on a student's continuation to graduate education – do not meet the bar of support that African American students may seek.

Rather than assuming that students should change their expectations for what faculty relationships should entail, it would behoove colleges and universities to start by providing incentives for faculty to critically examine how they relate to students. Do faculty establish shared expectations for how mentoring or advising relationships will work? Current studies suggest that establishing shared expectations at the outset of a mentoring relationship is vital to student satisfaction and success (Huskins, et al., 2011). Are faculty attuned to the nuances of mentoring across race, gender, and/or social class? Research clearly indicates that the socio-cultural dynamics introduced through cross-race, cross-gender, and cross-class mentoring relationships present special concern (Patton & Harper, 2003; Reddick, 2012), but due to inequalities in the composition of the professoriate, may be difficult to avoid. Esnard et al. (2015) give the name "productive tensions" to these dynamics and note that they can be very powerful in building social capital in mentoring networks.

Finally, how – if at all – do institutions of higher education engage with students' families as a resource in encouraging student success? Are student affairs professionals trained to see encouraging students' continuation to graduate school as part of their role, or does it happen on an ad hoc basis? Our literature review suggests that for African American students who do go on to graduate education, support from key relationships in several areas of life was essential. Encouraging and institutionalizing networks of support therefore holds potential to advance educational opportunities for prospective African American graduate students, and to do so in a way that honors the collectivist framework within which many African American students pursue their goals.

Notes

1 Following the bachelor's degree, students in the U.S. may pursue 1–2 year master's degrees, 2–4 year professional degrees, and/or 4+ year Ph.D. programs.
2 This data was obtained from the Integrated Survey Data, SESTAT Public 2010, which aggregates underrepresented racial/ethnic minority groups under the umbrella category, "under-represented minorities." While it is not possible to observe attainment patterns from specific racial/ethnic groups, the data displays a telling portrait of inequalities among Asian, Whites, and underrepresented groups.
3 Note that due to very low numbers of Latinos and African Americans obtaining doctorates in some fields, that NCES has aggregated Latino and Blacks into a single category as a way of protecting their anonymity.
4 Although aspirations do not guarantee enrollment or attainment (Reynolds & Johnson, 2011), educational aspirations and expectations are among the strongest predictors of who pursues postsecondary degrees (Eagan et al., 2013; Heller, 2001; Nevill & Chen, 2007).

5 Society's "educational debt" is defined as the sum of "foregone resources that we could have (should have) been investing in (primarily) low income [students], which deficit leads to a variety of social problems (e.g. crime, low productivity, low wages, and low labor force participation)" (Haveman, 2006 as cited in Ladson-Billings, 2006).

References

Astin, A. W. (1977). *Four Critical Years: Effects of College on Beliefs, Attitudes, and Knowledge*. San Francisco, CA: Jossey-Bass.

Astin, A. W. (1993). *What Matters in College? Four Critical Years Revisited*. San Francisco, CA: Jossey-Bass.

Barefoot, B. O. (2008). Collegiate transitions: The other side of the story. *New Directions for Higher Education* (144), 89–92.

Barnett, M. (2004). A qualitative analysis of family support and interaction among Black college students at an ivy league university. *Journal of Negro Education, 73*(1), 53–68.

Barlow, A. E. L., & Villarejo, M. (2004). Making a difference for minorities: Evaluation of an educational enrichment program. *Journal of Research in Science Teaching, 41*(9), 861–881.

Bauer, K. W., & Bennett, J. S. (2003). Alumni perceptions used to assess undergraduate research experience. *Journal of Higher Education, 74*(2), 210–230.

Bersola, S. H., Stolzenberg, E. B., Love, J., & Fosnacht, K. (2014). Understanding admitted doctoral students' institutional choices: Student experiences versus faculty and staff perceptions. *American Journal of Education, 120*(4), 515–543.

Bettinger, E. P., Long, B. T., Oreopoulus, P., & Sanbonmatsu, L. (2012). The role of application assistance and information in college decisions: Results from the H&R block FAFSA experiment. *The Quarterly Journal of Economics, 127*(3), 1205–1242.

Boyer, E. L. (1987). *College: The Undergraduate Experience in America*. New York, NY: Harper and Row.

Buchmann, C., DiPrete, T. A., & McDaniel, A. (2008). Gender inequalities in education. *Annual Review of Sociology, 34*, 319–337.

Carson, L. R. (2009). "I am because we are" Collectivism as a foundational characteristic of African American college student identity and academic achievement. *Social Psychology of Education, 12*(3), 327–344.

Carter, D. F. (1999). The impact of institutional choice and environments on African American and White students' degree expectations. *Research in Higher Education, 40*(1), 17–41.

Carter, D. F. (2001). A dream deferred? *Examining the Degree Aspirations of African American and White College Students*. New York, NY: Routledge Falmer.

Chen, R., & Bahr, P. (2012). Investigating the effects of undergraduate indebtedness on graduate school application and enrollment. Paper presented at the annual meeting of the Association for the Study of Higher Education. Las Vegas, NV.

Chickering, A. W., & Risser, L. (1993). *Education and Identity* (2nd Edition). San Francisco, CA: Jossey-Bass.

Collins, R. (2002). Credential inflation and the future of universities. In S. Brint (Ed.), *The Future of the City of Intellect: The Changing American University* (pp. 23–46). Stanford, CA: Stanford University Press.

Eagan, M. K., Hurtado, S., Chang, M. J., Garcia, G. A., Herrera, F. A., & Garibay, J. C. (2013). Making a difference in science education: The impact of undergraduate research programs. *American Educational Research Journal, 50*(4), 683–713.

Esnard, T., Cobb-Roberts, D., Agosto, V., Karanxha, Z., Beck, M., Wu, K., & Unterreiner, A. (2015). Productive tensions in a cross-cultural peer mentoring women's network: A social capital perspective. *Mentoring & Tutoring: Partnership in Learning, 23*(1), 19–36.

Fine, M., Schwebel, A. I., & James-Myers, L. (1987). Family stability in Black families: Values underlying three different perspectives. *Journal of Comparative Family Studies, 18*(1), 1–23.

Fleming, J. (1984). *Blacks in College: A Comparative Study of Students' Success in Black and White Institutions.* San Francisco, CA: Jossey-Bass.

Foster, M. (1993). Othermothers: Exploring the educational philosophy of Black American women teachers. In M. Arnot & K. Weiler (Eds.), *Feminism and Social Justice in Education: International Perspectives* (pp. 101–123). Washington, DC: Falmer Press.

Fries-Britt, S., & Griffin, K. (2007). The Black box: How high-achieving Blacks resist stereotypes about Black Americans. *Journal of College Student Development, 48*(5), 509–524.

Fries-Britt, S., & Turner, B. (2002). Uneven stories: Successful Black collegians at a Black and White campus. *The Review of Higher Education, 25*(3), 315–330.

Griffin, K. A. (2013). Voices of the "Othermothers": Reconsidering Black Professors' relationships with Black students as a form of social exchange. *The Journal of Negro Education, 82*(2), 169–183.

Guiffrida, D. A. (2005). Othermothering as a framework for understanding African American students' definitions of student-centered faculty. *Journal of Higher Education, 76*(6), 701–723.

Harper, S. R., Patton, L. D., & Wooden, O. S. (2009). Access and equity for African American students in higher education: A critical race historical analysis of policy efforts. *The Journal of Higher Education, 80*(4), 389–414.

Hathaway, R. S., Nagda, B. R., & Gregerman, S. R. (2002). The relationship of undergraduate research participation to graduate and professional education pursuit: An empirical study. *Journal of College Student Development, 43*(5), 614–631.

Hearn, J. C. (1987). Impacts of undergraduate experiences on aspirations and plans for graduate and professional education. *Research in Higher Education, 27*(2), 119–141.

Heller, D. E. (2001). *The States and Public Higher Education Policy: Affordability, Access, and Accountability.* Baltimore, MD: John Hopkins University Press.

Herndon, K., & Hirt, B. (2004). Black students and their families: What Leads to Success in College. *Journal of Black Studies, 34*(4), 489–513.

Hirt, J. B., Amelink, C. T., & Schneiter, S. R. (2004). The nature of student affairs work in the liberal arts college. *Journal of Student Affairs Research and Practice, 42*(1), 94–110.

Hirt, J. B., Strayhorn, T. L., Amelink, C. T., & Bennett, B. R. (2006). The nature of student affairs work at historically Black colleges and universities. *Journal of College Student Development, 47*(6), 661–676.

Huskins, W. C., Silet, K., Weber-Main, A. M., Begg, M. D., Fowler Jr, V. G., Hamilton, J., & Fleming, M. (2011). Identifying and aligning expectations in a mentoring relationship. *Clinical and Translational Science, 4*(6), 439–447.

Ishiyama, J. (2007). Expectations and perceptions of undergraduate research mentoring: Comparing first generation, low income White/Caucasian and African American students. *College Student Journal, 41*(3), 540.

Kuh, G. D., & Hu, S. (2001). The effects of student-faculty interactions in the 1990s. *Review of Higher Education, 24*, 309–332.

Ladson-Billings, G. (2006). From the achievement gap to the education debt: Understanding achievement in US schools. *Educational Researcher, 35*(7), 3–12.

Lammers, W. J. (2001). An informal seminar to prepare the best undergraduates for doctoral programs in psychology. *Teaching of Psychology, 28*(1), 58–59.

Littlejohn-Blake, S. M., & Darling, C. A. (1993). Understanding the strengths of African American families. *Journal of Black Studies, 23*(4), 460–471.

Louque, A. (1999). Factors influencing academic attainment for African-American women PhD recipients: An ethnographic study of their persistence. *Negro Educational Review, 50*(3), 101–108.

Love, P. G. (1995). Exploring the impact of student affairs professionals on student outcomes. *Journal of College Student Development, 36*(2), 162–170.

Malcom, L. E., & Dowd, A. C. (2012). The impact of undergraduate debt on the graduate school enrollment of STEM baccalaureates. *The Review of Higher Education, 35*(2), 265–305.

Mawhinney, L. (2011). Othermothering: A personal narrative exploring relationships between Black female faculty and students. *The Negro Educational Review, 62*, 213–232.

McCallum, C. M. (2012). "Understanding the Relationships and Experiences That Contribute to African Americans' Decision to Enroll in Doctoral Education." PhD diss., Center for the Study of Higher and Postsecondary Education, University of Michigan.

McCallum, C. M. (2015a). "Mom made me do it": The role of family in African Americans' decisions to enroll in doctoral education. *Journal of Diversity and Higher Education, 2*(8), 1–14.

McCallum, C. M. (2015b). Turning graduate school aspirations into enrollment: How student affairs professionals can help African American students. *New York Journal of Student Affairs, 15*(1), 2–18.

Millett, C. M. (2003). How undergraduate loan debt affects application and enrollment in graduate or first professional school, *Journal of Higher Education, 74*(4), 386–415.

Mullen, A. L., Goyette, K. A., & Soares, J. A. (2003). Who goes to grad school? Social and academic correlates of educational continuation after college. *Sociology of Education, 76*(2), 143–169.

Nettles, M. T. (1991). Racial similarities and differences in the predictors of college student achievement. In W. R. Allen, E. G. Epps, & N. Z. Haniff (Eds.), *College in Black and White* (pp. 75–94). Albany, NY: State University of NY Press.

Nevill, S. C., & Chen, X. (2007). The path through graduate school: A longitudinal examination 10 years after bachelor's degree (NCES 2007–162). U.S. Department of Education. Washington, DC: National Center for Education Statistics.

Nobles, W. W. (2006). *Seeking the Sakhu: Foundational Writings for an African Psychology*. Chicago, IL: Third World Press.

Nobles, W. W. (2010). African philosophy: Foundations for Black psychology. In F. W. Hayes III (Ed.), *A Turbulent Voyage: Readings in African American Studies* (pp. 280–292). Lanham, MA: Rowman & Littlefield Publishers.

Oyserman, D., Coon, H. M., & Kemmelmeier, M. (2002). Rethinking individualism and collectivism: evaluation of theoretical assumptions and meta-analyses. *Psychological Bulletin, 128*(1), 3.

Page, S. E. (2008). *The Difference: How the Power of Diversity Creates Better Groups, Firms, Schools, and Societies.* Princeton, NJ: Princeton University Press.

Pascarella, E. T., & Terenzini, P. (1991). *How College Affects Students.* San Francisco: Jossey-Bass.

Pascarella, E. T., & Terenzini, P. T. (2005). *How College Affects Students* (Vol. 2). K. A. Feldman (Ed.). San Francisco, CA: Jossey-Bass.

Patton, L. D. (2009). My sister's keeper: A qualitative examination of mentoring experiences among African American women in graduate and professional schools. *Journal of Higher Education, 80,* 510–537.

Patton, L. D., & Harper, S. R. (2003). Mentoring relationships among African American women in graduate and professional schools. *New Directions for Student Services* (104), 67–78.

Perna, L. W. (2004). Understanding the decision to enroll in graduate school: Sex and racial/ethnic group differences. *Journal of Higher Education, 75*(5), 487–527.

Posselt, J. R., & Black, K. R. (2012). Developing the research identities and aspirations of first-generation college students: Evidence from the McNair scholars program. *International Journal for Researcher Development, 3*(1), 26–48.

Posselt, J. R., & Grodsky, E. (forthcoming). Graduate Education and Social Stratification. *Annual Review of Sociology.*

Radford, A. W., Berkner, L., Wheeless, S. C., & Shepherd, B. (2010). *Persistence and Attainment of 2003–04 Beginning Postsecondary Students: After 6 Years* (NCES 2011–151). Washington, DC: U.S. Department of Education, National Center for Education Statistics.

Reddick, R. J. (2012). Male faculty mentors in black and white. *International Journal of Mentoring and Coaching in Education, 1*(1), 36–53.

Reynolds, J. R., & Johnson, M. K. 2011. Change in the stratification of educational expectations and their realization. *Social Forces, 90*(1), 85–109.

Roseboro, D. L., & Ross, S. N. (2009). Care-sickness: Black women educators, care theory, and a hermeneutic of suspicion. *Educational Foundations, 23,* 19–40.

Schwartz, R. A., Bower, B. L., Rice, D. C., & Washington, C. M. (2003). "Ain't I a woman, too?": Tracing the experiences of African American women in graduate school. *Journal of Negro Education, 72*(3), 252–268.

Seymour, E., Hunter, A. B., Laursen, S. L., & Deantoni, T. (2004).Establishing the benefits of research experiences for undergraduates in the sciences: First findings from a three year study. *Science Education, 88*(4), 493–534.

Stack, C. (1974). *All Our Kin: Strategies for Survival in a Black Community.* New York: Harper and Row.

Stolzenberg, R. M. (1994). Educational continuation by college graduates. *American Journal of Sociology, 99*(4), 1042–1077.

Taylor, R. J., Chatters, L. M., Woodward, A. T., & Brown, E. (2013). Racial and ethnic differences in extended family, friendship, fictive kin, and congregational informal support networks. *Family Relations, 62*(4), 609–624.

Triandis, H. C. (1995). *Individualism and Collectivism.* Boulder, CO: Westview Press.

Triandis, H. C., Bontempo, R., Villareal, M. J., Asai, M., & Lucca, N. (1988). Individualism and collectivism: Cross-cultural perspectives on self-ingroup relationships. *Journal of Personality and Social Psychology, 54*(2), 323.

U.S. Census Bureau (2013). Current Population Survey (CPS), 1970–2013. http://www.census.gov/cps/

U.S. Department of Education, National Center for Education Statistics. (2014). *The Condition of Education 2014: Educational Attainment* (NCES 2014–083).

Wakeling, P. (2007). White faces, black faces: Is British sociology a white discipline? *Sociology, 41*(5), 945–960.

Walker, V. S., & Tompkins, R. H. (2004). Caring in the past: The case of a southern segregated African American school. In V. Siddle Walker and J.R. Snarey (Eds.), *Race-ing Moral Formation: African American Perspectives on Care and Justice* (pp. 77–92). New York: Teachers College Press.

Wartman, K. L., & Savage, M. (2008). Parental involvement in higher education: Understanding the relationship among students, parents, and the institution. *ASHE Higher Education Report, 33*(6), 1–125.

Weidman, J. C. (1989). Undergraduate socialization: A conceptual approach. In J. C. Smart (Ed.), *Higher Education: Handbook of Theory and Research* (Vol. 5, pp. 289–322). New York, NY: Agathon Press.

Williams, M. R., Brewley, D. N., Reed, R. J., White, D. Y., & Davis-Haley, R. T. (2005). Learning to read each other: Black female graduate students share their experiences at a White research institution. *The Urban Review, 37*(3), 181–199.

Zhang, L. (2005). Advance to graduate education: The effect of college quality and undergraduate majors. *The Review of Higher Education, 28*(3), 313–338.

Chapter 12

Participation and access in higher education in Russia

Continuity and change of a positional advantage

Anna Smolentseva

In the last two decades massification has been the dominant trend in the development of higher education in Russia, but it has also been puzzling. With the breakdown of the Soviet Union in 1991, the entire social, political and economic structure in Russia has collapsed. No Soviet industry was thriving and demanded higher educated staff, no jobs were now assigned to the higher education graduates as it was in the USSR.

Under these circumstances the first few years of the new country showed a decline of the interest of the population in higher education, but after that the enrollments started to climb up very fast without any obvious reason. From 1995 to 2008 the number of students multiplied by 2.6 times and only a demographic downturn in the school leaver age group slowed down the process. However, many countries in the world have also experienced rapid recent growth in higher education, albeit a little later than Russia. Expansion has been the principal aspect of higher education (Trow 1973; Altbach et al. 2009). This expansion has deep and multifaceted impacts on all dimensions of higher education and society.

The 2010 national census data indicate that the share of the population with higher education credentials is rising: among 35- to 39-year-olds it was 33 per cent, for the 30–34 age cohort it was 38 per cent, for the 25–29 age group it was already 43 per cent and for 20- to 24-year-olds it had reached 40 per cent (Vserossiskaya perepis' . . . 2010). In future the indicators for the youngest cohort will almost certainly rise, as more complete a qualification or decide to enroll.

The dramatic change in the new system happened at the beginning of the transition to the market economy: it was an introduction of tuition fees. In the country, where in the socialist past higher education used to be a free right of citizens, now higher education turned into a service or a commodity. The tuition fees were introduced in the public sector for full-time and part-time education, while keeping tuition-free places subsidized by government, and in the newly established private sector operating on the tuition-fee basis. The transition proved to be substantial. Currently, the majority of students pay tuition fees – in 2012, 61 per cent of students in total, and 55 per cent of the students enrolled in the public sector (Statistika obrazovania . . . 2013).

This chapter will try to unpack the process of massification of higher education and the dynamics of increasing participation and equality of opportunity in the context of Russia. It will draw on conceptual approaches to massification of higher education in relation to expanding educational opportunities; discuss the dynamics of the social process of massification of higher education in relation to Russia; provide empirical evidence on the limited equalization of opportunity, and conclude with remarks on the Soviet legacy, and on the respective roles of continuity and change in the development of participation patterns in higher education.

Conceptual approaches to understanding of massification and access in higher education

In his seminal work American sociologist Martin Trow (Trow 1973) identified growth as a key trend in the development of higher education systems in industrialized societies. He emphasized three different aspects of growth of higher education systems: (1) the rate of growth, which in turn affects (2) the absolute size of systems and individual institutions and (3) changes in the proportion of the relevant age cohort enrolled in higher educational institutions. Three phases in the development of higher education were defined: elite (where the students constitute up to 15 per cent of the relevant age cohort), mass (15–50 per cent) and universal, where the majority of the age grade get access to postsecondary education (over 50 per cent).

These stages in the expansion of higher education reflect qualitative changes in the nature and role of higher education. Society transforms from reproduction of the ruling social class at the elite phase, through training a broad range of professionals at the mass phase, to an adaptation of wider population to rapid social and technological changes in the universal phase. Higher education transforms from being a privilege at the elite stage, through a right for those with certain qualifications in mass systems, to an obligation in the universal access context. The transition from one stage to another does not eliminate institutions evolved in a previous stage, but promotes institutional differentiation with a diverse set of roles and missions in a changing society. Elite institutions might maintain their role during the mass and universal phases. Trow stated that a diversified system of higher education reflects the status hierarchies in society and becomes an effective way to buttress the existing class structure.

Also in the 1970s, Austrian-British economist and journalist Fred Hirsch developed the concept of positional good (Hirsch 1976), which as applied to higher education means that higher education provides its holder with a relative advantage in competition for labor and social statuses. The value of positional goods is defined by its scarcity at each level of position. These are rivalrous and excludable goods. Positional goods are intrinsically inter-dependent which means that more investment in education by one person reduces the value of the positional investments of others; hence one individual wins only at the expense of another. Considering higher education as a positional good highlights the mutual interdependence of all members of a society and thus the social limitations of the meritocratic ideal. Systems that are constantly producing status on a competitive basis cannot ensure social justice. This suggests that further discussion could focus on how to organize an educational system so as to minimize the risks associated with the market approach and reduce inequalities.

The concept of higher education as a positional good has four important implications. First, in the process of massification, when the number of educated people with a given level of credential increases, the value of that credential must decline (Hirsch 1976; Marginson 1997). Sociologists have observed the same trend: Collins (1979, 2002) notes the high credentialism of American society in the 1970s. He argues that credentials inflation is a process more determined by supply than demand. The massification of education, along with credentialism, is not driven by higher demand in the labor market for graduate skills, but is rather a self-reproducing process generated by public pressure to expand access to higher education.

Second, under massification, while the positional value of credentials declines, the relative advantage of some groups over others is maintained. This proposition finds support in sociological research. It echoes Trow's elaboration of the maintenance of the social hierarchy in a diversified system of higher education, in the mass and especially universal phases. The same conclusion is suggested by the sociological model of 'effectively maintained inequality'. Once at a given level of education saturation has been achieved, quantitative inequalities in the odds are replaced by qualitative inequalities in the odds of getting on the more selective track (Lucas 2001; Ayalon and Shavit 2004). Hence, in a mass and especially universal access system, where a majority of age cohort attends higher educational institutions, social justice regarding access to higher education means not the accessibility of higher education as such, but the odds of access to certain forms of higher education, produced within specific institutions, that are associated with educational hierarchy and social advantage. The question regarding equity in higher education that is increasingly being asked in different countries is not access, but access to what? (e.g. Bastedo and Gumport 2003; Shishkin 2004, Eggins 2010; Brennan and Patel 2011).

Third, the positional good concept is helpful in understanding the nature and implications of vertical differentiation of higher educational institutions and the widening of the gap between elite and non-elite sectors (Marginson 1997). The invisible hand of market does not work in education markets. Normal market rules do not work in the elite higher education sector. The leaders of elite education accumulate their resources, reputation and symbolic capital over decades. They choose students, students do not choose institutions. The elite segment does not expand to meet all possible demand – thereby preserving the selectivity which is at the heart of positional value. Only in lower-segment (mass) higher education does the competition work on the basis of the normal economic rules, driving efficiency and an orientation to catering for students' needs. Attempts to improve educational quality in this segment are underestimated, because in terms of positional competition, these institutions are locked within lower-status positions (Marginson 1997).

Fourth, massification and the vertical diversification of higher education lead to the stratification of the student body across different institutional types. Students are stratified by social background, motivations and life chances. While there are no data or instruments that would allow us to assess the value added by the education in different types of institutions, the difference between them can be assessed in various ways. If prestigious ('up-market') institutions attract on the basis of their social status and the reproduction of social capital, non-prestigious ('down-market' institutions) work at expanding educational opportunities for lower social status groups who value accessibility, lower costs, convenience and academic aspects of learning (Brennan and Patel 2011).

The above conceptual lenses illuminate the social dynamics of the process of massification, identifying the interdependence of the processes of massification and social equity in higher education. The chapter will now explore these factors in relation to massification in higher education in Russia.

Massification and its drivers in Russia

The Soviet project incorporated political, economic and cultural agendas; and education was assigned a key role in the social and professional training of new generations and overall transformation of the society. Education was considered as an arena for the formation of the 'new (Soviet) man' who should combine a number of ideological and moral attributes: 'The Communist transformation of the society is intrinsically linked to the formation of a new man in which there is a harmonious combination of spiritual wealth, moral purity, and physical perfection' (Ob ukreplenii . . . 1958, p. 3). Along with that, higher education was as a strategic instrument for the economic and technological progress of the country (Smolentseva 2016).

Government policy put a great emphasis on the development and expansion of the higher education system from the beginning of the Soviet era. As a result, Trow's mass phase of higher education, the level of 15 per cent, was achieved in the Soviet period by the 1960s. Participation was 13 per cent in 1960. By the time of the breakdown of the USSR about a quarter of the age cohort were enrolled in higher education (Smolentseva 2012). The efforts of the Soviet government to develop the higher education system created the preconditions for the further leap towards the universal participation during the turbulent post-Soviet time.

At the beginning of the reform period, international experts estimated the level of participation of the USSR population as much lower than in Western Europe and argued for the development of a non-state sector of education, and user fees in the public sector (Heyneman 2010), as two methods of expanding access. Both were introduced in the early 1990s. There was a short-term decline in the enrollments in the 1990s following the dissolution of the USSR and the ongoing economic and political crisis. However, the higher education system expanded rapidly from 1995 onwards (Table 12.1). In 1991 there were 2,762,000 students, in 2000 that number was 4,741,000 and it reached 7,513,000 by 2008,

Table 12.1 Number of students and institutions in Russian higher education

	1991	1995	2000	2005	2006	2007	2008	2009	2010	2011	2012	2013	2014
Students (total), thousands	2,762	2,790	4,741	7,065	7,310	7,461	7,513	7,419	7,050	6,490	6,074	5,647	5,209
Public, %	100	95.1	90.1	84.8	83.9	83.2	82.8	82.7	83.0	84.0	84.7	84.3	84.6
Private, %	—	4.9	9.9	15.2	16.1	16.8	17.2	17.3	17.0	16.0	15.3	15.7	15.4
Institutions (total)	519	762	965	1068	1090	1108	1134	1114	1115	1080	1046	969	950
Public	519	569	607	655	660	658	660	662	653	634	609	578	548
Private	—	193	358	413	430	450	474	452	462	446	437	391	402

Source: Russian Federation Federal State Statistics Service. www.gks.ru. ' — ' means non-applicable, as private sector did not exist. Percents are calculated by author.

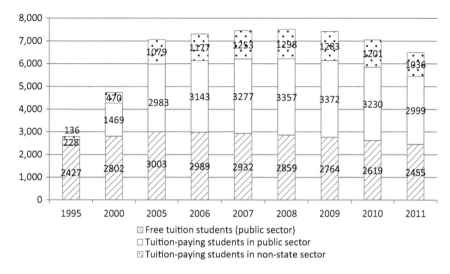

Figure 12.1 Privatization of costs in higher education as a driver of massification: number of tuition-free and tuition-paying students in public and private sectors, 1995–2011, thousands people

Source: Russian Federation Federal State Statistics Service. www.gks.ru.

the peak. Since then, the absolute number of students has been affected by demographic decline in the relevant age group.

The low birth rates of the 1990s led to a notable decline of the relevant age cohort and subsequently the student populations. Numbers in the 15–19 age cohort fell by 45 per cent between 2003 and 2013 (calculated by author using data from Rossiiskiy statisticheskii ezhegodnik 2010, 2013). In response to the demographic situation, the government has gradually lowered the number of tuition-free places in higher education, from 3 million in 2005 to about 2.5 million in 2011 (Indikatory obrazovania 2013), a reduction of about 17 per cent.

The data in Figure 12.1 show that the expansion of the 1990s and 2000s was accompanied by the partial privatization of costs, mainly in the tuition-charging part of the public sector. The government financial contribution to massification was not that significant: over the 10 years from 1995 to 2005, budgeted enrollments increased by only 20 per cent. The main increase in the number of students was associated with the growth of the fee-paying sector within public higher education. Emerging non-state institutions were unable to effectively compete with the public sector. Between 1995 and 2005, the number of tuition-paying students in public institutions almost doubled, increasing by 92%. Non-state enrollments also nearly doubled (87%), but in absolute numbers the size of the non-state sector was one third that of the tuition-charging programs in public institutions.

The introduction of user fees in the public sector, and the growth of the non-state higher education sector, were neoliberal reforms common to most of the post-Soviet countries (Smolentseva 2012). Support for such reforms was (and is) constructed normatively on the basis that these policies simply 'work' better, that economic globalization is exogenous, or that such market liberalization is 'inevitable' on the basis of international values (Fourcade-Gourinchas and Babb 2002). The low public funding of education contributes to privatization. According to UNESCO comparisons of the level of per capita GDP per tertiary student, Russia is in the bottom 10 countries (2007–2010) (UNESCO Institute for Statistics 2011). As a result, the expansion of higher education has not been accompanied by proportional growth in funding, nor in the number of academic staff. All these outcomes have notably affected the quality of higher education (Smolentseva 2016).

The fastest-growing segment of higher education was the part-time sector, rather than full-time students. More than half of the total student population now consists of part-timers. The student body includes 44 per cent studying in the public sector full-time, 40 per cent part-time in the public sector, 2 per cent attending the private sector full-time, and 14 per cent part-time in the private sector (Statistika obrazovania . . . 2013). In the Soviet period, the part-time sector had been large (42 per cent in 1990). Combining work and study was considered an effective way of improving the qualifications of the working population. The result of post-Soviet growth was that it became even larger. From 1995 to 2008, while the full-time enrollments doubled, the part-time enrollments quadrupled, constituting 54 per cent of total enrollments in 2008.

Massification and its escalation in the post-Soviet period is a complex social phenomenon. It can be explained by several factors. First, as noted, a comparatively high level of participation was already achieved in the Soviet time, which created the preconditions for further growth. Despite the fact that the proletariat was the hegemonic class in the USSR, as reflected in its social status, monetary and non-monetary benefits, Soviet policy contributed to the promotion of the value of education. By the end of the Soviet period participation in higher education had become a mass phenomenon and started to become a social norm for certain social groups.

Second, after the breakdown of the Soviet system, the structural transformation of the Soviet economy called for new occupations, skills and knowledge. Re-training in order to receive a new qualification became popular. Third, the economic returns to higher education have been relatively high, especially for women, at the level of OECD countries (Gimpelson and Kapeliushnikov 2011). The higher-educated workforce enjoyed better labor market outcomes, including lower unemployment rates, better working conditions and higher incomes. Fourth, noting that the higher education market tends to be driven more by supply than by demand (Marginson 1997), public higher educational institutions struggling with severe cuts in public funding had a strong motivation to expand numbers and increase total funds even if funding per student was in decline.

Finally, another key factor was the social status of non-manual work occupations and the potential for social mobility. In Soviet society, higher education was associated with the prestige of non-manual work, despite government efforts to emphasize the prestige of manual occupations. Even in the Soviet time, the social groups have prevailed in higher education (Konstantinovsky 1999). The break-up of the old social structure in the 1990s reinforced the need to maintain or strengthen one's social status and life chances. By the early 2000s sociologists observed that higher education had become a social norm (Dubin et al. 2004; Shishkin 2004). Even among groups that had not traditionally shown much interest in obtaining higher education qualifications, such as the rural population, higher education aspirations have grown.

The implications of massification: equity, credential inflation, stratification

The previous section suggested that among the implications of the massification of higher education in Russia have been credential inflation, continued inequality and the maintenance of the social hierarchy via the stratification of institutions, along with the differentiation of the student body. This section will explore some of the evidence for these trends.

The Soviet model promoted an egalitarian ideal of society. The system provided a range of special-entry arrangements for members of the rural population, for those directed to study by their industrial enterprises or collective farms and for those returning to education. However, to some extent, equal opportunities were a myth, one propagated by Soviet sociologists.

In the 1960s/1970s Shubkin and Konstantinovsky showed that the higher education system and the formation of the student body involved complex social process which form the accumulation and interiorization of knowledge, develop motivation for study and work and foster the elaboration of views and attitudes. To a large extent these operations depend upon the social characteristics of individuals – their place of residence, family background, peers, educational experience. They are also shaped by media. Sociologists found that despite the rhetoric of social mobility as well as some achievements in that area, there was a tendency for social groups – workers, peasants and intellectuals – to perpetuate themselves (Konstantinovsky 1999; Routkevich 2002). Subsequent analysis of educational differentiation by Gerber and Hout (1995), Gerber (2000) and Wong (2001) demonstrated also the influence of parents' educational attainment, occupational status and Communist Party membership in reproducing social groups and social status across generations. Government policy introduced special measures aimed to control the social composition of students at higher educational institutions, but this proved to be unsuccessful. The attrition rates amongst students admitted by special-entry arrangements were comparatively high, as it was more difficult for them to reach and maintain the required levels of academic achievement (Konstantinovsky 1999; Routkevich 2002). Hence, Soviet society was not free of the social barriers that were traditional elsewhere around the world. However, one form of traditional inequality, the low rate of participation of women, was overcome. By the end of the Soviet period more than half of all students were women.

In the post-Soviet period inequality of access to higher education has not been part of the policy agenda and has not been subjected to a thorough scholarly analysis. Available studies have shown that despite the expanding higher education system and higher participation rates, the factors shaping unequal opportunity persist: differences in the socio-economic status of families; area of residence; and type of secondary school attended, which is dependent upon the cultural capital of the family that chooses the school (Konstantinovsky 1999; Shishkin 2004; Roschina 2006; Konstantinovsky 2008). These studies also point to the stratification of higher education between different levels of institutional status, and the socially advantaged social composition of enrollments in the elite subsector of higher education (Roschina 2006).

Recent data on the social background of students shows to what extent the higher-educated social class is reproduced today in Russian society (Figure 12.2). The share of students who come from families with higher-educated parents is more than double the proportion of higher-educated people in the 40- to 59-year-old population. For example, while only 21.9 per cent of 40- to 59-year-old men have a higher education diploma, almost half of all students (45.8 per cent)

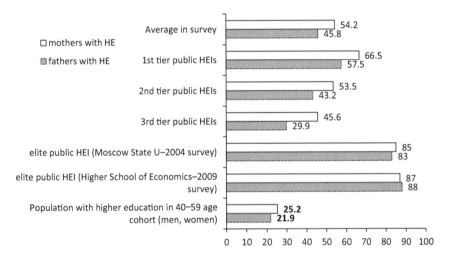

Figure 12.2 Parental education of full-time higher education (HE) students, %

Sources of data: Monitoring of Economics of Education (conducted by National Research University – Higher School of Economics); for average in survey: public and private HEIs, full-time students; for three tiers of HEIs: survey data, 2011; public HEIs (*N* = 37), 1,288 full-time students.[1] Population with higher education in 40–59 age cohort: National Census (2010). Data on Moscow State University 2004: Gasparishvili and Toumanov (2006). Data on Higher School of Economics: Higher School of Economics Center for Institutional Research (2009).

belong to families where the father has higher education. The most striking data are those that reveal the social differentiation of higher education. The top tier institutions attract students from the most educated families (57.5 per cent of students have fathers with higher education). The middle tier also draw significantly on the educated part of the population (43.2 per cent), while institutions with the lowest prestige absorb mostly first-generation students in higher education (29.9 per cent).

The elite sector is especially selective. At Moscow State University and the Higher School of Economics, more than 80 per cent of students are from higher-educated families. This trend has been long-standing. In a 1994 survey of first-year Moscow State University students, over 80 per cent (fathers 84%, mothers 83%) originated from higher-educated families (Vasenina and Sorokina 2002). A century ago, parental education was an important characteristic of student body at this institution: 26 per cent came from families where the father had higher education, and 6 per cent from families where the mother had higher education (Gasparishvili and Toumanov 2006).

It can be supposed that most prestigious and tuition-free places are occupied by the representatives of socially advantaged groups, while non-elite and non-free places have to be taken by the rest. However, according to this data, the social makeup of those studying for free and those paying for education does not significantly differ by parental education and social status (workers, specialists, etc.). That could be partly associated with the multiplicities of social dimensions and the ambiguity of social structure of post-Soviet society, which means inconsistency of different aspects of social status (Lenski 1954), such as income, education, occupation as well as the stratification within educational and occupational groups. The results can also be associated with the inaccuracy of the instrument measuring social status in this survey. The limited sample does not allow us to develop a further analysis while controlling for variables, nor to be conclusive about whether there is less or more inequality.

In relation to current data it is important to more closely investigate social differentiation among students and graduates in the different tiers of institutions. Third tier institutions, that are less selective, tend to work at providing opportunities for previously underserved populations. But we lack data about what kind of opportunities they provide.

In an international comparative perspective, Russia appears as one of the national systems that tend to reproduce social groups, rather than one of the systems that are more socially inclusive, with relatively high levels of intergenerational mobility. A methodology developed by Patrick Clancy (2010) uses Eurostudent 2011 survey data to compare the relative odds of accessing higher education where parents have higher education versus those without higher education; and also compares the odds for students whose parents are from 'other' occupational groups versus parents from 'blue-collar' occupational groups. This analysis indicates that Russia has a higher level of inequality than most of the 22 European countries in the survey (Russian case data is calculated by author,

Smolentseva 2012). Interestingly, not all post-Socialist countries exhibit the same level of inequality. The situation looks better in Slovenia, the Czech Republic and the Slovak Republic. Not all countries with universal access to higher education tend to be socially unequal to the same extent as Russia: the outcome seems to be more equitable in Finland, Norway, Slovenia.

Another methodology designed to assess the degree of social inclusion, also based on Eurostudent data, uses a simple comparison between the ratios for the higher-educated social group (higher-educated father to respective population indicator) and the lowest-educated social group (lowest-educated father to population indicator) (Haaristo et al. 2012). This again suggests that Russia is among countries with an unequalizing higher education system. Russia has low representation of the lower-educated group and substantial overrepresentation of the higher-educated group (Russian case data is calculated by the author, Smolentseva 2012).

The two methodologies provide similar results. In both cases the group of countries with more equitable access remains the same, including the Netherlands, Finland, Switzerland and Ireland, while Russia persistently demonstrates that its huge higher education system fails to represent the social composition of the society.

As in many other countries in the world, the question now being asked about Russian higher education is not simply whether there is access, but what is gained by achieving access. In the mass and universal stages of participation in higher education, the issue is not how to get into higher education, but what articulates access to higher education of differing qualities (even though there is no consensus on the definition of 'quality'); and where these different higher education trajectories lead to, in terms of social, economic, psychological outcomes for individuals and society.

There is no research data in Russia in relation to credential inflation, but there are policy and societal concerns about the massification of higher education. The massification of doctoral education in the same period of the 1990s–2000s in which ordinary higher education diplomas were being massified might indicate a growing social need to gain higher positional value in the educational credential (Smolentseva 2007). There is also evidence from other national contexts that lower-level higher education degrees are not competitive nor popular in a mass system of higher education (Kember 2010; Parry 2012).

Following Hirsch's insights (1976) that in order to maintain the value of the positional good it becomes necessary to restrict access to this level of education and to develop a vertical hierarchy to enhance the relative advantage associated with more prestigious institutions, the Russian government has talked about the overeducation of the population, and the low quality of educational programs and institutions, exacerbated by demographic decline; and tried to both limit or reverse the expansion of the system, and strengthen the hierarchy of credential value.

In higher education 'excellence programs' tend to stimulate major research institutions which traditionally belonged to the elite sector, or lead to investment in new to-be-elite institutions. In Russia this approach resulted in the selection on a competitive basis of 27 institutions in 2009 and 2010 that received special funding of up to USD 60 million per institution. These HEIs received the status of national research universities. Ten federal universities were established by merging various regional institutions during 2006–2014. Two universities were granted special status and separate funding arrangements: Moscow State University and St. Petersburg State University. In 2012, 15 universities were selected to receive additional funding towards the achievement of a goal set by the President of the Russian Federation, 5 Russian universities in the top 100 in the global rankings. Differentiation of funding will certainly lead to a further gap between elite and non-elite HEIs (Carnoy 2011). Stratification of the student body, mirroring and reproducing social stratification of the population, might also be strengthened.

Concluding remarks: continuity and change in participation patterns in Russian higher education

In Russia, the massification of higher education can be partly explained by the increasing importance of the positional advantages associated with higher education, in a society in which the Soviet system of social status has been discontinued and a new system of status is being built, on the basis of post-Soviet rules which are still evolving. However, as in the Soviet time, the most educated and socially advantaged groups keep their privilege over participation in higher education, especially in the elite segment.

It is plausible to argue that the increasing stratification and differentiation of higher education is a result of the reforms of the last two decades. The idea of education as a service, and the educational system as a market of educational services, was established in the early 1990s (Smolentseva 2016), though at that moment it could be considered largely as derived from the withdrawal and/or incapability of the state to carry on an effective educational policy and support it financially.

Higher education expansion, largely driven by family aspirations and resources, has probably reached its ceiling in absolute terms when the size of the relevant age population started to decline in 2008. A system that was based to a large extent on private investments in higher education began to contract. A similar trend, the contraction of a previously expanded higher education system, can be observed in other post-Socialist countries, such as Poland, with the same replacements of private financing towards more public provision (see Kwiek 2014).

The situation in Russian higher education may reflect the generally high level of social inequality in modern Russian society. The expansion of higher education participation, which might have led to increasing social opportunities through higher education, in fact has aided the reproduction of remarkable social disparities. After the end of the Soviet era the Gini coefficient of disposable income in Russia increased from 0.26 to 0.42 (1990–2012), with the most of the increase taking place in the early 1990s during the privatization process. Few emerging economies have experienced such a radical change in such a short time (Ukhova 2014).

Nevertheless, it is important that some social groups previously underrepresented in higher education were able to gain access in the process of system expansion. However, research is needed to understand what kind of opportunity the increasingly stratified system of higher education has created. The conceptual approaches employed for this paper have highlighted the social dead-end of positional competition, the further vertical stratification of higher education institutions, and emphasis on elite higher education. It is essential to pay more attention to the needs of the mass sub-sector of higher education, which serves the majority of the population, so they will not be overlooked. Apparently, there is also a need for a new policy approach, which does not reduce higher education to its economic value in terms of market and quasi-market, but understands education as a developmental process of learning, and embraces the other social dimensions and benefits which higher education brings to societies, groups and individuals.

Note

1 The institutions in the sample were divided into three groups depending on the average national test score of students enrolled at tuition-free basis. For first tier institutions an average score was set at 70 and higher, for second tier, between 60 and 69 and for the third tier 59 and lower (the maximum score at any subject test is 100).

References

Altbach, P., Reisberg, L., Rumbley, L. (2009). *Trends in Global Higher Education: Tracking an Academic Revolution*. Paris: UNESCO 2009 World Conference on Higher Education.

Ayalon, H. & Shavit, Y. (2004). Educational Reforms and Inequalities in Israel: The MMI Hypothesis Revisited. *Sociology of Education 77*, 103–120.

Bastedo M. & Gumport P. (2003). Access to What? Mission Differentiation and Academic Stratification in U.S. Public Higher Education. *Higher Education, 46*(3), 341–359.

Brennan, J. & Patel, K. (2011). Up Market or Down Market: Shopping for Higher Education in the UK. In P.N. Teixeira and D.D. Dill (Eds). *Public Vices, Private Virtues: Assessing the Effects of Marketisation in Higher Education*. Rotterdam: Sense Publishers. pp. 315–326.

Carnoy, M. (2011). As Higher Education Expands, Is It Contributing to Greater Inequality? *National Institute Economic Review, 215*, 34.

Clancy, P. (2010). Measuring Access and Equity from a Comparative Perspective. In H. Eggins (Ed.). *Access and Equity: Comparative Perspectives*. Rotterdam: Sense Publishers. pp. 69–102.

Collins, R. (1979). *The Credential Society: An Historical Sociology of Education and Stratification*. Cambridge, MA: Academic Press.

Collins, R. (2002). Credential Inflation and the Future of Universities. In Steven Brint (Ed.). *The Future of the City of Intellect: The Changing American University*. Stanford: Stanford University Press, pp. 23–46.

Dubin, B., Gudkov L., Levinson, A., Leonova, A. & Stuchevskaya, O. (2004). Dostupnost' vysshego obrazovania: sotsial'nye i institutsional'nye aspekty [Accessibility of higher education: social and institutional aspects]. In. S.V. Shishkin (Ed.). *Dostupnost' vysshego obrazovania v Rossii [Accessibility of Higher Education in Russia]*. Moscow: Independent Institute for Social Policy, pp. 24–71.

Eggins, H. (Ed.). (2010). *Access and Equity: Comparative Perspectives*. Rotterdam: Sense Publishers.

Fourcade-Gourinchas, M., & Babb, S. (November 2002). The Rebirth of the Liberal Creed: Paths to Neoliberalism in Four Countries. *American Journal of Sociology, 108*(3), 533–579.

Gasparishvili, A., & Toumanov, S. (2006). *Moskovskii student sto let nazad I nyne* [Moscow student 100 years ago and now]. *Otechestvennye zapiski, 3*(30), 230–239.

Gerber, T.P. (2000). Educational Stratification in Contemporary Russia: Stability and Change in the Face of Economic and Institutional Crisis. *Sociology of Education, 7*(34), 219–246.

Gerber, T.P. & Hout, M. (1995). Educational Stratification in Russia during the Soviet Period. *The American Journal of Sociology, 101*(3), 611–660.

Gimpelson, V. & Kapeliushnikov, R. (Eds.). (2011). *Rossisskii rabotnik: obrazovanie, professia, kvalifikatsia [Russian Worker: Education, Profession, Qualification]*. Moscow: Higher School of Economics.

Haaristo H., Orr D. & Little B. (2012). *EUROSTUDENT Intelligence Brief: Is Higher Education in Europe Socially Inclusive?* Retrieved from http://www.euro student.eu/download_files/documents/IB_HE_Access_120112.pdf

Heyneman, S. (Spring 2010). A Comment on the Changes in Higher Education in the Former Soviet Union. *European Education, 42*(1), 76–87.

Hirsch, F. (1976). *Social Limits to Growth*. Cambridge: Harvard University Press.

Indikatory obrazovania [Indicators of Education] (2013). *Number of Students in Higher Education by Sources of Funding*. Moscow: HSE Publishing House, p. 98.

Kember, D. (2010). Opening Up the Road to Nowhere: Problems with the Path to Mass Higher Education in Hong Kong. *Higher Education, 59*(2), 167–179.

Konstantinovsky, D. (1999). *Dinamika neravenstva* [The Dynamics of Inequality]. Moscow: Editoral URSS.

Konstantinovsky, D. (2008). *Neravenstvo i obrazovanie* [Inequality and Education]. Moscow: Editoral URSS.

Kwiek, M. (2014). Structural Changes in the Polish Higher Education System (1990–2010): A Synthetic View. *European Journal of Higher Education, 4*(3), 266–280.

Lenski, G. (1954). Status Crystallization: A Non-Vertical Dimension of Social Status. *American Sociological Review, 19*(4), 405–413.

Lucas, S. (2001). Effectively Maintained Inequality: Education Transitions, Track Mobility, and Social Background Effects. *American Journal of Sociology, 106*, 1642–1690.

Marginson, S. (1997). *Markets in Education*. Sydney: Allen and Unwin.

Ob ukreplenii svyazi shkoly s zhizn'yu i o dal'neishem razvitii sistemy narodnogo obrazovania v SSSR. (1958) Zakon SSSR [On strengthening links between school and life and further development of the system of national education. The Law of the USSR]. Moscow.

Parry, G. (2012). Higher Education in Further Education Colleges. *Perspectives: Policy and Practice in Higher Education, 16*(4), 118–122.

Roschina, Y. (2006). Ch'i deti uchatsya v rossiiskikh elitnykh vuzakh? [Whose children are studying at elite Russian universities]. *Voprosy obrazovania, 1*, 347–369.

Rossiiskiy statisticheskii ezhegodnik [Russian statistical yearbook] (2010). Federal Statistical Agency: Moscow.

Rossiiskiy statisticheskii ezhegodnik [Russian statistical yearbook] (2013). Population by age groups. Retrieved from http://www.gks.ru/bgd/regl/b13_13/IssWWW. exe/Stg/d1/04–06.htm. Accessed 20 May 2014.

Routkevich, M.N. (2002). *Sotsiologia obrazovania i molodezhi: Izbrannoe (1965–2002) [Sociology of Education and Youth: Selected Papers (1965–2002)]*. Moscow: Gardariki.

Shishkin, S. (Ed.). (2004). *Dostupnost' vysshego obrazovania v Rossii* [Accessibility of Higher Education in Russia]. Moscow: Independent Institute for Social Policy.

Smolentseva, A. (2007). The Changing Status of the PhD Degree in Russia: An Academic Attribute in the Non-Academic Labor Market. *European Education, 39*(3), 81–101.

Smolentseva, A. (2012). Access to Higher Education in the Post-Soviet States: Between Soviet Legacy and Global Challenges. Paper commissioned and presented at Salzburg Global Seminar, October 2–7, Salzburg, Austria. Retrieved from http://www.salz burgglobal.org/fileadmin/user_upload/Documents/2010–2019/2012/495/ Session_Document_AccesstoHigherEducation_495.pdf

Smolentseva, A. (2016). Transformations in the knowledge Transmission Mission of Russian Universities: Social vs Economic Instrumentalism. In David M. Hoffman and Jussi Välimaa (Eds.). *Re-Becoming Universities? Critical Comparative Reflections on Higher Education Institutions in Networked Knowledge Societies*. Dordrecht: Springer. pp. 169–200.

Statistika obrazovania v tsifrakh [Statistics of education in numbers] (2013). Moscow: NII Respublikanskii issledovatel'skii nauchno-konsultatsionnyi tsentr ekspertizy.

Trow, M. (1973). *Problems in the Transition from Elite to Mass Higher Education: Carnegie Commission on Higher Education*. Berkeley, CA: Carnegie Commission on Higher Education.

Ukhova, D. (2014). After Equality: Inequality Trends and Policy Responses in Contemporary Russia. Oxfam discussion paper. May 2014.

UNESCO Institute for Statistics in EdStats (July 2011). Note: Figures are for the most recent year with data available. Data were not available for 106 countries. Retrieved from http://siteresources.worldbank.org/EXTEDSTATS/ Resources/3232763–1194387694925/TertiaryEd.zip

Vasenina, I. & Sorokina, N. (2002). *Vysshee obrazovanie v sovremennom mire* [Higher Education in Contemporary World]. In *Chelovek i sovremennyi mir* [Man and Contemporary World]. Moscow: Infra, pp. 418–440.

Vserossiskaya perepis' naselenia [National census] (2010). Retrieved from http:// www.gks.ru/free_doc/new_site/perepis2010/croc/perepis_itogi1612.htm

Wong, Raymond (2001). Egalitarianism versus Social Reproduction: Changes in Educational Stratification in Five Eastern European Countries [On line]. Paper to be presented at the Research Committee on Social Stratification and Mobility (RC28) of the International Sociological Association at Mannheim, Germany, April 26–28. Retrieved from http://www.mzes.uni-mannheim.de/rc28/papers/Wong_isa.zip

World Bank (2016). Education Statistics. Retrieved from http://data.worldbank. org/data-catalog/ed-stats.

Chapter 13

Can Holistic and Contextualised Admission (HaCA) widen access at highly selective universities?

Experiences from England and the United States

Anna Mountford-Zimdars

Introduction

Large parts of the present book rightly focus on the challenge of different groups in society accessing any form of higher education at different rates and the causes for such differences: there is a strong focus on the persistent link between social origin and attainment in education and differential transition rates and the social, economic and cultural causes underlying it. In contrast, this chapter only looks at admission to the internationally most highly ranked US and UK universities where applications by far outstrip the supply of available places. This group includes universities like Stanford, Harvard, Oxford, Edinburgh and University College London. The challenge of admission here is not so much that students who are not admitted to one of these institutions will fail to gain any place for study in higher education. To be roughly in the ballpark to even apply to these universities, applicants generally have an attainment record that makes them eligible for admission to a wide range of institutions. Instead, admission and access to elite institutions raises the question of what *type* of higher education different social groups can access and also of whether and how these universities select new undergraduates in a social context of inequality.

This chapter introduces and describes the idea of Holistic and Contextualised Admissions (HaCA), why it is used, who benefits and then discusses criticisms and limitations of HaCA. It concludes that HaCA can enhance enrolment in highly selective higher education for disadvantaged groups. To realise its full potential, however, HaCA needs to be part of an integrated approach that encompasses support and outreach prior to higher education and continues throughout students' progression within higher education into further study and employment. In using HaCA, it seems prudent for policy makers and practitioners to bear in mind the context that gives rise to the need for HaCA in the first place and to keep a focus on the meta-stories of social inequalities while making useful practical changes to make elite admissions more accessible to a wider range of applicants. The chapter is based on a wider exploration of admissions issues in

England and the US (Mountford Zimdars 2016) and a UK national report on contextualised admissions (Moore et al. 2013).

The meaning of Holistic and Contextualised Admissions

In both the US and the UK, HaCA has a strong association with selective universities in a context where demand for places vastly exceeds available places for study. However, the basic logic of HaCA can be useful for universities that are not selective and looking to perhaps find potential among students without traditional entrance qualifications (SPA 2015).

The basic idea of HaCA is that it enables universities to consider a wide range of factors when admitting students – usually, HaCA is focused on undergraduate admissions. For these applicants, a standard consideration in admission is previous academic attainment, i.e. grades in schools and predicted grades and achievement in any additional admissions tests. HaCA broadens such academic considerations to include looking at other aspects of applicants' prior lives, experience and achievement. The US term 'holistic admission' means considering a "broader range of factors in the admission decision" (NACAC 2011). Each applicant is considered holistically. In Harvard's description of its holistic admission policy:

> While academic accomplishment is important, the Admissions Committee considers many other factors – strong personal qualities, special talents or excellences of all kinds, perspectives formed by unusual personal circumstances, and the ability to take advantage of available resources and opportunities.
>
> (Harvard College 2015)

Historically, the origins of holistic admission at elite US universities in the early 20th century had exclusionary rationales. HaCA was used to justify not admitting academically qualified applicants from certain groups – such as Jewish applicants (Karabel 2005).

Today, US institutions use holistic evaluation to admit students with a range of qualities and accomplishments, including sports and artistic achievements and HaCA is more associated with a social mobility and social justice agenda. This is indicated by the policy being less popular with the political right than with the left. Holistic admission also allows universities to admit an overall ethnically diverse cohort of new undergraduates. However, HaCA also justifies admitting students with a particular link with the university, for example because their parents have given money to the institution.

In UK, the idea of contextualising the prior academic attainment of applicants is traced back to at least the 1960s and 1970s (Zimdars 2007, p. 234).

The term and systematic use of 'contextualised admissions', however, is a more recent term that has really taken off in England in the 21st century. Prominent in mainstreaming the term was the recommendation in the Schwartz Report (2004) that contextualised admissions should be used as part of fair admissions. The first university to systematically adopt an official contextualised admissions policy was the University of Edinburgh in 2004 (University of Edinburgh 2015, p. 4). The use has since spread across the Russell Group and other HE providers.

While holistic admission in the US evaluates all aspects of an applicant's non-academic talents and personal attributes and contexts, contextualised admission in the UK means primarily looking at applicants' academic attainment in the context of their school as well as the context of their geographic area and family. This facilitates evaluating whether an applicants' prior attainment reflects their true potential for academic success in higher education or whether perhaps their potential is higher than indicated by their grades. UK contextualised admissions means the systematic use of objective:

> contextual information (meaning information collected via the application process) and contextual data (meaning data matched to applicants, including through outreach) . . . as part of the undergraduate admission process, in order to assess an applicant's prior attainment (academic or otherwise) and potential to succeed in higher education in the context of the circumstances in which their attainment has been obtained.
>
> (Moore et al. 2013, p. 6)

Why use Holistic and Contextualised Admissions?

This section describes the range of conceptual rationales and arguments marshalled in support of HaCA. These can be broadly categorised as social justice, diversity, civicness, economic and social mobility and practical rationales.

For some supporters of HaCA, the primary driver is rooted in social justice considerations and that contextualising applicants is the right thing to do in itself. For example, the Universities of Edinburgh and Manchester in the UK, both early adopters and leaders in contextualised admission, root their contextualised admissions policies in a social justice framework.

A related argument is how having a diverse student body is a laudable educational goal in itself. This argument is frequently voiced in the US but less dominant in the UK. The support letter for an admissions case that reached the Supreme Court of the US regarding the University of Texas Austin's consideration of diversity within its admissions decisions is illustrative. Signed by a range of private US universities, the amici cuiriae letter argued:

> Universities continue to have a compelling interest in ensuring that their student bodies reflect a robust diversity that enables them to offer a learning

environment that enriches the educational experience for all students and also prepares them to be active, capable citizens and leaders in a complex and heterogeneous nation and world.

(Brief of Brown University et al. as Amici Curiae
Supporting Respondents 2012, p. 3)

There is further evidence that a diverse student body creates a vibrant university life as well as subsequent civic engagement. Bowen and Bok's landmark study *The Shape of the River* (2000) demonstrated how students from racial minorities – some admitted with lower grades under affirmative action policies – disproportionately participated in volunteering and civic life later on, thus demonstrating societal returns to their higher education experience.

Discussions of social returns, in turn, relate also to the economic argument that not admitting students into (elite) higher education who have particular potential to contribute to university life and later on, to society, employment and to the economy, is a waste of talent and human resources. Such economic and social mobility based arguments enjoy wide political support in the UK. In both the UK and the US, there is evidence that school achievement is closely related to socio-economic differences between communities as well as the effects of qualitative differences between schools and grades. Those from privileged schools and families achieve more highly than those from less advantaged backgrounds (e.g. BIS 2011). HaCA gives a chance of gaining admission to elite universities to relatively high-achieving but educationally and socio-economically disadvantaged applicants. Evidence in the UK shows that students admitted from worse performing schools matched on grades outperform their private school–educated counterparts once at university (HEFCE 2003; Ogg et al. 2009; Hoare and Johnston 2011; Taylor et al. 2013; Lasselle 2014; but see Partington et al 2011).

There is also a practice-based rationale for using HaCA. US and UK universities engage in a range of outreach activities that encourage and support disadvantaged students – defined in different ways – to consider and apply to selective universities. However, outreach work is not always linked to university admissions decisions. Using HaCA allows institutions to translate their outreach efforts into a higher chance of admission for those who participated in outreach schemes. This is useful for the students and the universities as these students are more likely to take up their offer for a place and are more likely to stay in higher education than similar applicants who were not part of outreach schemes (Bridger et al. 2012). Furthermore, the Office for Fair Access in the UK gives universities targets of increasing the intake of students from disadvantaged socio-economic groups and state schools. Being able to translate outreach efforts into enrolled students helps universities meet those targets.

US universities feel that their alumni and the media would be concerned if the representation of e.g. ethnic minority students and athletes dropped among admitted students. HaCA helps ensure that a reasonable number of these students are admitted. US holistic admission is also used for preferential admission of children whose parents have contributed financially to the institution. However, this policy does not fall under the umbrella of widening access but meets financial institutional objectives.

Who benefits from HaCA?

Giving special consideration through HaCA is based on a framework of various considerations that includes social background, educational, geographic/geodemographic and personal circumstances. In the UK, contextualised admission is always focused on the applicants whereas we have already seen that holistic admissions in the US is also mindful of institutional objectives such as having sports-teams that win and maintaining good relationships with donors.

Empirical research has shown how holistic admission has benefitted Black students in the US (Grodsky 2007) and those with first nation status. However, there is also research showing that students of Asian origin need to achieve higher grades compared with Whites to be admitted to elite universities (Espenshade and Radford 2009). Holistic admission has also enhanced admissions chances to selective universities for children of former graduates and financial donors (Golden 2006), for recruited athletes (Lincoln 2004) and those with special talents (Fetter 1995; Stevens 2007) as well as those who have overcome adversity such as low family income. It has increased the geographic representation of students recruited from across all US states as well as internationally. The top tier of US universities practicing holistic admission – including all Ivy League institutions – are needs blind meaning they will admit students without considering their ability to pay and then meet the required costs of housing, tuition fees and incidentals for students.

Work in England has shown how contextualising attainment results in "adjustment sponsorship" (Mountford-Zimdars 2015) or enhanced admissions chances for those educated in state schools. There has also been an increase in enrolment of students from lower socio-economic groups and areas with historically low progression to higher education and some ethnic minority students have higher transition rates into higher education than White groups; the enrolment rate of those who participated in outreach has increased (Moore et al. 2013). However, it has been more challenging to increase the representation of students in higher education who have a background of being a refugee and who have been in foster or state care, largely because hardly any students with this profile achieve sufficiently highly to be potentially eligible for highly selective higher education.

Many UK universities find that contextual flagging of applicants has increased their overall representation of disadvantaged students year-on-year. It remains a research challenge, however, to evaluate how many individual students have been admitted through contextualised admission who may not have been admitted without it in light of the complex factors that impact on admissions and transition to higher education.

Discussion and critique

This section discusses criticisms of HaCA and responses to them.

In the US, holistic admission is under attack from the political right as well as the political left. The political right takes issues with the historic connection between holistic admission and affirmative action. Recent lawsuits against race-sensitive or diversity policies are born out of this critique that fears reverse discrimination for Whites (e.g. inter alia Fisher v. University of Texas at Austin et al. 2013).

The political left is most offended by how holistic admissions in the US allow for 'legacy' admission of those who are giving money to institutions or who have a link with the institution and how this can perpetuate existing advantages and disadvantages. Arguably HaCA could be used as a smokescreen hiding a continued association between social origin and grades in school (Machin 2006) and the 'surface' rather than 'deep' meritocracies of liberal democracies (Turner 1966): by allowing some flexibility in elite admission, HaCA may (perhaps inadvertently) confer legitimacy to a system of elite and non-elite institutions and structural inequalities and focus attention away from the fact that most disadvantaged students participate in the lower prestige forms of education in any stratified higher education system (e.g. Brint and Karabel 1989). HaCA might then give an illusion of social mobility for the many, when in reality it might only enhance opportunity for a few outstanding disadvantaged students. The counter-argument is that not doing anything at all will certainly not enhance the situation.

Criticism or suggestions for enhancement of HaCA have also come from within the practitioner community in admission and outreach. This can concern disagreement regarding which groups are flagged for special consideration as well as issues around data quality and reliability for identifying disadvantage. Taking into account whether or not someone has successfully completed an outreach programme can also be controversial as it can mean that other students with similar previous disadvantages but without the support of an outreach programme may not experience the same advantages in admission. US holistic admissions approaches are more flexible with regards to the complex individual circumstances than data-driven contextual flagging. A related criticism is that research and discourses on HaCA, perhaps surprisingly, do not generally consider the effect of not being admitted into selective higher education on disadvantaged students who were supported and encouraged to apply and who then miss out on a place at their preferred university. While being mindful of these complexities and genuine issues, the alternative of not doing anything will certainly do even less to make elite higher education more accessible for a wider range of potential students.

There is also a criticism that contextualised admission does not go far enough and that the university experience itself and curricula in higher education need to change. An example of an initiative that has just done this is King's College London 'Extended Medicine Programme'. The first of its kind, it was introduced in 2001 and contextualised not only admissions (eligibility is restricted to state school students, now also first in family in higher education) but the entire first three years of the medical degree programme are contextualised: students admitted to the programme enjoy additional study support and a changed work-load for their first two years and benefit from peer and staff mentoring throughout their degree (King's College 2015). This example shows that the choice between HaCA and other support is not an either-or choice but that a range of initiatives to enhance access and progression can provide wrap-around support for students.

Another criticism is that HaCA may not be 'widening' participation to those who would not participate in higher education otherwise. Those who are admitted through HaCA at highly selective universities would have been very likely to secure a place at alternative institutions in higher education. While this is true, there is a paradox that elite higher education in the US and at a handful of UK university is usually a lot cheaper for poor students than higher education at other universities because of the higher and more generous availability of scholarships at elite institutions related to their larger endowments and also the lower overall prevalence of low-income students compared with less selective universities. HaCA at elite universties might thus entice some students into higher education who would not otherwise have gone. Furthermore, diversifying the student body at elite higher education is arguably worthwhile in itself in countries that have a strong hierarchy of universities like the US and the UK and where there are differential returns in the labour market to different types of higher education.

A related concern is that even when disadvantaged students benefit from HaCA, there is some evidence for the UK that students from private school and middle-class families reap higher earnings from their elite higher education than disadvantaged students (Macmillan et al 2015). This highlights again that HaCA cannot fully combat the reproduction of class that take place in society beyond academia. On the upside, there are opportunities for universities to link HaCA to supporting student progression within higher education, to making a difference to students while they are in universities and to support transitions after university (see e.g. Mountford-Zimdars et al. 2015).

Finally, a meta-criticism is that HaCA is only relevant in marketised HE systems with elite institutions and selective admissions based on prior attainment – recent interest in HaCA in e.g. Ireland and Australia is illustrative (Geoghegan 2014). Countries that have more accessible or less hierarchical higher education systems to start with arguably do not need HaCA or not the versions of HaCA used in the US and the UK. For example in the German higher education model students have the right to participate in higher education as long as they pass their school-leaving examination, the Abitur. Few subjects have enrolment restrictions and there are no tuition fees. Even in this general 'open access' model of higher education, advantages in enrolment are given to students who need to live locally due to family commitment or disability and students who have taken time out since school. The Danish and Scandinavian approach is to pay all students to participate in higher education with the stipend eliminating family economic resources as a predictor of who participates (e.g. Thomsen 2012).

Even when countries face situations where there are more potentially eligible students than there are higher education places, HaCA is not the only possible response. For example the Dutch medical lottery gives a weighted chance of being admitted to study medicine for students within different bandings of school-leaving grades (Stone 2015). Reasoning, good and bad, is thus eliminated from decisions. Instead of the context-conscious approach taken by HaCA, the lotteries are context blind.

Empirically disentangling the relative merits of different higher education systems can be a challenge although Shavit et al.'s 2007 landmark book goes some way to mapping equality in access across systems. Broadly speaking, different systems, inevitably, have different advantages and drawbacks. Open access policies, for example are fairer at the point of entry in allowing everyone to enrol who wishes to do so. However, when there is a high drop-out as it occurs in Germany, some UK higher education providers or community colleges in the US, such access opportunities do not always translate into improved employment and life-chances. This does not genuinely benefit students as access without success is no opportunity. This contrasts with the high retention rates of close to 100 per cent for all students, including disadvantaged ones, at highly selective UK and US institutions. Simultaneously, HaCA ultimately tends to apply at the margins of admissions processes without changing the structure of inequality in countries.

Conclusion

This section highlights two key findings from this chapter. The first finding relates to the use of HaCA in the US and the UK and the second finding relates to the effectiveness of HaCA.

First, HaCA in the UK and the US needs to be understood within contexts of relatively high economic inequality when compared with other liberal democracies combined with highly stratified higher education systems where graduate employment outcomes depend not only on participating in higher education but the prestige of the institution attended. HaCA then is a way to acknowledge that treating all applicants for higher education the same does not provide equality of opportunity in admission. By contextualising applicants and their achievements, HaCA allows some students who would have not been able to participate in elite higher education to do so.

So, by way of a second conclusion is HaCA the answer to the access challenge? To conclude, HaCA and other admissions policies can only ever be a partial answer to the access challenge. Creating a more socially just and inclusive higher education system requires an integrated approach that joins up outreach and early year works that raise attainment rather than just aspirations with admission and support at university and into employment or further study. As part of such an integrated approach, HaCA can play a crucial part in making educational journeys that little bit fairer. At the same time, while working towards continuously enhancing the possibilities of HaCA, practitioners and scholars need to be mindful that HaCA is an interim measure that would be obsolete if societies succeeded in creating greater opportunities for all regardless of the accident of educational, geographic and personal contexts.

References

BIS (2011), *Analysis of Progression Rates for Young People in England by Free School Meal Receipt and School Type*. London: Department for Business, Innovation and Skills. Available at: https://www.gov.uk/government/uploads/system/uploads/attachment_data/file/32585/11–1082-widening-participation-higher-education-aug-2011-v3.pdf

Bowen, W., and Bok, D. (2000), *The Shape of the River*. Princeton, NJ: Princeton University Press.

Bridger, K., Shaw, J., and Moore, J. (2012), *Fair Admissions to Higher Education Research to Describe the Use of Contextual Data in Admissions at a Sample of Universities and Colleges in the UK, Final Report for Supporting Professionalism in Admissions (SPA) Programme*. Cheltenham: SPA.

Brief of Brown University et al. (August 2012), As Amici Curiae Supporting Respondents. Fisher v. University of Texas. (No. 11–345).

Brint S. G., and Karabel J. (1989), *The Diverted Dream: Community Colleges and the Promise of Educational Opportunity in America, 1900–1985*. New York: Oxford University Press.

Espenshade, T. J., and Radford, A. W. (2009), *No Longer Separate, Not Yet Equal: Race and Class in Elite College Admission and Campus Life*. Princeton: Princeton University Press.

Fetter, J. H. (1995), *Questions and Admissions: Reflections on 100,000 Admissions Decisions at Stanford*. Stanford, CA: Stanford University Press.

Fisher v. University of Texas at Austin et al. (2013), No. 11–345.

Geoghegan, P. M. (2014), 'The Irish Experiment: Undergraduate Admissions for the 21st Century'. In Stead, V. (ed) *International Perspectives on Higher Education Admission Policy: A Reader*, New York: Peter Lang Publishing, pp. 39–47.

Golden, D. (2006), *The Price of Admission: How America's Ruling Class Buys Its Way into Elite Colleges – and Who Gets Left Outside the Gates*. New York: Random House.

Grodsky E. (2007), Compensatory Sponsorship in Higher Education. *American Journal of Sociology* 112(6), pp. 1662–1712.

Harvard College (2015), What we look for. Available at: https://college.harvard.edu/admissions/application-process/what-we-look

HEFCE (2003), Schooling effects on higher education achievement HEFCE 2003/32. Available at: www.hefce.ac.uk/pubs/hefce/2003/03_32.htm

Hoare, A., and Johnston, R. (2011), Widening participation through admissions policy – a British case study of school and university performance. *Studies in Higher Education* 36(1), p. 21.

Karabel, J. (2005), *The Chosen: The Hidden History of Admission and Exclusion at Harvard, Yale, and Princeton*. Boston: Houghton Mifflin.

King's College (2015), Extended medical degree programme. Available at: http://www.kcl.ac.uk/prospectus/undergraduate/emdp/details, accessed 5.09.2015.

Lasselle, L. (2014), School grades, school context and university degree performance: Evidence from an elite Scottish institution. *Oxford Review of Education* 40(3), pp. 293–314.

Lincoln, C. (2004), *Playing the Game: Inside Athletic Recruiting in the Ivy League.* White River Junction, VT: Nomad Press.

Machin, S. (2006), Social Disadvantage and Education Experiences, OECD Social Employment and Migration Working Papers no. 32.

Macmillan, L., Tyler, C., and Vignoles, A. (2015), Who gets the top jobs? The role of family background and networks in recent graduates' access to high-status professions. *Journal of Social Policy* 44, pp. 487–515.

Moore, J., Mountford-Zimdars, A., and Wiggans, J. (2013), Contextualised Admissions: Examining the Evidence Report of Research into the Evidence Base for the Use of Contextual Information and Data in Admissions of UK Students to Undergraduate Courses in the UK, Report to Supporting Professionalism in Admissions August 2013.

Mountford-Zimdars, A. (2015), Contest and adjustment sponsorship in the selection of elites: Re-visiting Turner's mobility modes for England through an analysis of undergraduate admissions at Oxford University. *Sociologie* 62(2), pp. 157–176.

Mountford-Zimdars, A. (2016), *Meritocracy and the University: Selective Admission in England and the U.S.* London and New York: Bloomsbury.

Mountford-Zimdars, A., Sabri, D., Moore, J., Sanders, J., Jones, S., and Higham, L. (July 23, 2015), *Causes of Differences in Student Outcomes, Higher Education Funding Council for England, HEFCE.* London: Bloomsbury.

National Association for College Admission Counseling (NACAC) (2011), State of college admission report. NACAC. Available for purchase at: http://www.nacac-net.org/research/PublicationsResources/Marketplace/research/Pages/Stateof-CollegeAdmission.aspx

Ogg, T., Zimdars, A., and Heath, A. (2009), Schooling effects on degree performance: A comparison of the predictive validity of aptitude testing and secondary school grades at Oxford University. *British Educational Research Journal* 35(5), p. 781.

Partington, R., Carroll, D., and Chetwynd, P. (2011), *Predictive Effectiveness of Metrics in Admission to the University of Cambridge.* University of Cambridge. Available at: http://www.admin.cam.ac.uk/offices/admissions/research/a_levels.html

Schwartz, S. (2004), *Fair Admissions to Higher Education: Recommendations for Good Practice.* Nottingham: DfES.

Shavit, Y., Arum, R., and Gamoran, A. (eds) (2007), *Stratification in Higher Education.* Stanford: Stanford University Press.

Stevens, M. (2007), *Creating a Class: College Admissions and the Education of Elites.* Boston: Harvard University Press.

Stone, P. (2014), Access to Higher Education by the Luck of the Draw. In Mountford-Zimdars, A., Sabbagh, D. and Post, D. (eds) (2014) *Fair Access to Higher Education: Global Perspectives.* Chicago: University of Chicago Press, pp. 248–270.

Supporting Professionalism in Admissions (SPA) (2015), *SPA's Use of Contextualised Admissions Survey Report 2015 (with HEDIIP).* Cheltenham: SPA.

Taylor, T., Rees, G., Sloan, L., and Davies, R. (2013), Creating an inclusive higher education system? Progression and Outcomes of Students from Low Participation Neighbourhoods at a Welsh University. *Contemporary Wales* 26, p. 138.

Thomsen, J. P. (2012), Exploring the heterogeneity of class in higher education: Social and cultural differentiation in Danish University Programmes. *British Journal of Sociology of Education* 33(4), pp. 565–585.

Turner, R. H. (1966), Acceptance of Irregular Mobility in Britain and the United States. *Sociometry* 29, pp. 334–352.

University of Edinburgh (2015), *Student Recruitment & Admissions Briefing: Contextual Data in Undergraduate Admissions at the University of Edinburgh.* Edinburgh: University of Edinburgh.

Zimdars, A. (2007), *Challenges to meritocracy? A study of the social mechanisms in student selection and attainment at the University of Oxford.* DPhil. University of Oxford.

Chapter 14

Diversifying admissions through top-down entrance examination reform in Japanese elite universities

What is happening on the ground?

Beverley Anne Yamamoto

The notion that Japanese university-bound students face an almost unprecedented period of 'examination hell' during upper secondary school in order to pass difficult admissions tests has been transmitted well beyond the borders of this island nation. The image of students in pristine uniforms, sitting tidily behind small wooden desks, packed 40 or more in a classroom, all studying diligently for exams, is an enduring one. Yet, in the context of a declining population and the over-expansion of new universities in the early 1990s, Japan is now experiencing an era of so-called full admissions, or *zennyū jidai*, where there is a place for any student wanting to advance on to an institution of higher education. Competition remains only at the top in the prestigious national and elite private universities. Lower-tier and even medium-tier institutions are competing with each other for too few students and have already made changes in how they admit students. With the mathematics of admissions against them, many lower-tiered universities cannot meet quotas.

While competition may remain fierce at the top of the Japanese university hierarchy, even here the elite institutions are under pressure to diversify admission procedures. This is less about meeting quotas and more about 'nurturing' (*ikusei*) a certain kind of graduate. In order to create the next generation of leaders, top-tier universities are under pressure to play a role in nurturing 'global *jinzai*' or global human resources who, it is hoped, will give Japan a competitive edge in the global market place. As such, universities are under pressure to recognise scholastic abilities nurtured in a wider variety of educational settings, in Japan and overseas, as well to take into account learner competencies and attributes that have hitherto not been a part of the admissions process.

The pressure is coming from the Ministry of Education, Culture, Sports Science and Technology (MEXT) which in turn is under pressure from the business sector, as well as the Ministry of Finance and the Cabinet Office. They argue that in an era of intense global business competition and the 'informationisation' (*jōhōka*) of society, schools and universities should be responding by creating global *jinzai* (Central Council for Education, 2014: 1; Council for the Promotion of Human Resources for Globalization Development, 2011). Diversification of the admissions process offers the possibility of a more nuanced concept of objectivity and equity/fairness (*heikōsei*) in competition for places at top-tier universities (Central Council for Education, 2014: 5). Nevertheless, critics counter that the 'new concept of scholastic ability' (*atarashii gakuryokukan*) promoted by the Central Council for Education and MEXT, with its emphasis on 'more complex and subjective considerations such as students' motivations and personal concerns and interests, or varying ways of "discovering and solving problems"' (Kariya, 2013: 15) will result in differences of cultural capital within the home having an even greater influence on the outcome of selection processes at secondary and post-secondary levels (Kariya, 2013: 15).

This chapter offers an overview of some of the key currents and discourses around university admissions and access in Japan focusing particularly, but not exclusively, on the top-ranked institutions. It then takes as a case study, Osaka University, a top national university, to dig a little deeper into practice by pointing to some of the issues that face those involved in reforming admissions on the ground. Key questions addressed in this chapter are:

1   What vision does the discourse of 'diversifying admissions' encompass and what are its limits?
2   How are practitioners on the ground implementing top-down, admissions reform policy in these early stages of the reform process? In what way is admissions practice changing?
3   What equity issues arise or are likely to arise as a result of both discourse and practice on admissions?

Diversity of the HE sector in Japan

The HE sector in Japan is marked by considerable diversity, with four types of post-secondary institutions (see Table 14.1): universities offering four-year undergraduate degree programs as well as graduate master's and doctoral programs;

Table 14.1 Higher education institutions in Japan by management type, student numbers by gender (figures as of 1 May 2014)

	Total	National	Public	Private	Students Total (1,000)	Male (1,000)	Female (1,000)
Universities	781	86	92	603	2,855	1,635	1,220
Graduate schools	623	86	77	460	251	173	78
Junior colleges	352	–	18	334	137	16	121
Colleges of technology	57	51	3	3	58	48	10
Specialized vocational colleges	3,206	10	195	3,001	659	294	365

Source: Statistics Bureau, 2015, table 16.1.

junior colleges offering two-year associate degrees; colleges of technology, or *kōsen*, offering 'high-level vocational qualifications' (Newby et al., 2009: 11), and special vocational training colleges offering five-year programs that straddle upper and post-secondary (Ishida, 2007: 63–64; Newby et al., 2009: 11–12). These institutions may be funded at a national level, at a prefectural or city level (referred to as public universities) or privately usually through educational foundations that may also include primary and secondary schools.

The University of Tokyo was the first (est. 1877) of nine imperial universities to be established in Japan and its colonial territories and remains Japan's most prestigious university through to this day (University of Tokyo, 2015).

By 1939 another six imperial universities had been created in mainland Japan, including Osaka University. In addition, one had been created in Korea, today Seoul National University, and one in Tawian, today National Taiwan University, while under Japanese rule. Post-war reforms meant that the seven mainland imperial universities became national universities (*kokuritsu daigaku*), but remained under direct control of MEXT. Today these seven institutions continue to carry the prestige of being 'former imperial' universities. These are 'comprehensive, multi-faculty, predominantly research-led institutions' that are able to compete on an international level (Newby et al., 2009: 14). They are highly competitive in terms of entrance, particularly at the undergraduate level.

Today there is a total of 86 'national' universities including the seven former imperial universities. These generally have highly competitive entry requirements, subsidised tuition and low academic staff ratios. While highly competitive, the expectation has always been that anyone can enter, regardless of background, if they work hard and are able to pass the entrance examinations (Kariya, 2013: 104).

In addition to the national universities, there are another 89 public universities (*kōritsu daigaku*) run by municipalities. While not as prestigious, they still rank above many of the private universities. Each has a 'particular local or regional focus . . . and/or are of a specialist professional or technical character' (Newby et al., 2009: 14). Charging low tuition, they are attractive to students from a variety of backgrounds.

The majority of universities in Japan are private and these institutions enrol the bulk (2.1 million) of Japan's 2.8 million undergraduate students. The private universities vary greatly in status, with some top institutions that are highly competitive to enter while others are unable to meet government designated quotas. The number of private universities continued to increase into the 1990s even though Japan was already experiencing population decline (Newby et al., 2009: 15). While private universities receive subsidies from MEXT, they rely heavily on examination and tuition fees to survive. The third- and even some second-tier institutions are squeezed by a lack of students in this 'full admissions' era (Kinmonth, 2005: 113).

Not only are there a large number of institutions with different funding bases, there is also a well-noted range of quality (Eades, 2005: 297–299). As a result, while we may be in an era of 'full admissions', the value of the education received and its currency value as social capital is far from equal even at the university level.

The distinctive features of the Japanese HE sector

Ishida Hiroshi (2007: 64–67) identified four distinctive features of the HE sector in Japan: a high level of gender segregation, hierarchy, but low mobility between the layers, strong control by central government and direct entrance for most students to university after graduation from high school.

Gender segregation

Women are more likely than men to choose to go to junior college than four-year university (Table 14.2). At peak levels of enrolment in 2004, 90 percent of the 234,000 students enrolled in junior colleges were female (Ishida, 2007: 64). Offering 'non-technical courses in home economics, education and the humanities' (Ishida, 2007: 64), junior colleges are regarded by many parents, students and employers as the perfect post-secondary location for women (Jolivet, 1997: 45).

Women are underrepresented in the most prestigious universities, and especially in the STEM subjects. They are overrepresented in the humanities, in health sciences, other than medicine and dentistry, and in home economics and early education (Gender Equality Bureau, Cabinet Office, 2015: Chapter 8).

Lack of mobility between institutions

Although it is possible to 'top up' an associate degree from a junior college and qualifications from the vocational colleges to degree level (Newby et al., 2009: 16), there is little movement between these four tiers of post-secondary institutions. As a result, where students enter the system matters (Ishida, 2007: 65–66). Despite most universities offering the possibility of transfer at the beginning of the third year, there is relatively little movement. The difficulty of the entrance exams acts as a barrier to transfer to more competitive universities (Ishida, 2007: 66).

Ministry control

The Japanese HE sector is under the strict supervision of MEXT (Ishida, 2007: 66). The NUCs now have greater decision making powers, but in a recent OECD country report it was noted that the reins are still kept overly tight (Newby et al.,

Table 14.2 Advancement rates from high school to university and/or junior college (percentage of the age cohort)

2015	Total	Male	Female
University and junior college	54.5	52.1	56.9
University	51.5	55.4	47.4
Junior college	5.1	1.1	9.3

Source: e-stats, 2015: Table nen004.

2009: 19). As the current demand for admissions reform makes clear, the government and MEXT can still heavily influence fundamental decisions made by universities.

Dependent on the government for funding, control of universities takes place in a number of ways, not least the linking of major funding to particular goals and requirements. The latest Super (Top) Global University funding is a case in point, and it is through this that the top-tier universities are being persuaded to diversify their admissions. While private universities may have to raise tuition fees to generate income and manage budgets, they are not 'private' in the sense of having autonomy over what they offer or how they offer it. Whether national, public or private, 'the basic control mechanism has not changed until the present time' (Ishida, 2007: 66).

Few second chances

A final distinctive feature of the Japanese HE sector is that 'the transition from secondary to postsecondary schools is sequential' (Ishida, 2007: 66), meaning that students rarely take a break unless seeking to re-sit entrance exams for prestigious programs.

The point of entry is important. If a student enters at junior college level, they are unlikely later to go on to university. If they enter a university that is ranked low, it is unlikely they will be able to move up to a more prestigious institution later. Thus, students get stuck at the level they enter post-secondary education, and this in turn impacts their future career trajectory.

Access to higher education in Japan and equity issues

The background to the *zennyū* (full admissions) phenomenon is the expansion of the upper secondary and then post-secondary sector in the late 20th century. By the 1980s, the advancement rate to high school had reached 95 percent for males and 93 percent for females (Gender Equality Bureau, 2015: 25). As Japanese high schools are 'sharply ranked by difficulty of entry' (Kariya, 2013: 11), this change was epochal, establishing 'educational *selection* as a mass phenomenon' (Kariya, 2013: 12, emphasis added).

The universalisation of upper secondary education was followed by a steady increase in high school students going to university or junior college from 23.6 percent in 1970 (17.1 percent going to university and 6.5 percent to junior college) to the levels seen in Table 14.2. While Ishida depicts the expansion of higher education as one of the major transformations that took place in post-war Japan (Ishida, 2007: 63), Kariya argues that in terms of selection it only built on the more significant transformation of the universalisation of high school education (Kariya, 2013: 12), resulting in both increased opportunities for students, but also refinement in selection practices with nearly universal selection at secondary level.

Tsuneyoshi demonstrates that for the privileged, selection through entrance examinations has shifted even further down the school system (Tsuneyoshi, 2013: 166). In the more affluent urban centres, where there is stiff competition to enter prestigious private combined junior/high schools, education selection often starts at primary level and is more extreme in that it is often separated from what students study as part of the National Curriculum (Tsuneyoshi, 2013: 166). Thus notwithstanding where it takes place, the late 20th century saw the rapid expansion of 'social selection by way of education' so that today it is a mass phenomenon in Japan (Kariya, 2013: 11).

Expansion of higher education and persistence of social inequalities

While the 1990s saw the expansion of HE, inequalities in access to post-secondary education were not reduced. Today, parental education continues to have a strong impact on a student's educational attainment. Ishida investigated the 'changes and stability of educational opportunities' at the post-secondary level across the country across four age cohorts, taking into account the hierarchy of institutions in Japan concluding that

> [T]he impact of parental education was substantial and persistent across cohorts. Sons and daughters of parents with low levels of education were disadvantaged at virtually all stages of educational advancement. This finding suggests that in addition to economic and social resources, parents' cultural resources are highly consequential to the educational achievement of their offspring.
>
> (Ishida, 2007: 85)

The exception to the above trend was the gender gap in post-secondary education, which 'had been reduced substantially in the postwar period' (Ishida, 2007: 84). By the early 1970s, young women were as likely as young men to complete high school education and by the 1990s they were almost as likely to go on to university as their male peers. Nevertheless, as discussed above, gender segregation has remained (Arimoto, 2015: 1).

The persistence of inequality of access to higher education should not come as a surprise. The expansion of the HE sector in the 1980s and 1990s was not accompanied with a specific policy to reduce the inequalities in access to higher education (Ishida, 2007: 85). Socio-economic background received little attention in educational research or policy making as it was felt that that if you worked hard anyone could get into a good university. Where differences in ability were acknowledged, the problem was framed as how to ensure that students with lower ability did not feel inferior (Kariya, 2013: 57–58).

In what was perceived to be a meritocratic system, the role of MEXT and the universities was to ensure that tests measured ability and not family background. Entrance examinations with multiple choice questions were regarded as objective and fair. They were regarded as class neutral and accessible to 'all who put their minds to working hard' (*ganbareba dekiru*). Yet, as Kariya Takehiko argues, this idea has served to hide 'social class disparities in education opportunity from sight' rather than remedy them (Kariya, 2013: 104).

It is noteworthy, therefore, that the current discourse around admissions generated by MEXT and the Central Council for Education, a policy think tank, challenges the idea that examination testing is fair and objective. It demands universities radically re-think what is 'fair' and 'meritocratic' in an era of diversity and globalisation.

The movement to reform university admission in top-tier universities

Admissions reform: Gakuryoku and AO admissions

Universities are asked to change how they carry out admissions, meaning how and what is used to assess students in the selection process. This may be viewed as a response to the new and emerging concepts of learning that focus not only on knowledge acquisition, but also that of skills, competencies and attitudes and the newly articulated ideal of attracting students with diverse learning backgrounds. At a basic level, it is a reaction to changes in demographics that have made competitive university admissions a practice of the past for many institutions.

When competition remained in the system, Japanese university admissions practices focused heavily on assessing students' *gakuryoku* or basic scholastic ability, which in the national and public universities were measured by two layers of written examinations, one managed centrally by MEXT (the Central National University Admissions Examination – hereafter 'Centre Exam') and the second set institutionally by universities.

In an era of full admissions, however, third- and even second-tier universities have moved to more flexible admissions procedures focusing on the Admissions Office Entrance Examinations (AO *nyūshi*), which amounts to selection based on documentary screening and an interview. It is looked on as a way that less competitive universities do 'selection' in an attempt to meet quotas (Katase, 2008: 31; Kinmonth, 2005: 121). As Kinmonth astutely notes, 'AO *nyūshi* – a blend of American and Japanese terminology is an oxymoron in that typically no "entrance examination" (*nyūshi*) as such is required' (Kinmonth, 2005: 121). For less competitive institutions, the screening is no longer to assess academic ability, but a ritual exercise that is practiced in order to give the impression that universities are selecting students, when the reality is that students and/or those advising them are selecting the universities. In these institutions admissions has moved from 'selection to seduction' (Kinmonth, 2005).

On the student side, the rigours of 'examination hell' remain only for those with elite aspirations. For the vast majority, the university application and selection process has been reduced to a consideration of 'the relative attractiveness of competing admission offers from a large number of colleges and universities desperate to fill places and generate enough tuition revenue to avoid bankruptcy' (Kinmonth, 2005: 106). With competition taken out of the system, high schools, which previously had focused almost exclusively on examination preparation, find themselves no longer totally sure what their role should be.

The call for admissions reform

Despite the hitherto low status of AO admissions in Japan, elite institutions are under pressure to diversify admission procedures by incorporating or expanding AO admissions in order to recognise scholastic abilities nurtured in a wider variety of educational settings in Japan and overseas, as well as to take into account learner competencies, experiences and attributes that have not been part of the admissions process.

Those in the pro-reform lobby argue that the current Centre Exam system focuses too much on testing the reproduction of narrowly defined 'basic knowledge' (*kiso gakuryoku*) and does not encourage students to be inquirers, risk takers, communicators, internationally minded or output any of the other 21st-century learning competencies that are generally recognised as being integral to global *jinzai* or a global elite class (Resnik, 2008: 147, 153). The desire to see schools and universities produce global *jinzai* has led to a government-led project to introduce the International Baccalaureate Diploma into 200 high schools (upper secondary level) in Japan (see Yamamoto et al., 2016).

In 2013, the Education Rebuilding Council released a report on the transition from upper secondary (high school) to post-secondary (university) and noted the importance of universities introducing multifaceted and comprehensive assessments and evaluations for student selections and university admissions (Education Rebuilding Council, 2013: 7). This report encouraged universities to go beyond assessing students' scholastic abilities in admission screening, to include competencies, motivations and readiness to enter college, as well as previous activities and experiences.

Following on from this, the Central Council for Education (2014) also issued a report about the need to reform the current entrance examination system in the elite national universities. It calls for critical thinking, decision-making and communication skills to be taken into account over and above basic scholastic abilities or *gakuryoku* (Central Council for Education, 2014: 15).

The Council also criticises the lack of transparency around admissions policy even though universities and departments are now required to produce an Admissions Policy for students and other stakeholders. These are criticised as being overly abstract and largely disconnected from the admissions practice (Central Council for Education, 2014: 11).

Surprisingly, the government-level discourse on admissions points out that the hitherto system is exclusive rather than inclusive. The Central Council for

Education argues that admissions practice has not recognised or valued the achievements or possible contribution of students who have studied outside the mainstream national curriculum, including students from international schools in Japan or those who have studied overseas; students who have gone straight out into society and worked and students with disabilities, among others. The Council calls for admissions to recognise the full range of student learning prior to university, formal and non-formal, and to measure a students' 'solid academic capabilities' (*tashikana nōryoku*) rather than simply scholastic ability as measured by *gakuryoku* tests (Central Council for Education, 2014: 1).

Finally, the report argues that with universities and faculties/departments within universities setting different standards of admission, procedures are overly complex and burdensome, thus calling for the professionalisation of admissions with staff trained to evaluate scholastic ability and more general selection methods (Central Council for Education, 2014: 27). This is not entirely new for private universities, but in the elite national universities admissions has been one of many rotated administrative responsibilities.

The same report also outlined ways in which the current system of admissions negatively impacts education both at high school and university levels. It proposes a refocus for middle-stratum high schools (*chūkan sō*), away from entrance examination preparation towards developing knowledge, critical thinking skills, communication skills and decision-making skills (Central Council for Education, 2014: 4).

The Council also notes that in high schools where 'disparities in home environment and income have meant that the majority of students find the "hitherto *gakuryoku* model" overly challenging, the task of just graduating students is already more than many of these schools can cope with' (Central Council for Education, 2014: 4). The implication is that students are poorly prepared for entrance into universities, that in turn are poorly prepared to teach such students.

Plans to abandon the Centre Examination

As a part of a major reform of the admissions process, the current format of the Centre Examination will be abandoned and a new means of testing potential entrants for admissions will be implemented by 2021. Designated institutions will be piloting the new exam in its first stage from 2017 so there is great anticipation and debate about what it will look like. The new test has been tentatively named the *Daigaku kibōsha gakuryoku hyōka tesuto* ("Evaluative Test of Scholastic Ability for Those Desiring to Enter University") (Central Council for Education, 2014: 15–18).

The new test will evaluate at multiple levels using all or many of the following: essay, interviews, presentations, group debate, high school transcripts, records of experiments or study projects conducted at schools, personal statement about motivations for wanting to study at university, plan of study, qualifications and certificates. By evaluating in multiple ways, the selection team will be able to assess the 'solid academic capabilities' of the candidate (Central Council for Education,

2014: 27). The new admissions exam will take into account not only knowledge and skills, but also critical thinking, decision-making capabilities, judgement, autonomy, diversity and collaborative skills.

At the same time, the high schools will be required to assess their students using the tentatively named *kōkō kiso gakuryoku tesuto* ("High School Test of Basic Academic Abilities"), which will assess students on a 10-point scale in a variety of areas. The aim is to measure in an objective way what students themselves have achieved academically while in high school. Through the use of such a test it is expected that student motivation will be stimulated (Central Council for Education, 2014: 17). To date, there has been no standardised test for students leaving either lower or upper secondary education. The results of this test should also be used in the new university admissions testing.

Recent university funding, especially the Top Global University (originally called Super Global University initiative) funding, has been linked specifically to expanding the range of assessment in admission. The 37 universities that were awarded funding are required to recognise alternative forms of university entrance certification including the International Baccalaureate, the Advanced Placement Test and to use these instead of the scholastic ability (*gakuryoku*) tests.

The response of Osaka University – *Sekai Tekijuku Nyūshi*

This section considers how practitioners on the ground are implementing top-down admissions reform policy in these early stages of the reform process.

In 2014, Osaka University was one of 13 universities awarded Type A funding from the Top Global University project funding indicating it has capacity to be ranked in the top 100 of international universities within the next 10 years (MEXT, 2014).

In line with its application, Osaka University established a Global Admissions Office (GAO)[1] with staff hired specifically to engage in the recruiting and selection of students from overseas or from schools offering the International Baccalaureate Diploma in Japan. GAO seeks through a 'comprehensive screening process' to 'develop outstanding graduates with a high sense of ethics and international-mindedness, capable of displaying leadership in a variety of fields' (GAO Osaka University, 2015). GAO is tasked with screening students from overseas for both Japanese- and English-language taught programs, for short-term programs and students who have been educated in programs outside or within Japan but who have studied programs that go beyond the Japanese national curriculums. The latter category includes students who have taken the International Baccalaureate Diploma, or studied at a school offering the Super Global High School program or at a Super Science High School. The additional study these students have undertaken cannot be measured adequately through the current Centre Exam system. The emphasis within GAO is on admissions that involves comprehensive screening, especially interviewing and essay submissions.

GAO is charged not only with selection, but also knowledge production around admissions. Its role is to 'study and research secondary school education systems, national common examinations, and university entrance examinations and systems' around the world (Osaka University, 2015). It is tasked with creating a new entrance examination for privately funded international students, as well as the collection and analysis of data and information about university admissions overseas, including the responsibilities and qualifications of admissions staff.

The framing of the GAO mission represents the professionalisation of admissions procedures at a university level hitherto not seen at Osaka University and few other national universities. However, with funding of the office based at the moment on temporary funding, the sustainability of this model is questionable. In addition, given the substantial power over admissions that remains at the school or faculty level, it is also debatable whether a small team of temporary staff can implement radical changes to admissions.

Alongside GAO and with considerable overlap, a new category of *Sekai Tekijuku Nyushi* or World *Tekijuku* Admissions has been created to select 25 percent of the student population across faculties and departments, using a form of AO admissions. This is overseen by a World *Tekijuku* Admissions Committee made up mostly of tenured professors seconded from different faculties. Each faculty or school had to propose alternative methods of screening students for *Tekijuku* Admissions to that of the two-tiered Centre Exam plus faculty-level exam.

The expectation held by many of us already involved in 'special admissions' for the undergraduate international programs taught in English was that the International Baccalaureate Diploma and a number of other internationally recognised examinations that serve as university entrance certification would be recognised so that a candidate would not have to take the Japanese Centre Exam. However, the first round of International *Tekijuku* Admissions suggests a reluctance to abandon it in the case of admissions for Japanese nationals or international students if schooled in Japan and entering regular Japanese-language instruction programs. Instead, there has been a layering on of demands so that the Centre Exam plus other requirements has been set.

A newly emerging idea is that of *gakuryoku* AO *nyūshi*, or admissions using a combination of the Centre Exam and the more holistic AO *nyūshi*. Students will have to get a certain score on the Centre Exam and then submit an internationally recognised university entrance certification, as well as school recommendations, project work and an IELTS/TOEFL score as evidence of English proficiency very much higher than required of students applying for programs delivered in Japanese through the traditional *gakuryoku* (two layers of testing) route.

There is a reluctance to move away from the known. While MEXT, among others, are pushing for reform of admissions, on the ground many key stakeholders are not convinced that there is a need. Unlike many universities, Osaka is still able to be highly selective and there is considerable confidence that we are able to get the most talented students following existing admissions practices.

Furthermore, key faculty members involved in *Tekijuku* Admissions do not want to change course content in any way or make adjustments in terms of teaching style. Again, there is confidence and comfort in the system as it is. A more diverse learning environment may be regarded as desirable by MEXT, but for those who would have to teach and adjust to such an environment it is perhaps an unwelcome challenge. Indeed, overall there is reform fatigue with so many changes being imposed from above.

Another area of concern is the maintenance of the reputation of the university as the 'quality' of the institution is measured by the 'quality' of the students entering, captured through their Centre Exam and *hensachi* scores. There is perhaps an unease that if 25 percent or more of students are coming in through alternative routes – some see it as a 'back door' – that the status of the university could be affected. In an attempt to ensure 'quality' as well as to comply with MEXT stipulations, old and new methods are being combined in a way that could work against diversity.

Clearly, the new World *Tekijuku* Admissions is a work in progress by people who are not specialists in AO – or international admissions. While those involved in GAO are supposed to be specialists, the lines of authority between these two groups working on admission is confused and poorly defined. In the future it is expected that the research and knowledge production generated by GAO will inform how AO admissions are done in the university as a whole. Yet decisions about how the practice of selecting students is conducted may not change if key stakeholders at the faculty level are not convinced.

The first round of *Tekijuku* Admissions could be interpreted as a stand against top-down admissions reform. While claiming to be holistic, the new *Tekijuku* Admissions will ensure that only a trickle of students can enter using this route. Those who will be able to meet requirements set by faculty-level World *Tekijuku* Admissions screening may end up being limited to those with enormous economic, social and cultural capital. How we select students is a highly sensitive and emotive area of debate internally and one that can garner strong opinions. Ideas of fairness, reliability and quality assurance are at the heart of discussions, but for some only the present model displays these essential elements.

What equity issues arise or are likely to arise as a result of both discourse and practice on admissions?

I would like to conclude this chapter by addressing the final question about equity of access. The intention of the proposed admissions reform is to stimulate both high school and university educational practice, by assessing students on a wider range of indicators than has hitherto been the case in top-tier universities. It is also to bring 'selection' based on essential skills, competencies and knowledge for institutions lower down the HE hierarchy. Over the past 20 years a noted disparity in educational attainment has opened up at the secondary level, with a divide between those students who have the motivation and resources (intellectual, economic, social and psychological) to compete for a place in a top university, and those who do not have elite university aspirations. We know that the cost of acquiring the out-of-school support in the form of *juku* education that is usually required to get a place in a top-tier university is prohibitively high for some families.

Attempts have been made over the past 20 years to make high school accessible to all students regardless of parental background (Yamamoto et al., 2016). Yet, *juku* attendance has become an essential part of entrance examination preparation, with 64 percent of students in lower secondary school attending these supplementary institutions that in fact lead to a 'double schooling' situation (Mawer, 2015: 131–132). On top of this, an increasing number of university students are having to take out loans to attend university. With interest accrued, there is concern that an increasing number of university students are defaulting on these loans when they graduate (Ouchi, 2015: 69). While the proportion of students receiving 'scholarships' (*shōgakukin*), which in fact are loans, had long been steady at roughly 20 percent through to the mid-1990s, this rose dramatically thereafter to reaching 52.5 percent in 2012 (Ouchi, 2015: 70–71).

Ouchi Hirokazu, in a study of student loan uptake and loan default, argues that the changes that occurred in the 1990s were not only quantitative but also qualitative (Ouchi, 2015: 71). The inappropriately named *scholarships* went from being 'something used by a small number of students from economically deprived families to over half of all students going to university' (Ouchi, 2015: 71). One of the reasons for this change is the massification of higher education resulting in more students continuing on to university from families that are not particularly well off. In addition, many young women who previously would have attended the cheaper two-year junior colleges are now taking four-year courses at more expensive universities (Ouchi, 2015: 72–73).

At the same time, since 1995 there has been a steady decline in the average income of households supporting students. While in 1994, the peak for household income, the average household income was 6.64 million yen, by 2012 this had dropped to 5.37 million yen. As a result of 'the decrease in household income of those supporting tuition fees and the lifestyle of university students' over half the population are now taking out loans (Ouchi, 2015: 74). Most of these loans accrue interest and repayment begins from when the student reaches 23 years of age regardless of income and are paid back over 15 years. Most students graduate at age 22 (Ouchi, 2015: 78). An increasing proportion of student loans are being extended beyond 15 years by graduates attempting to survive on very low incomes (Ouchi, 2015: 80).

The rising cost of *juku* and of university education in the face of declining household incomes means that for the poorest 18-year-olds university is already prohibitively expensive. If in addition, economic and social capital is needed to navigate the system prior to university entrance due to changes to the admissions system, we may find that family background has an even greater impact on university entrance.

Abandoning the Centre Exam and university-based entrance exams that require high-level memorisation and exam technique may help those who cannot afford *juku* to join the competition. However, if a written entrance examination measuring *kiso gakuryoku* is not abandoned, the need for supplementary schooling may not lessen. If then along with this, additional demands such as expensive English proficiency testing, overseas experience, internships and other experiences that require cultural and social capital are layered on top, the admission reforms could, counter to expectations, serve to further reproduce social divisions and obstruct social mobility.

For the proposed reform of admissions outlined by MEXT and articulated by the Central Council for Education to realise their aims, monitoring data needs to be collected to see what impact these changes bring. At different levels of the system, who benefits and who loses? At the same time, attention needs to focus not only on the point of entry, but the impact of diversification of admissions on the ideal content and delivery of teaching and learning. As educators, we should be working to help students realise the potential they bring to university, whether viewed as knowledge, skills, competencies, experiences or motivations. As the Central Council for Education envisions, reform needs to extend to both high school and university education. Those involved in admissions need to monitor through data collection the impact of these reforms on access to education by family background. This would be a radical step forward.

Conclusion

We have seen how Japan has a highly diverse and hierarchical HE sector, with access structured by class, age and gender. Hitherto, enormous trust has been placed on the reliability and efficacy of *gakuryoku* testing at a single point in time just before university entrance. In the context of demographic changes, globalisation and the informationisation of society, the current system has been breaking down. Many lower-level institutions, rather than selecting students, are attempting to 'seduce' them into entering. The idea of AO admissions in these institutions is something of a smokescreen, giving the appearance that selection is going on when in fact it is not. Yet, with huge real and perceived differences in 'quality' between institutions, just getting to university does not necessary mean that much.

For some students, the reality of full admissions makes high school something of a nonsense: why bother studying when learning has been defined in terms of learning for exams? It is also clear that the schools themselves are not entirely sure what they are supposed to be teaching their pupils in this age of full admissions. On the other hand, the continued use of *gakuryoku* testing through university entrance exams for the more competitive is similarly seen to negatively impact the learning that occurs at high school. The call is for a wider range of knowledge, skills, competencies and experience to be recognised and valued in the selection process. It is expected that this will diversify access to top universities.

As we have seen, however, there are still many obstacles to be overcome in order for the vision contained in the Central Council for Education's report to be realised and for admissions to diversity in a way that brings equity and fairness. Diversifying admissions should not be mistaken with adding more items of examination in the selection process. Adding items for assessment that add further burdens on to the current *gakuryoku* testing regime may further polarise admissions by excluding those from non-privileged backgrounds, and those who would like to come back to study at a later stage in their life course. The reform of the admissions system needs to be properly monitored to make sure we know who is benefiting or not from the changes.

Note

1 The Global Admissions Office was renamed the Center for the Study of Higher Education and Global Admissions as of September 1, 2016.

References

Arimoto, A. 2015. Introduction: The changing academic profession in Japan: Its past and present. In Arimoto, A., Cummings, W., Huang, F., Shin, J.C. (eds.). *The Changing Academic Profession in Japan*. London: Springer, pp. 1–26.

Central Council for Education. 2014. Atarashii jidai ni fusawashii kōdaisetsuzoku no jitsugen ni muketa kōtōgakkō kyōiku, daigakukyōiku, daigakunyūshi senbatsu no ittaiteki kaikaku ni tsuite [Holistic reform of high school education, university education, and university admissions and selections in order to establish the high school and university connection suitable in this new age]. Retrieved from: http://www.mext.go.jp/b_menu/shingi/chukyo/chukyo0/toushin/__icsFiles/afield-file/2015/01/14/1354191.pdf (Accessed 15 May 2015).

Council for the Promotion of Human Resources for Globalization Development. 2011 *Gurobaru jinzai ikusei suishin iinkai chūkan matome* (Council for the Promotion of Human Resources for Globalization Development Interim Report). Retrieved from: http://www.kantei.go.jp/jp/singi/global/110622chukan_matome.pdf (Accessed 21 December 2015).

Eades, J. 2005. The Japanese 21st center of excellence program: Internationalisation in action? In Eades, J. S., Goodman, R., Hada, Y. (eds.). *The 'Big Bang' in Japanese Higher Education: The 2004 Reforms and the Dynamics of Change (Japanese Society Series)*. Victoria: Trans Pacific Press, pp. 295–323.

Education Rebuilding Council. 2013. *Kōtō gakkō kyōiku to daigaku kyōiku tono setsuzoku daigaku nyūgakusha senbatsu no arikata ni tsuite (Dai 4 ji teigen)* [Connections between high school and university education: Concerning the way students are examined for university entrance (Fourth round of recommendations]. Retrieved from: http://www.kantei.go.jp/jp/singi/kyouikusaisei/pdf/dai4_1.pdf (Accessed 21 December 2015).

e-stats. 2015. *Gakkō kihon chōsa* (Basic school survey). Retrieved from: http://www.e-stat.go.jp/SG1/estat/List.do?bid=000001015843. (Accessed 26 November 2015).

GAO Osaka University. 2015. *Global Admissions Office*. Retrieved from: http://www.osaka-u.ac.jp/en/academics/ed_support/gao/office (Accessed 17 October 2015).

Gender Equality Bureau, Cabinet Office. 2015. *Women and Men in Japan, 2015: Gender Equality Bureau, Cabinet Office.* Retrieved from: http://www.gender. go.jp/english_contents/pr_act/pub/pamphlet/women-and-men15/index.html (Accessed 2 December 2015).

Ishida, H. 2007. Japan: Educational expansion and inequality in access to higher education. In Shavint, R., Arum, R., Gamoran, A. (eds.). *Stratification in Higher Education.* Stanford, CA: Stanford University Press, pp. 63–86.

Jolivet, M. 1997. *Japan the Childless Society?* London: Routledge.

Kariya, T. 2013. *Education Reform and Social Class in Japan: The Emerging Incentive Divide.* Abingdon Oxfordshire: Routledge.

Katase, K. 2008. *AO nyūshi ni kansuru shiron: Kyōyō gakubu ni okeru AO nyūshi nyūgakusha no seiseki no suii wo jirei ni* [A note on Admission Office entrance: Based on a case study of the scores of applicants for the Faculty of Liberal Arts]. Tohoku Gakuin University Education Research Institute 8, pp. 31–45. Retrieved from: http://www.tohoku-gakuin.ac.jp/facilities/institute/education/pdf/pub08_03. pdf (Accessed 15 May 2015).

Kinmonth, E. H. 2005. From selection to seduction: The impact of demographic change on private higher education in Japan. In Eades, J. S., Goodman, R., Hada Y. (eds). *The 'Big Bang' in Japanese Higher Education: The 2004 Reforms and the Dynamics of Change (Japanese Society Series).* Victoria: Trans Pacific Press, pp. 106–135.

Mawer, K. 2015. 'Casting new light on shadow education: Snapshots of *juku* variety'. *Contemporary Japan* 27(2), pp. 131–148.

MEXT. 2013. *Heisei 26 nendo kokkōritsu daigaku nyūgakusha senbatsu no gaiyō* [Year of 2014 Descriptions of university admissions at national and public universities]. Retrieved from: http://www.mext.go.jp/b_menu/houdou/25/09/1339253. htm (Accessed 15 May 2015).

MEXT. 2014. *Selection for the FY 2014 Top Global University Project*, Press Release. MEXT, September 2014.

Newby, H., Weko, T., Breneman, D., Johanneson, T., Maassen, P. 2009. *OECD Reviews of Tertiary Education: JAPAN.* Pairs: OECD.

Ouchi, H. 2015. Nihon no shōgakukin mondai (The issue of university student scholarships). *The Journal of Educational Sociology* 96, pp. 69–86.

Resnik, J. 2008. The construction of the global worker through international education. In Resnik, J. (ed). *The Production of Educational Knowledge in the Global Era.* Rotterdam: Sense Publishers, pp. 147–167.

Tsuneyoshi, R. 2013. Junior high school entrance examinations in metropolitan Tokyo: The advantages and costs of privilege. In DeCocker, G., Bjork, C. (eds). *Japanese Education in an Era of Globalization.* New York: Teachers College, Columbia University, pp. 164–182.

Statistics Bureau, Ministry of Internal Affairs and Communications eds. 2015. *Statistical Handbook of Japan, 2015.* Tokyo: Statistics Bureau, Ministry of Internal Affairs and Communications.

University of Tokyo. 2015. *About UTokyo: Chronology.* Retrieved from: http:// www.u-tokyo.ac.jp/en/about/chronology.html. (Accessed 22 September 2015)

Yamamoto, BA, Saito, T, Shibuya, M, Ishikura, Y, Gyenes, A, Kim, V, Mawer, K and Kitano, C. 2016. *Implementation and Impact of the Dual Language International Baccalaureate Diploma Programme (DP) in Japanese Secondary Schools.* Bethesda, MD, USA. International Baccalaureate Organization. Retrieved from: http:// www.ibo.org/research/programme-impact-research/diploma-studies/. (Accessed 20 September 2016).

Chapter 15

The mobility imperative

English students and 'fair' access to international higher education

Rachel Brooks and Johanna Waters

Introduction

Studying overseas for higher education can now offer financial benefits to English students, when compared with enrolling at a domestic university. Indeed, undergraduate tuition fees in England are currently the highest in Europe (European Commission, 2012), with only Australia, Canada and the US offering 'more expensive' degrees. Within an increasingly competitive international market, many European universities appear to offer particularly good value for money and, since the introduction of higher tuition fees in England in 2012, have often actively targeted English students. It is not, however, only financial concerns which may cause English students to look abroad. It has been suggested that for those students who fall short of the ABB threshold at A-level (at which universities have been able to offer as many places as they like)[1] but are keen to study at a high-status university, overseas universities may seem more accessible than their Russell Group counterparts (Collinson, 2012).

Given this context, in this chapter we draw on two main sources of evidence to assess the extent to which access to international higher education, on the part of English students, can be considered 'fair'. We first consider the characteristics and social location of young adults from England who have either studied for a degree overseas, or were seriously considering doing so. Here, our analysis is based on 85 in-depth qualitative interviews. Second, we draw on a detailed analysis of 40 school websites to explore the messages that students in England are given about overseas study, and the extent to which this varies by both school type and social location. We conclude by arguing that while there is some evidence that specific types of international mobility, such as the work placement scheme offered as part of the Erasmus programme, may be available to students from a wider range of backgrounds (Deakin, 2014), access to the majority of mobility opportunities remains socially differentiated, and a realistic possibility for only a small and privileged minority of young people.

Background

It is now well documented that international student mobility brings considerable advantage to both the host country and institution. Within the UK, for example, recent research has demonstrated the very significant economic contributions made by overseas students, both to individual institutions, through the fees they pay, and to the wider community they live in. Indeed, it is estimated that, in 2011–12, international students studying at UK higher education institutions paid £3.9 billion in tuition fees and £6.3 billion in living expenses (BIS, 2013a). International students increase the cultural diversity of campuses and classrooms, thus enabling home students to develop their inter-cultural skills and understanding of other cultures (Jones and Brown, 2005). In addition, they can help to ensure the viability of some programmes, particularly postgraduate programmes in science, technology, engineering and mathematics, which tend to recruit relatively poorly among 'home' students (UUK, 2014). Benefits are also derived in the longer term, through the political and economic links that are forged between the UK and the home nation of those who are internationally mobile (BIS, 2013b). As a result, we have seen the emergence of an increasingly competitive global market for internationally mobile students.

The market is also driven by the actions of *sending* countries. While the UK has been reluctant to promote whole degree mobility (presumably because of a desire to ensure that students pay their fees in the UK rather than elsewhere), it has strongly encouraged mobility as part of a degree (what is often referred to as 'credit mobility') (e.g. UKHE International Unit, 2013). Non-governmental organisations are also involved in facilitating outward mobility. In the UK, the Sutton Trust operates a scheme to encourage students from disadvantaged backgrounds to study in the US. Moreover, at the regional level, the European Commission has set a target for 20 per cent of graduating students within European Higher Education Area having had an international mobility experience as part of their studies by 2020 (CEC, 2009). Whole degree mobility has also been actively encouraged by some nation-states. For example, Ye and Nylander (2015) show how the Singaporean government sponsors elite mobility to the universities of Oxford and Cambridge in the UK through the provision of scholarships (and institutional support via a number of elite colleges within Singapore). It does this, Ye and Nylander argue, 'in exchange for highly specialised professional expertise designed to uphold key functions within the state' (p.26) when the graduates enter the Singaporean labour market on their return (scholarship-holders are required to take up jobs in the civil service).

Considerable advantage also accrues to *individuals* who pursue their degree overseas, although this is differentiated by both sending nation and destination. In addition to the potential financial advantages of moving to a country charging lower fees, discussed above (see also Brooks and Waters, 2011), and the opportunity to gain access to elite institutions (Brooks and Waters, 2009), there is now a substantial body of literature that has documented the labour market advantages of those in possession of an overseas degree. First, an overseas education can provide access to educational qualifications that are more highly valued than their domestic equivalents. For example, Rizvi (2000) has argued that, in Malaysia, overseas qualifications have a particularly high status within the labour market; this thus encourages a large number of students to move abroad – often to Australia – to study for their degree. An overseas education can, however, offer more than simply a high status form of qualification. Indeed, Waters (2007) suggests that it is access into an elite culture, derived from association with other internationally mobile students, which is most significant – in the case of her research, for those entering the labour market in Hong Kong, after studying abroad. It is, however, important to recognise that these advantages are not played out in the same way for all international students. Indeed, Sin (2013), focussing, like Rizvi, on Malaysia, has contended that a more nuanced analysis is needed; not all overseas degrees have equal impact within the labour market. She demonstrates how overseas-educated graduates were sometimes disadvantaged by not having accumulated as much local cultural capital as those who remained in Malaysia for higher education and, in some cases, this made it more difficult to secure jobs with Malaysian employers that expected 'a more submissive interaction style, indicative of Asian reverence for authority and seniority' (p.860), rather than the more confident and assertive approach that may be developed during a Western higher education. Nevertheless, in general terms, an overseas education tends to be highly valued in economies across the world, and is sought by many students as a means of securing 'distinction' within increasingly congested national labour markets (Bodycott, 2009; Singh and Doherty, 2008; Wiers-Jensen, 2011).

An overseas education is also seen as facilitating entry to *global* labour markets. Brown et al. (2011) have argued cogently that the 'war for talent' has become globalised; prestigious graduate employers are increasingly recruiting internationally. This focus on foreign talent was justified, by their respondents, 'on grounds of an aging workforce, skill shortages in key areas such as engineering and science, or the benefits of rubbing shoulders with the best of the best as a way of lifting everyone's game' (p.91). It has led to, Brown et al. argue, the targeting of elite universities worldwide, and a concomitant disregard for national loyalties. Indeed, they cite the case of a leading financial services company, which targets just eight globally ranked universities, only one of which was in the UK, despite a significant proportion of the company's activities being located in London. This type of approach is actively encouraged by those universities positioned highly in global league tables, as they also benefit from being associated with other elite institutions and perceived as a route to elite, transnational careers. Thus, as Brown et al. (2011) note, leading corporations and elite universities 'have engaged in a tango that enhances each other's brands' (p.95). For individual students with ambitions to enter the corporate world, accessing an elite higher education institution becomes increasingly important. As such institutions tend to be concentrated in the Anglophone world, and particularly the US, mobility for study is often required.

Empirical studies that have focussed specifically on the impact of study abroad on employment have indeed documented that it often has significant career benefits both in the short- and long-term, in many different parts of the world, and in relation to both credit and whole degree mobility (Bracht et al., 2006; Potts, 2015). Moreover, such studies have also indicated that mobile students often also benefit in terms of their wider learning – developing interpersonal and communication skills, an increased ability to work with those from other cultures and enhanced problem solving and analytical skills (Murphy-Lejeune, 2002; Potts, 2015; Roberts et al., 2010). Teichler (2004) has argued that overseas study can be an effective means of challenging students' attitudes and engrained perspectives 'because of an all-embracing confrontation . . . [with] a culture different from that at home' (p.11), while the benefits derived from informal learning outside the classroom, during a period abroad, have also been noted (Baláž and Williams, 2004).

To consider in more detail the extent to which access to international student mobility, and the associated benefits outlined above, can be considered 'fair', we draw on two studies that we have conducted over recent years. The first part of our analysis below considers the characteristics and social location of young adults from England who had either studied for a degree overseas (in the previous five years), or were seriously considering doing so (in the next year or two). Here, our analysis is based on 85 in-depth qualitative interviews (see Brooks and Waters (2009) for further details of the methodology employed). Second, we draw on a detailed analysis of 40 school websites to explore the messages that students in England are given about overseas study, and the extent to which this varies by both school type and social location. (For a detailed discussion of the methods employed in this second study, see Brooks and Waters (2015) and Waters and Brooks (2015).)

British students and overseas study

In this section, we discuss the findings of our qualitative analysis of the decision-making of young adults in England around international higher education. We were interested in understanding both the characteristics of young people who were seriously considering – or had undertaken – undergraduate studies abroad, and their motivations for doing so. Our data suggested that access to overseas opportunities is not available to all pupils – there is quite a marked social differentiation when it comes to international higher education (see Waters, 2006). This was most striking at the undergraduate level; only the most privileged individuals are exposed to the possibility, or given the opportunity, to study abroad. We begin by discussing the pertinent social structures that appeared to enable overseas study, before moving on to consider students' motivations for considering this (still relatively unusual) educational pathway.

It was notable that, with few exceptions, students who had chosen to study abroad had received a significant level of support from those around them. In particular, schools played an important role in providing a necessarily supportive environment. In no small part, this was attributable to the fact that most pupils had attended/were attending a fee-paying private school, with all the additional resources that that implies. The cultural capital possessed by elite and more 'expensive' schools attracted 'recruiters' from Ivy League universities, who visited the schools and gave talks to pupils on studying abroad. A school attended by one student offered a 'pre-SAT' test to its pupils, in order to prepare them for the exam required by North American universities for entry onto their undergraduate and graduate programmes (the SAT).[2] These structures made international study *a possibility* – whereas for pupils not attending such elite institutions, it is likely that they would 'not even think' of applying to a university overseas, let alone actually go through with it.

In addition to the important role played by schools, other aspects of students' home 'habitus' made overseas study a possible, if not favourable, option. Several students described the important role played by other family members in introducing to them the possibility of overseas study. One individual had been taken on a 'universities tour' of the East Coast of the United States with her parents before deciding to apply to an American university – another had holidayed in Boston, Massachusetts, as a child, staying with her parents' friends in Cape Cod. This, she claimed, had undoubtedly influenced her decision to study in America. From our sample, it was apparent that students who had chosen to pursue an international education had done so amidst a great deal of support, whether from their school, friends or family.

Schools had their own reasons for encouraging applications to top (usually US Ivy League) universities abroad. As we have written elsewhere (see Brooks and Waters, 2009), one key motivation for pursuing study abroad at the undergraduate level was the opportunity it provided for a 'second chance' at, or alternative route to, academic success (cf. Bourdieu, 1996). It was surprisingly common amongst our sixth-former and undergraduate sample to find that individuals had applied to Oxbridge and failed to secure a place at their preferred UK university. Furthermore, any other (non-Oxbridge) UK university was seen as simply 'not good enough' for them – Ivy League institutions in the US offered an 'honourable substitute' to Oxbridge. These findings reflect what Bourdieu (1986) has written in relation to the emergence of new institutes of management in France, where he claims that these institutes provide academically 'less successful' students with a 'second chance'. He proceeded to describe these institutes as 'honourable substitutes' for the most prestigious qualifications. This is what we have found in relation to international education – that in many cases it provided an honourable substitute to Oxbridge, as the following quotations illustrate:

> I got rejected by two of my top unis, I got rejected by Oxford and I got rejected by Durham and kind of at the moment it's just like if I don't get

a place in the States I don't feel like going to uni for the first year anyway, maybe trying to re-apply.

(Kamil, attending co-educational sixth-form college)

In the summer I was, I had decided, I'd got my A Level results and I was like right I'm going to, I definitely want to take a gap year, I'd decided on that, I definitely want to re-apply [to Oxford], this is what I want to do. And as I was looking at places in England that I wanted to re-apply to, I was looking at league tables and I was just looking at an international league table and then I just thought to myself, well that would be quite interesting if I did that.

(Jessica, sixth-former, private girls' school)

One interviewee admitted that he had been very lazy and spoilt at school. He had not worked hard, and the opportunity to go to Canada to study offered him a 'blank sheet'. He said: 'I left school with five GCSEs, two Bs and three Cs – very, very poor. I didn't make any effort, I didn't try, I didn't study, I could not be bothered. I had no . . . I was very lazy and unmotivated. I had no desire. I grew up in a very spoilt environment, so of course, why did I have to do anything, you know? The world was going to come to me.' (Richard, completed higher education in Canada). He continued:

I don't think I had a future plan, to be honest. My future plan was to avoid working and sleep late! And that fitted in well because of course it meant a guaranteed four year pass out of employment. At the time that was a massive motivation. I just didn't want to work and I wanted to find any way possible to avoid doing anything I didn't want to do.

Richard spent six years in Canada completing an undergraduate degree, funded by his parents, and now works for a large beauty chain based in the UK as head of marketing. His case was perhaps the starkest example of how an overseas degree offered a second chance at success for highly privileged but not necessarily hard-working or high-achieving individuals.

As we have observed in papers elsewhere (Brooks and Waters, 2009; Waters and Brooks, 2010), in contrast to how the literature portrays the vast majority of 'international students', motivations amongst our UK sample were not always explicitly linked to concerns with employability. One individual described studying abroad as a 'big juicy adventure'. Two others talked about it being a very personal decision that they were doing 'for themselves'. Another described it as potentially 'life changing'. For a small number, it was little more than a chance to have some fun, whilst also providing the opportunity to put off (for a short time) the inevitable drudgery of getting a job and becoming independent. Again, these findings seem inevitably to point to a level of privilege attached to international higher education amongst English students that implies that overseas study is anything but a 'level playing field' when it comes to access and social equality. Nevertheless, there is some evidence to suggest that *graduate-level* overseas study has the potential, at least, to be more socially inclusive (partly as a consequence of increased funding opportunities for fewer potential applicants).

Although our sample makes no claims to be representative, our findings have been borne out, however, by the results of a much larger subsequent survey conducted by Allan Findlay and colleagues at the universities of Dundee and Sussex (see, for example, Findlay et al., 2012). Whilst dealing with a far larger sample, they also concluded that international study tends, on the whole, to exacerbate rather than alleviate inequalities in educational opportunities within the UK.

Elite schools and support for overseas study

In this section, we discuss the findings of a different project examining the 'public faces' of elite schools in England. Our primary source of data was their webpages (as described above) – the websites of 40 different 'elite' schools were analysed – 20 state and 20 private, selective and non-selective. We were particularly interested in uncovering the different geographies that schools represented. One aspect of this concerned the ways in which international issues were displayed (or not), and this included, for some schools, support given to and celebration of overseas university applications and successes. There were very obvious and somewhat surprising differences between 'school types' (state and private, academically selective and socially 'influential') and the amount of support and encouragement they give pupils with regards to making an overseas university application. Our findings can be summarised as follows: state schools were far more willing to celebrate internationalisation (in its various guises) on their webpages, and yet they seemed to have far fewer pupils applying to and securing places at elite overseas universities (this was assumed from the absence of data), compared to the most expensive and ostensibly influential private schools. As we will go on to discuss below, this no doubt relates in part to the discrepancy in resources available to schools to support international applications. These resources were often described, in some detail, on high-fee elite schools' webpages, and were notable by their absence from the websites of state and 'cheaper' private schools.

In the earlier section, we discussed the structures of support (the enabling environment) provided by certain schools to pupils considering overseas study.[3] Likewise, the websites of the schools that we examined in this second project described the various ways in which they 'supported' and 'encouraged' applications to overseas universities by their pupils. Some of these findings mirror closely what young people in our earlier study (discussed above) told us. For example, two schools ('private influential #1'[4] and 'private influential #8') provided a 'SAT preparation course' at the school. One of these schools sends on average around 13 pupils a year to overseas universities, including to the US, which would seem to be a significant number. Another school, also in this category, boasts that it holds 'many talks every year' from admissions tutors at top universities in the US ('private influential #4'). Its website illustrates specifically which US universities pupils were successful in gaining entry to. 'Private influential #8' claims to provide 'specialist guidance' for applications to universities in the US through an 'expert advisor'. Nine percent of 'leavers' in 2012 at this school went abroad for university. Another school hosted a 'US universities visit', where admissions tutors from four Ivy League universities 'gave an informative talk, explaining the application process and describing undergraduate life at a major US university'. More than 60 pupils and their parents were said to have attended the talk ('private influential #10'). Between 2007 and 2013, as many as 70 pupils at this school secured a place at a top US higher educational institution.

Unlike the students we talked to in the earlier project, schools' websites do not give any particular reason *why* they encourage overseas applications, other than the fact that many US universities are ranked amongst the best in the world. However, they do place far greater emphasis on Oxbridge applications and successes than on international applications (as suggested by the relative prominence given to these options on their web pages). There was a strong implication that elite UK universities remain by far the 'best' and preferred option for privileged pupils, and Ivy League universities are an 'honorable' (if second-best) substitute. Here, we see strong resonance with Bourdieu's (1996) contention that the new institutes of management that had emerged in France offered 'a second chance, as it were, to students who have not received from the academic world the recognition they had been anticipating' (p.217) and thus helped to secure the reproduction of social advantage.

Unsurprisingly, however, schools did not make explicit reference to any notion that pupils applying to the US had 'failed' to gain entry to Oxbridge. This is something that we can infer from the findings of our earlier project, where pupils had told us that this was the case.

Without exception, these schools also organise and run expensive and elaborate trips abroad for pupils (expeditions), which may or may not have a direct bearing on the decision to apply overseas for university entrance. Five of the schools we surveyed have 'branch campuses' in the Middle East or East Asia. Again, we can only speculate on whether this has any direct bearing on the propensity of pupils to apply overseas when thinking of university applications. However, it does expose them to the idea of internationalisation and the possibility of an alternative educational future.

What our analysis showed was that these aspects, related to overseas university applications, were almost exclusively associated with high-fee, highly influential private schools, and were almost universally *absent* from the state schools we analysed. The exception to this was a small number of news stories featuring pupils who had been successful in securing scholarships to overseas universities. Most state schools and less expensive private schools simply did not provide any information (numbers of pupils successfully applying to universities abroad, descriptions of support available, etc.) on overseas study within their webpages at all. This was a notable and telling absence.

It would seem, therefore, that an inequality persists when it comes to the opportunities afforded to individuals by overseas study, especially at the undergraduate level. Within England, the resources are simply not in place within most state schools to support pupils who wish to apply abroad. Any pupil who does want to take this route will have to do so independently – a tall undertaking for any young person. It would be interesting to compare these findings to data for state/private-sector schools elsewhere in Europe and the world, as the question of whether the UK is exceptional in this regard is a moot one. This leads inevitably to the issue of the reproduction of social inequalities in relation to higher education. Is there any evidence to suggest that students who study abroad are actually *advantaged* by these overseas opportunities later in life? Our findings in relation to this question have, in fact, been mixed. Whilst there has been, in the literature at large, an assumption that overseas study is inherently beneficial (particularly when it comes to the accumulation of cultural capital and employability – see Waters, 2006), our study of those English young people who went abroad suggests that some had actually felt disadvantaged on return to the UK, when attempting to enter the job market. They complained that their foreign credentials were not sufficiently recognised or valued in the UK context. British institutions are perhaps particularly insular when it comes to understanding and appreciating foreign academic credentials, and also demonstrate a propensity to valorise British qualifications above all else. Our respondents described employers not understanding overseas qualifications and/or not appreciating why they had decided to study abroad (see Brooks et al., 2012, for a fuller discussion). At the same time, however, the CV- and life-enhancing potential of a period spent abroad should not be underestimated, conferring in many cases significant cultural capital. It is not always possible to relate directly and unproblematically the relationship between credentials, employability and overall 'success' in life.

Conclusion

In this chapter, we have drawn on data from interviews with UK students and an analysis of the websites of UK schools to explore the ways in which access to international HE is currently played out, and the motivations of those who embark on a degree overseas. We have demonstrated how social structures, particularly the school a young person attends and the habitus of their family, can strongly influence a decision to study abroad. Moreover, we have suggested that overseas study can offer a 'second chance' at 'success' for highly privileged but not necessarily hard-working or high-achieving students – noting that this was sometimes allied to a desire for adventure, rather than any concern about enhancing future employability. Here, we noted similarities with Bourdieu's (1996) arguments about the function of new institutes of management in France. Our website analysis revealed an interesting paradox – that although state schools were much more likely than their private counterparts to celebrate internationalisation in an explicit manner on their webpages, they seemed to have far fewer pupils both applying to and securing places at overseas universities. Perhaps most important, stark differences emerged between the two sectors (state and private) in the resources available to support a decision to apply overseas, with significantly fewer on offer to those in state schools, irrespective of whether their school was selective or comprehensive in its intake. Such differences are socially significant because, although the evidence about the direct labour market advantage of an overseas education (to UK students) remains rather unclear, it is undoubtedly the case that a period of overseas study enhances, at the very least, the cultural capital of mobile students.

UK policy documents outline a strong 'mobility imperative': all higher education students are encouraged to take advantage of opportunities to become mobile, and engage in some form of study or work abroad during their degree (UKHE International Unit, 2013). Nevertheless, there is no acknowledgement in such documents that access to these opportunities is currently socially patterned, with those from more privileged backgrounds much more likely to pursue both whole degree and credit mobility than their less privileged peers. Although in some parts of the world, where local labour markets are perceived to offer few prospects, educational mobility may be a more everyday occurrence (Cairns, 2014), on the whole, it remains a relatively elitist pursuit. Deakin's (2014) work on the Erasmus work placement scheme, offered to higher education students, has indicated that the possibility of earning a salary 'can overcome the financial barrier associated with studying abroad and, therefore, [has] the potential to attract students from lower socio-economic groups who are not financially supported by their families' (p.35) and thus widen participation. However, our data suggest that access to the majority of mobility opportunities remains socially differentiated, and a realistic possibility for only a small and privileged minority of young people.

Notes

1 This threshold, which removed restrictions on the number of high-grade students universities were able to recruit, was introduced in 2012. From 2015, however, there has been no restriction on the number of students universities can recruit at any grade level.
2 Although not all the students in our sample had chosen to study in North America, this was by far the most popular destination (see Brooks and Waters (2009) for a full list of destination countries).
3 We have no evidence to suggest that 'international' opportunities for higher education were offered to and taken up by only those who were 'international' pupils.
4 We refer to each of the schools in the sample in terms of their type of school (and their number among schools of the same type). 'Private influential' refers to the category of private schools that are deemed to have a significant influence on public life in the UK, and appear in the Sutton Trust's list of most influential private schools (see Sutton Trust, 2012). The other categories used in our research were 'High-performing private' and 'High-performing state'.

References

Baláž, V. and Williams, A. (2004) 'Been there, done that': International student migration and human capital transfers from the UK to Slovakia, *Population, Space and Place*, 10, 217–237.

Bodycott, P. (2009) Choosing a higher education study abroad destination: What mainland Chinese parents and students rate as important, *Journal of Research in International Education*, 8, 3, 349–373.

Bourdieu, P. (1996) *The State Nobility: Elite Schools in the Field of Power* Stanford, CA, Stanford University Press.

Bracht, O., Engel, C., Janson, K., Over, A., Schomburg, H. and Teichler, U. (2006) *The Professional Value of Erasmus Mobility* Final report presented to the European Commission, Directorate-General Education and Culture.

Brooks, R. and Waters, J. (2009) A second chance at 'success': UK students and global circuits of higher education, *Sociology*, 43, 6, 1–18.

Brooks, R. and Waters, J. (2011) Fees, funding and overseas study: Mobile UK students and educational inequalities, *Sociological Research Online*, 16, 2. Available online at: http://www.socresonline.org.uk/16/2/1.html

Brooks, R. and Waters, J. (2015) The hidden internationalism of elite English schools, *Sociology*, 49, 2, 212–228.

Brooks, R., Waters, J. and Pimlott-Wilson, H. (2012) International education and the employability of UK students, *British Educational Research Journal*, 38, 2, 281–298.

Brown, P., Lauder, H. and Ashton, D. (2011) *The Global Auction* New York, Oxford University Press.

Cairns, D. (2014) *Youth Transitions, International Student Mobility and Spatial Reflexivity* London, Palgrave.

Collinson, P. (2012) Save £25,000 at university and join the 'tuition fee refugees', *The Guardian*, 17 August 2012. Available online at: http://www.guardian.co.uk/money/2012/aug/17/save-25000-university-tuition-fee-refugees

Commission of the European Communities (CEC) (2009) *Promoting the Learning Mobility of Young People* COM (2009) 329 Final. Brussels, Commission of the European Communities.

Deakin, H. (2014) The drivers to Erasmus student work placement mobility: A UK student perspective, *Children's Geographies*, 12, 1, 25–39.

Department of Business, Innovation and Skills (BIS) (2013a) *International Education: Global Growth and Prosperity* London, BIS. Available online at: https://www.gov.uk/government/publications/international-education-strategy-global-growth-and-prosperity

Department of Business, Innovation and Skills (BIS) (2013b) *The Wider Benefits of International Higher Education in the UK (Research Paper Number 128)* London, BIS. Available online at: https://www.gov.uk/government/publications/international-higher-education-in-the-uk-wider-benefits

European Commission (2012) *National Student Fee and Support Systems, 2011/12*, Education, Audiovisual and Culture Executive Agency (European Commission). Available online at: http://eacea.ec.europa.eu/education/eurydice/documents/facts_and_figures/fees_and_support.pdf

Findlay, A. M., King, R., Smith, F. M., Geddes, A. and Skeldon, R. (2012) World class? An investigation of globalisation, difference and international student mobility. *Transactions of the Institute of British Geographers*, 37, 1, 118–131.

Jones, E. and Brown, S. (eds) (2005) *Internationalising Higher Education* London, Routledge.

Murphy-Lejeune, E. (2002) *Student Mobility and Narrative in Europe: The New Strangers* London, Routledge.

Rizvi, F. (2000) International Education and the Production of Global Imagination, In: Burbules, N. and Torres, C. (eds) *Globalisation and Education: Critical Perspectives* New York, Routledge, pp. 205–225.

Roberts, A., Chou, P. and Ching, G. (2010) Contemporary trends in East Asian higher education: dispositions of international students in a Taiwan university, *Higher Education*, 59, 149–166.

Potts, D. (2015) Understanding the early career benefits of learning abroad programs, *Journal of Studies in International Education* (Advance online access).

Sin, I. L. (2013) Cultural capital and distinction: Experiences of the 'other' foreign student, *British Journal of Sociology of Education*, 34, 5, 848–867.

Singh, P. and Doherty, C. (2008) Mobile students in liquid modernity: Negotiating the politics of transnational identities. In: Dolby, N. and Rizvi, F. (eds) *Youth Moves; Identities and Education in Global Perspective* New York, Routledge.

Sutton Trust (2012) *The Educational Backgrounds of the Nation's Leading People.* London, The Sutton Trust.

Teichler, U. (2004) The changing debate on internationalisation of higher education, *Higher Education*, 48, 5–26.

UKHE International Unit (2013) *UK Strategy for Outward Mobility* London, UKHE.

Universities UK (2014) *International Students in Higher Education: The UK and Its Competition* London, UUK. Available online at: http://www.universitiesuk.ac.uk/highereducation/Pages/InternationalStudentsInUKHE.aspx

Waters, J. L. (2006) Geographies of cultural capital: Education, international migration and family strategies between Hong Kong and Canada. *Transactions of the Institute of British Geographers*, 31, 179–192.

Waters, J. L. (2007) 'Roundabout routes and sanctuary schools': The role of situated educational practices and habitus in the creation of transnational professionals, *Global Networks*, 7, 4, 477–497.

Waters, J. and Brooks, R. (2015) 'The magical operations of separation': English elite schools' on-line geographies and functional isolation, *Geoforum*, 58, 86–94.

Wiers-Jensen, J. (2011) Background and employability of mobile vs. non-mobile students, *Tertiary Education and Management*, 17, 2, 79–100.

Ye, R. and Nylander, E. (2015) The transnational track: State sponsorship and Singapore's Oxbridge elite, *British Journal of Sociology of Education*, 36, 1, 11–33.

Conclusion

Neil Harrison and Anna Mountford-Zimdars

Towards a new agenda for access research

In the preface, we set out our vision for this book. Rather than producing another collection of empirical studies around access to higher education, our aim was to bring together chapters which would primarily be useful to those researching in the field. We aimed to introduce a wider palette of theoretical perspectives and then to highlight some of the contemporary challenges that still demand the attention of the research community across the globe. Of course, we also hope that the book is useful to practitioners and policymakers, as well as to those teaching around social and educational inequality. However, the focus on supporting future research was what guided the inclusion of contributors and chapters.

This conclusion therefore draws out what we believe are some of the key insights to construct a fruitful onward research agenda and a wider programme of social action for access researchers. We begin by synthesising key ideas from the diverse theoretical perspectives in Section 2, before drawing on Sections 1 and 3 to frame some of the overarching challenges where research attention is needed.

Theoretical perspectives

We feel that strong research around access to higher education has to be rooted in social theory. We have attempted to showcase a diverse array of interdisciplinary perspectives and philosophical standpoints. This is partly to supplement (or maybe even disrupt) the pervasive dominance of Bourdieusian discourses around access, although Burke's chapter provides an excellent defence of the ground for Bourdieu's 'thinking tools' of field, capital and habitus in explaining patterns in access and the choices made by individuals.

The six theory chapters in Section 2 provide a rich variety of lenses for exploring the conceptual field. Placing this section at the heart of this book is rooted in our belief that policies and practices to increase access to higher education grounded in theory are more likely to effect change than *ad hoc* interventions without a clear causal purpose. This juxtaposition of different scholarly traditions is unusual as too often there is a tendency to see these different conceptual approaches and traditions as being in competition. This fragmentation can risk missing the opportunities for synthesis and positive critique that arise from combining different traditions.

Interestingly, there are a number of shared concepts between the theories presented within this book which we think are likely to be instructive. We would like to draw attention to four of these here:

1   **The connection between macro and micro levels.** Thompson's chapter provides a useful jumping-off point in outlining Boudon's work, where the key insight is perhaps that there are two distinct processes at work in determining the inequality within educational systems: that lower socio-economic groups achieve fewer qualifications (we will return to this shortly) and that, at a given level of qualification, they are less likely to choose to progress (or, as Harrison observes, maximise the status of their higher education). This juxtaposition of educational qualifications as a positional good determining the ability to demand higher education and the ability of individuals to make active choices within a democratic system is instructive, setting up a macro and micro level of access theory. Indeed, there is arguably not currently a unified theory of access that is able to account for both macro trends and changes as well as the micro decisions of potential learners in higher education.

2   **The role of individual choice.** Burke focuses mainly on the structural constraints on prospective students' choices and how these operate through Bourdieu's concepts of capital and habitus. Higher education is an uncertain path for those from less advantaged communities, subtly guided by the classed expectations of teachers and others. For Wilson-Strydom, agency is at the heart of the choice, but Sen's framework foregrounds the idea that the opportunities/capabilities available are part of the structures of inequality, such that the ability to choose higher education differs along with the value placed upon it by different individuals. Kahn's chapter uses Archer's typology of reflexivities to consider how individuals might accommodate the idea of higher education within their *modus vivendi*. He suggests that policy tends to situate higher education within a social mobility framework that appeals to autonomous reflexives who prioritise performance and status, and to a lesser extent to meta-reflexives whose primary concern is their positive role within the world. Conversely, individuals focusing on social relations within their community (communicative reflexives) and those who find decision-making problematic (fractured reflexives) are less likely to see themselves progressing to higher education unless 'advisers' help shape their choices. Simon similarly highlights the role of informed others as a means of managing complexity and shaping decisions which lie beyond the individual's experiences and Harrison argues that it is more advice that prospective students need, not more information.

3 **The changing and individual nature of risk.** The other recurring theme is the vital role of risk, although there are different views on how this impacts on prospective students. Brynin's chapter uses Beck's idea of the 'risk environment', where established certainties of career and identity have become complex and uncertain, but subverts many of the usual assumptions about disadvantaged young people. Rather than constructing higher education as a risky option for this group, Brynin builds a strong case that it is a safer option than early entry to the labour market – 'good jobs' have become graduate jobs. Thompson's chapter also tackles risk and specifically how social groups or individuals wish to avoid downward social mobility. This is not inconsistent with Brynin's argument, where the fear of low paid work or unemployment underpins a buoyant demand for higher education, whereas the middle classes are able to rely more on social capital alongside credentials to maintain their status. Risk is also associated with entry to elite higher education, where perhaps individuals' habitus acts as a barrier due to fear around being accepted into an alien and alienating environment. This is perhaps particularly true with Archer's communicative reflexives, who may choose forms of higher education based within their community, and are unlikely to leave it to study or graduate work. This is also linked to the availability and representativeness heuristics discussed in Harrison's chapter, where an absence of experience of elite universities constructs them as unfamiliar and based around stereotypes as socially excluding and academically exacting; he also highlights Kahneman's work on the complex and nonlinear nature of attitudes to risk.

4 **Access as a lived experience, not an entry point.** Both Wilson-Strydom and Kahn stress that thinking about access should not be confined to the entry process, but engage also with the nature and quality of students' participation within the system, their progression opportunities and how their higher education translates into social mobility and labour market outcomes. This relates to the previous discussions around elite higher education; furthermore Wilson-Strydom describes how two students ostensibly accessing the same manifestation of higher education may have quite different experiences with implications for social justice within this lived experience.

Contemporary challenges

The eight chapters in Sections 1 and 3 provide a whistlestop tour around the globe to demonstrate the ubiquity of access challenges and the commonalities in some of the ways in which they express themselves. In particular, five overarching themes emerge:

1 **Inequalities in school achievement.** In nearly all higher education systems, access is dictated in some way by a measure of school achievement (or other qualifications for mature entrants). However, admissions systems vested with

decades of confidence in their value for meritocratic sifting are now coming under more scrutiny, as discussed by Yamamoto and Mountford-Zimdars. It is well known that achievement is heavily influenced by family background and social group membership, but there remains insufficient appreciation of this within access research and practice. First, systems that enshrine historic privilege cannot be fair – and probably not even meritocratic. Second, school examinations are subject to manipulation (e.g. through additional tuition or 'hothousing') generating misleading measures of ability. Third, tests of learning at school may not be the best predictors for flourishing in higher education, with its differences in curriculum, pedagogy and purpose.

2   **Hierarchical systems and their natural conservatism.** The focus of access research has traditionally been around the proportions of various social groups progressing to higher education. However, Marginson highlights the strongly hierarchical nature of the higher education sector in many developed nations, with a minority of historical elite universities bolstered by a long tail of others striving for that elite status. While clear inroads in access have been made in general, the routes into the 'top' universities remain problematic for disadvantaged students. The challenge of access is no longer about just getting into higher education, but the type of institution and programme and where it is located. Furthermore, Yamamoto describes the pressures exerted on universities by the hierarchies in which they sit and the trappings of elitism surrounding them. Whatever the moral or governmental pressures, the inherent conservatism of maintaining a system which has placed one's own institution at the top is hard to resist. There is evidence in a number of chapters here of a rearguard action from policymakers, universities and individual academics in the name of preserving 'standards'.

3   **New frontiers of elitism.** There are two key examples within the book of new forms of elite education with differential rates of access. McCallum and colleagues discuss issues around African Americans accessing postgraduate education, while Brooks and Waters look at the ways in which privileged British young people use international study as an emerging means of maintaining their privilege – opposite sides of the same coin. Marginson sees this as an inevitable feature of highly competitive environments, with social elites finding new ways of obtaining positional advantage through education and Thompson reminds us of the usefulness of the effectively and maximally maintained inequality frameworks for understanding such patterns.

4   **Reaching remote and divided communities.** While there has always been research interest around marginalised communities and their demand for higher education, this has tended to be overwhelmed by more general concerns about young people in relatively mainstream settings. Jardine highlights the practical challenges of engaging with prospective students across long distances, as well as questioning the ethics of targeting communities whose need for higher education is moot and where outward migration could compromise their viability. Hendin and colleagues examine the attempts to extend

access to Palestinian Arabs in Israel despite the very obvious divisions, while Wilson-Strydom's chapter is built around the stark inequalities in South Africa and the legacy of apartheid. More broadly, this raises questions about the normative role of higher education and its ability to benefit marginalised communities without denuding them of their most able individuals.

5   **Access in the 'new economies' and the developing world.** The opening chapter from Chien and colleagues at UNESCO put the access challenge into a broader perspective by comparing developed and developing nations. While there are clear equality issues in the former, the comparisons with the latter demonstrate the scale of the challenges that remain around the world. There are opportunities for these nations to learn from existing research, but those developing most quickly are in danger of repeating the pseudo-meritocratic mistakes from elsewhere. Of the new global economies, Smolentseva's chapter on post-communist Russia demonstrates the ability of emerging social elites to dominate access and to construct their own hierarchies.

Towards a future research agenda

Returning to Boudon's classification of primary and secondary effects provides us with a context for framing a future research agenda which we consider to be vital. Taking the secondary effect first, despite decades of education as a discipline, we continue to lack a strong theoretical and empirical understanding of the messy route by which socio-economic disadvantage translates into educational disadvantage:

- Why do some children with high early achievement later fall off the pathway leading to higher education?
- Why do some make it 'against the odds' when presented with seemingly insurmountable barriers while similarly obstructed peers do not?
- What role do key influencers, including parents and teachers, play in attainment?
- To what extent can these trajectories be influenced by policy and practice?

These are not questions that are often engaged with by those researching access to higher education, yet addressing social differences in children's educational achievement is possibly the biggest step to closing the social gaps in higher education. Rather, there is something of a tendency to view the decision to seek higher education as a discrete act with limited history or context.

Turning to this decision, we have highlighted above the vital roles played by choice and risk, and these clearly deserve further research. The pervasive assumption that higher education is a risky option for those in disadvantage needs re-evaluating, along with the orthodoxy that more information is always the answer. There have always been 'pioneers' who have chosen to attend higher education despite their disadvantages and we believe that there is much to be learned from exploring the choices they made when others around them did not.

Research also needs to consider more what happens during and after higher education – in other words, the question not just of access, but of access to what? Differential access to 'experience enhancements' during higher education (e.g. internships or extra-curricular activities) contribute to students' ability to access to postgraduate education and higher-level career opportunities, especially within the congested graduate labour market in many developed nations. This raises conceptual questions around the dominant discourse that higher education enhances opportunities in later life for everyone. Conversely, we need a better understanding of how social elites safeguard against non-participation or lower attainment in higher education by flexing their social, cultural and economic capitals, thus still providing excellent life-outcomes for their children.

Further research is also needed to document choices and experiences of under-represented groups. Such work is well-represented in this book as vital in avoiding imprinting our own expectations of decision-making on these individuals. However, we also feel that more research is needed focusing on the home communities of students and exploring how higher education can support (or even undermine) these communities collective capacity, wellbeing and flourishing alongside offering individual benefits. We need a more holistic picture of the meaning of higher education for individuals, institutions and communities.

One contemporary research trend is focusing on the evaluation of interventions intended to improve access, such that concepts of good practice can evolve and be shared. We are positive about the intent behind this – to ensure that the limited funds available are put to the best use – but we are concerned that this 'what works' agenda can easily degenerate into a reductionist view of the access challenge as 'fixable' through a simplistic toolkit of motivational experiences for young people that does not respect the complexity of their lives or the enduring nature of social stratification. As noted above, such efforts also need strong contextualisation regarding differential school achievements.

Social activism and the challenge to institutions

Researching access to higher education is not a neutral position or act. It is grounded in a sensitivity to inequality and historic privilege, with an intent (whether explicit or tacit) to challenge those inequalities. We hope that this book has provided researchers – and maybe practitioners and policymakers – with some more weapons in their armoury. In addition, it is important that researchers feel connected to a global community of practice. This book showcased that there are similar challenges to address across the world beyond our own nations.

One particular role that researchers can play is challenging their own institutions on their policy and practice around access. This clearly already happens in many instances, but we hope this book might stimulate this further and in new directions.

Given the pedagogic and other expertise housed within universities, we believe there is a clear need for them to concern themselves more in remedying the disparities in the attainment of young people from disadvantaged backgrounds. This has generally been seen within the purview of schools and government, but its role in propelling young people towards higher education (of different types) is key. Harrison's chapter highlights the need for high-quality advice challenging assumptions, rather than ever more information or a focus on raising 'aspirations'; interventions with teachers and parents are likely to bear fruit. Similarly, Kahn reflects on those people who may 'choose themselves' out of higher education (or certain types thereof) due to their links to their community or their own anxieties about taking bold decisions – there is a clear role for institutions here.

As discussed above, hierarchical educational systems tend to be antagonistic towards innovation; elite institutions benefit from the status quo, while lower-status ones are constantly trying to play the game to move towards elite status. Nevertheless, there is a clear space for confident and values-driven institutions to rethink what they valorise during the admissions process and how this is operationalised. As Mountford-Zimdars describes, there are institutions who having willingly taken the risk of developing admissions policies that risk moving down league tables by accepting those with lower qualifications but higher potential. Contesting the nature of the prevailing admissions system is a positive research contribution.

The continuing access challenge

Inequalities in access to higher education are deeply embedded in their societies. We have mainly focused in this book on developed nations where the inequalities around higher education mirror steep stratification by social class, with ethnicity and gender also playing a part to a greater or lesser extent. By pulling together these contributions, we are hoping to prompt a new wave of research interest in the access challenge – one which is strongly grounded in theory and which takes a holistic perspective rather than focusing solely on policy and practice interventions late in secondary education. We are therefore encouraging the global research community to focus on both the individual's decision-making and on the societal structures that define the decisions available to them, as well as to take an active role in challenging the practices of their own institutions where they support questionable hierarchies and unjustifiable elitisms.

Index

academic staff 180–2, 211
accommodation during higher education 162, 166
admissions policy/process 61, 150, 162, 205–15, 216, 223–6, 229–30, 250
African American students 171–89
agency 45, 52, 57, 58, 116, 135–8, 245
Archer, Margaret 58, 130–5, 245–6
aspiration 74, 122, 136, 163, 164, 197, 228, 250
attainment 68, 71, 147, 153, 161, 162, 164, 175, 206–8, 210, 212, 221–2, 246, 248–9

Beck, Ulrich 57, 103, 110, 246
behavioural economics 88, 90–1, 93
Boudon, Raymond 67–8, 71–5, 248
bounded rationality 86–91, 94–7
Bourdieu, Pierre 51–63, 67, 71, 75, 79, 91, 104, 236, 239, 244, 245
Breen-Goldthorpe model 75–9
bursaries 96–7; see also scholarships

capabilities approach 113–24
choice and decision-making 52, 54, 74–5, 80, 85–8, 91, 92–6, 130, 136, 245, 250
civic engagement 208
collectivism 177, 178
competition 25–6, 39, 192, 206, 216, 218, 233
contextualised admissions 205–15, 223–4
contextualised data 162
credentialism 63
critical realism 129

cultural barriers 149, 152; and language 166
cultural capital 35, 53, 56, 61–2, 171, 177, 198, 217, 221, 234, 236, 240–1, 244, 249

disability 117, 160
discrimination 183
diversity: of students 117, 207, 222, 233; of universities 37–9
downward mobility 75–6, 78

early years 165, 212
economic capital/resources 53, 76, 78
economic development 5, 122, 145, 150, 151, 153, 154, 168, 248
educational opportunities 68, 79, 117–8
educational transitions 68, 75
effectively maintained inequality 27, 70–1, 76, 146, 192, 193, 210, 247
employment outcomes 60, 92–4, 101, 102, 108–10, 128–9, 153, 205, 212, 233–4, 240–1, 246, 249
entrance examinations 216, 220–2, 224, 229, 238, 247
equality 13–15, 17–21, 26, 33, 145, 158, 190, 197, 212, 217, 220, 227, 230, 232, 235; see also equity
equity 13–15, 17–21, 26, 33, 145, 158, 190, 197, 212, 217, 220, 227, 230, 232, 235; see also equality
ethnicity 36, 147, 148, 171–3, 206, 208–9, 250; see also race
evidence-based 164; evaluation of 167
expansion of higher education 25, 26, 101, 190–1, 195, 200–1

family 179, 180, 184, 207, 247
fictive kin 178, 180
field of study 94, 176, 177, 219
financial barriers 7, 13, 17, 93, 97,
    162–3, 171
foster care 209
funding for students 152, 164, 168, 171

gender 13, 76, 171, 173, 174, 198,
    219, 221
geography 40, 158–60, 165, 167–8,
    197, 207, 209, 213, 247
government funding 10, 44, 153, 159,
    160, 168
graduate/postgraduate education
    171–189, 238, 247, 249
Group of Eight 158, 162, 168

habitus 52, 54, 56–8, 60, 91, 95, 245
holistic admission 152, 205–15
human capital theory 78, 92, 101, 118–9

implicit student model 148, 149
inclusion 146, 154, 199, 200, 212,
    223, 246
indigenous/first nation peoples 159,
    160, 163, 209
inequality 79–80, 113, 143,
    151, 199, 201, 205, 212,
    221, 245, 250
information: advice and
    guidance 68, 97, 148, 152,
    153, 172, 184, 211, 238,
    245, 250; availability of 86–7,
    88–9, 90, 92–5
integration 146, 152
international mobility 8, 232–41, 249
investment 101, 102–3, 110
Ivy League 236, 239

Jewish students 145, 206

Kahneman, Daniel 85, 88–90

labour market 76, 92–3, 102, 104–5,
    105–8
legacy admission 206, 210
lottery 212

market economy 118, 190, 201, 208,
    211, 216
mass higher education 33, 35

maximally maintained inequality 27, 70,
    76, 192, 247
meritocracy 145, 221–2, 247–8
micro-macro link 245

national frameworks 146, 149–54,
    158–60, 163, 168
Nussbaum, Martha 113, 115,
    118–9, 120

OECD 151, 161
opportunity trap 104
outreach/pre-university programmes
    150, 152, 160, 164, 167, 205,
    208–10, 212

Palestinian Arab students 145–54, 248
parental education 35, 59, 198, 221
participation patterns/rates 33, 68–9,
    81, 128, 146, 147, 161, 167, 191,
    193–5, 220
part-time students 196
policy framing 146–7, 193, 196–7, 201,
    208, 216, 219, 222, 244
positional good 191–2, 200–1, 245
poverty 15–16
prestige (institutional)/elite
    institutions/stratification
    of higher education institutions
    35–41, 44, 69, 95–6, 97, 134,
    150, 179, 191, 192, 198–99,
    201, 205, 216, 217–9, 223–4,
    227, 229, 232–4, 236, 239,
    245–7, 250
primary and secondary effects of
    inequality 71–5, 80–1, 248
privatisation 190, 195–6, 201–2
professional service staff 182–3
progression and retention 25–6, 95,
    120, 154, 159, 205
prospect theory 88

race 36, 147, 148, 171–3, 206, 208–9,
    250; see also ethnicity
rational action 67–8, 74, 77,
    79–80
reflexivity 130–2, 136–8
refugees 209
religion 147
risk and risk aversion 75, 78–9, 87,
    88–9, 91, 103, 110, 246, 248, 250
role models 148, 164

rural/remote communities 40, 159, 161–8
Russell Group 109, 232

satisficing 87, 95
scholarships 149, 153, 162–3, 211, 228, 233; *see also* bursaries
secondary education/schools 21–5, 55, 59–60, 121, 146–8, 153, 161, 162, 164, 165, 167, 198, 208, 210–11, 217–8, 220, 223–5, 228, 232, 236–8, 240–41, 246–50
Sen, Amartya 113, 115, 118–9, 120, 123, 245
Simon, Herbert 85–8, 245
social activism 249
social capital 35, 53, 160, 163, 164, 171, 177, 179, 184, 221, 246, 249
social justice 59, 113, 114–5, 119, 120, 145, 150, 168, 192, 206–7, 212, 246
social mobility 42–5, 75–6, 133, 150, 153, 197, 199, 206–7, 210, 229

socio-economic differences/social origin/social class 34, 39, 51, 54, 58–9, 62, 77, 113, 121, 122, 134, 147, 159, 161, 163, 167, 168, 171, 197–8, 201, 205, 208–10, 221–2, 229–30, 232, 235, 241, 245–6, 246, 250
student experience 60, 94–6, 121–2, 123, 137
student loans 163, 228
support during higher education 152, 153, 160, 249

teaching and learning 55, 172, 207, 222, 227, 229, 235
technology interactions 166
theory-practice link 143
tuition fees 13, 41, 162, 190, 195, 199, 209, 211, 218, 223, 232–3, 236

universal access 192

 # Taylor & Francis eBooks

---

Helping you to choose the right eBooks for your Library

Add Routledge titles to your library's digital collection today. Taylor and Francis ebooks contains over 50,000 titles in the Humanities, Social Sciences, Behavioural Sciences, Built Environment and Law.

Choose from a range of subject packages or create your own!

Benefits for you

- » Free MARC records
- » COUNTER-compliant usage statistics
- » Flexible purchase and pricing options
- » All titles DRM-free.

 REQUEST YOUR FREE INSTITUTIONAL TRIAL TODAY

Free Trials Available
We offer free trials to qualifying academic, corporate and government customers.

Benefits for your user

- » Off-site, anytime access via Athens or referring URL
- » Print or copy pages or chapters
- » Full content search
- » Bookmark, highlight and annotate text
- » Access to thousands of pages of quality research at the click of a button.

eCollections – Choose from over 30 subject eCollections, including:

Archaeology	Language Learning
Architecture	Law
Asian Studies	Literature
Business & Management	Media & Communication
Classical Studies	Middle East Studies
Construction	Music
Creative & Media Arts	Philosophy
Criminology & Criminal Justice	Planning
Economics	Politics
Education	Psychology & Mental Health
Energy	Religion
Engineering	Security
English Language & Linguistics	Social Work
Environment & Sustainability	Sociology
Geography	Sport
Health Studies	Theatre & Performance
History	Tourism, Hospitality & Events

For more information, pricing enquiries or to order a free trial, please contact your local sales team:
www.tandfebooks.com/page/sales

 Routledge
Taylor & Francis Group

The home of
Routledge books

www.tandfebooks.com